W9-BKY-961

THE PERILOUS LIFE OF SYMPHONY ORCHESTRAS

The Perilous Life
of Symphony Orchestras

Artistic Triumphs and Economic Challenges

Robert J. Flanagan

Yale UNIVERSITY PRESS

NEW HAVEN & LONDON

SOUTH HUNTINGTON
PUBLIC LIBRARY
HUNTINGTON STATION, NY 11746

784.2068
7la

Published with assistance from the Louis Stern Memorial Fund.

Copyright © 2012 by Robert J. Flanagan.
All rights reserved.
This book may not be reproduced, in whole or in part, including illustrations, in any form (beyond that copying permitted by Sections 107 and 108 of the U.S. Copyright Law and except by reviewers for the public press), without written permission from the publishers.

Yale University Press books may be purchased in quantity for educational, business, or promotional use. For information, please e-mail sales.press@yale .edu (U.S. office) or sales@yaleup.co.uk (U.K. office).

Set in Ehrhardt type by Newgen North America.
Printed in the United States of America.

Library of Congress Cataloging-in-Publication Data
Flanagan, Robert J.
The perilous life of symphony orchestras : artistic triumphs and economic challenges / Robert J. Flanagan.
    p.   cm.
Includes bibliographical references and index.
ISBN 978-0-300-17193-8 (hardcover : alk. paper)
1. Symphony orchestras—Economic aspects.   I. Title.
ML3795.F548 2012
784.2068'1—dc23

2011022872

A catalogue record for this book is available from the British Library.

This paper meets the requirements of ANSI/NISO Z39.48–1992 (Permanence of Paper).

10 9 8 7 6 5 4 3 2 1

CONTENTS

ACKNOWLEDGMENTS

During the preparation of this study, I benefited from the comments and criticisms of many thoughtful and well-informed symphony musicians, orchestra managers, and board members in the United States and in Europe. I wish there were space to identify them all. I received valuable suggestions on specific topics from academic colleagues including Paul Dimaggio, Mel Reder, Greg Sandow, Lee Soderstrom, and James Van Horne. My wife, Susan R. Mendelsohn, and anonymous reviewers for the Yale University Press also provided valuable comments that helped shape the final manuscript. I am particularly grateful for the assistance of Bri' Godfrey at Stanford University and the staff at Yale University Press in preparing the manuscript for publication.

The study relies on data from several sources. The League of American Orchestras provided me with data on finances and operations of U.S. symphony orchestras and patiently responded to my questions about the definitions and interpretations of some variables. Opera America also generously provided similar information on its member organizations. These organizations provide data under the condition that researchers not publish information that would permit the identification of economic or operational data for individual performing arts organizations. I have willingly accepted this condition, as my main interest was in conducting statistical analyses of the data to determine industry-wide trends and regularities.

There is occasional mention of financial aspects of particular orchestras, but these comments do not use any information provided by the League or

Opera America. They rest instead on information found in publicly available tax returns (available for individual symphony orchestras and other not-for-profit organizations at www.guidestar.org, for example) or discussions in the print media.

Finally, I would like to thank the Graduate School of Business at Stanford University, my intellectual "home" since 1975, and the Netherlands Institute for Advanced Study, where much of the study of the economic issues facing European symphony orchestras was conducted during 2009, for providing financial support and environments that facilitated the completion of this work. Needless to say, none of the individuals or organizations mentioned above is responsible for the conclusions of the book.

THE PERILOUS LIFE OF SYMPHONY ORCHESTRAS

CHAPTER 1

Surpluses, Deficits, and Symphony Orchestras

On February 26, 2008, the New York Philharmonic Orchestra, the oldest symphony orchestra in the United States, played a remarkable concert in Pyongyang, the capital city of North Korea, as part of an effort to use cultural exchange to thaw diplomatic relations between the two countries. The program included the national anthems of each country, the prelude to act 3 of Richard Wagner's *Lohengrin*, Antonín Dvořák's "New World" Symphony, and George Gershwin's *An American in Paris*. The encores included compositions by Georges Bizet and Leonard Bernstein, along with a popular Korean folk song. Whatever the ultimate diplomatic effects, the concert itself was an artistic and popular triumph. The *Economist* (2008) reported, "The orchestra received a rapturous standing ovation. Even North Korea's most senior attendee, Vice-President Yang Hyong Sop, readily got to his feet."

About six weeks earlier, the board of directors of the Columbus, Ohio, symphony orchestra, which had presented a critically acclaimed performance in Carnegie Hall ten years earlier, announced that their orchestra was near bankruptcy. Faced with several years of deficits, the board proposed to save about $2.5 million in the following year's budget by reducing the number of full-time orchestra musicians from 53 to 31 and reducing the concert season from 46 to 34 weeks. Part-time musicians would be hired when necessary to fill the orchestra's ranks. The musicians' union subsequently rejected that proposal, citing the impact on the income of the symphony's musicians. In late September, following the cancellation of summer concerts and the 2007–8 concert season, the symphony's musicians ratified a new agreement that involved $1.3 million in reduced wages as well as forgone health and pension benefits. A later agreement negotiated in 2011 provided musicians with base pay equal to 64 percent of their pay in 2008 (Sheban 2011).

Both events were "typical" in the sense that, over longer periods, there are a significant number of U.S. orchestras that run surpluses and an even larger number that run deficits. Even the New York Philharmonic, one of the wealthiest symphony orchestras in the United States, faces significant economic challenges, with ever-growing expenses and declines in some types of performance revenue (Lubow 2004). Averaged over the 1987 through 2000 concert seasons, the financial balance for 63 large U.S. symphonies was negative (deficit), but the experience of individual orchestras was widely dispersed. Forty-six orchestras ran deficits on average, while 17 orchestras ran surpluses on average. But irrespective of their average position, all orchestras experienced considerable annual variation in their financial balance. In each year some orchestras ran significant surpluses, while others ran significant deficits, but none of the 63 orchestras had surpluses (or deficits) throughout the entire period. The next chapter sets out the foundation of the ongoing economic insecurity faced by symphony orchestras.

In year 2000 dollars, the overall financial balance for the median orchestra changed from a deficit of almost $49,000 in 1987 to approximate balance in 2000 following a strong growth of private contributions during the robust economy of the late 1990s. Most orchestras achieved their strongest financial position during 1997–99, when highly favorable general economic conditions prevailed. Finances again deteriorated during the recession that greeted the 21st century and the Great Recession that began in late 2007. This pattern signals the importance of general economic conditions on the financial health of orchestras, a phenomenon that receives more attention in chapter 3. But many other factors influence an orchestra's financial health, for whether general economic conditions are good or bad, financial outcomes vary enormously among individual orchestras.

The demise of several orchestras over the past 20 years further signals the financial pressures on the industry. Bankruptcies have included the Florida Philharmonic Orchestra (2003) and orchestras in Birmingham, Alabama (1993), Oakland (1994), Sacramento, California (1996), San Diego (1996), San Jose, California (2002), Tulsa (2002, following a reorganization in 1994), Honolulu (2009), Louisville, Kentucky (2010, following a near miss in 2003), Syracuse, New York (2011), and Albuquerque, New Mexico (2011). Some of these orchestras eventually reorganized and reopened—usually with a different name and distinctly weaker finances. Two other orchestras, Denver and New Orleans, entered bankruptcy and later reformed as labor cooperatives—the Colorado and Louisiana symphony orchestras, respectively. Nor have the difficulties been limited to regional orchestras. In October 2010 the Detroit Symphony Orchestra's musicians struck following disagreements with management about how to address a serious financial deficit. With the strike unresolved in February 2011, the management of the orchestra canceled what was left of the 2010–11 concert season. After further negotiations, the musicians and management reached an agreement that permitted an abbreviated concert season to begin in mid-April 2011. Two foundation gifts failed to alleviate serious financial pressures facing the Philadelphia Orchestra, which filed for bankruptcy in April 2011—the first such action by a major U.S. orchestra.

What explains these disparate experiences? Why are many symphony orchestras living on the edge, while others are in a comparatively secure financial position? Answering these questions requires an understanding of the economic environment in which symphony orchestras exist and of the main institutions that influence that environment. Understanding the environment is partially a matter of appreciating why the flows of revenues received and expenses incurred by symphony orchestras look so different from the revenues and expenses of a typical business organization. Chapter 4 explores these revenues and expenses. Happily, there is more than an accounting exercise involved. Understanding the underlying forces clarifies why most orchestras must be organized as not-for-profit organizations and why even the advantages of this form of organization do not guarantee financial health.

More than accounting is at stake also because the revenues and expenses of symphony orchestras reflect decisions by individuals and institutions whose motivations must be explored to fully understand the economic environment of orchestras. Performance revenues rest importantly on attendance decisions—why some people choose to attend an orchestra performance while others opt instead for competing uses of their leisure time. Chapter 5 explores the prospects for raising performance revenues. Much of the salary expense incurred by orchestras reflects the outcome of collective bargaining negotiations between symphony management and unions representing artistic and nonartistic personnel. Chapter 6 examines the growth and structure of pay within and between U.S. orchestras.

For reasons that will become apparent, symphony orchestras, most other performing arts groups, colleges and universities, and many other nonprofit organizations must rely upon income that does not flow from their normal operations. The flow of such nonperformance income to orchestras depends upon a variety of complex decisions. Government support reflects how and why governments decide to support the arts, for example. The nature of public support of U.S. orchestras discussed in chapter 7 contrasts sharply with the approach to government support taken elsewhere in the world (chapter 10). Private nonperformance income depends on the capacity and motivation for philanthropy by individuals, businesses, and foundations (chapter 8). A board of trustees is responsible for the general governance of a symphony orchestra, including its financial performance. The board's investment and management of an orchestra's endowment determine both the annual flow of investment income and the availability of endowment resources to support future activities (chapter 9). This book tries to integrate the economic facts with the motivations and behaviors underlying the revenues and expenses of symphony orchestras.

Viewed superficially, foreign orchestras may seem to escape the financial challenges faced by their U.S. counterparts. Elsewhere in the world, symphony orchestra bankruptcies are unheard of, for example. Yet no orchestra in the world earns enough to cover its operating expenses; no orchestra is self-supporting. Instead, orchestras around the world face common economic challenges with different sources of nonperformance income. The absence of bankruptcies abroad reflects the prominent role of governments in providing subsidies to orchestras and other performing arts. Chapter 10 assesses the scope of government support abroad and discusses how a system of government subsidies influences an orchestra's performance revenues and expenses.

Care must be taken in selecting organizations for a representative industry study. A study of symphony orchestras should include organizations that represent the diversity of organizational experience and account for most of the sector's activity. If one were to choose the largest symphony orchestras at the beginning of the study period (1987 in this case), the study would lose information on emerging orchestras that later grew into musical and economic significance. If one were to choose the largest orchestras at the end of the period (2005 in this case), the study would lose information on musical organizations that have declined or even disappeared during the study period. Such biases from the selection of a sample are potentially serious, since both growing and declining orchestras can yield important information on the sector's economic challenges.

To preserve such information, the sample analyzed in this book includes every symphony orchestra that was one of the largest 50 symphonies in the United States (based on budget size) for at least two years during the 1987–88 through the 2005–6 concert seasons. Each symphony that met this requirement remains in the sample throughout the 19-year period, irrespective of its rank in other years. Stable, ongoing organizations dominate the sample; the majority of the orchestras reported data for 18 or 19 years during the period. But the selection procedure retains some orchestras whose economic health declined during the period (and hence would not be in the largest 50 symphonies late in the period), along with growing orchestras that moved into the "top 50" category late in the period. This approach produced a sample of 63 symphony orchestras (listed in the appendix to this chapter), representing over 70 percent of orchestra revenues and expenditures in the United States. If there is a group that is slighted by this procedure, it is the smallest symphony orchestras. As it happens, these orchestras are likely to submit incomplete data at irregular intervals—factors that would have limited their weight in the analyses anyway. The analysis also relies on U.S. government data on local market characteristics, such as population and per capita income, and data on the operations and finances of competing performing arts organizations.

CHAPTER 2

Why Are Surpluses
So Difficult to Maintain?

The permanent orchestra season has, as usual, been financially a bad one all over the country. With the end of April . . . come the bills for those who pay the piper. . . . There is always a deficit, which public-spirited guarantors are called upon to pay year after year. A permanent orchestra, it seems pretty well established by American experience, is not at present a paying institution, and is not likely immediately to become so. . . . [Nevertheless,] the prevailing note of the guarantors of the America Orchestras is one of hopefulness. Things are coming on; the public is being educated; it will support the orchestras in larger and larger numbers till they are finally . . . self-supporting.

This quote from a *New York Times* article could have been written in the early years of the 21st century. As it happens, it appeared a century earlier in a review of the financial results of the 1902–3 concert season (Aldrich 1903). In it we can see a number of themes that remain salient today. First, no symphony orchestra earns enough from performances to cover its performance expenses. Second, that fact is not likely to change in the foreseeable future. Third, the survival of orchestras depends on the resources provided by "guarantors." And, finally, the hope persists that building audiences will make orchestras self-supporting.

A century later, the durability of the economic challenges facing symphony orchestras worries pessimists, while the continued survival of most major symphonies may encourage complacency among optimists, who conclude that solutions to chronic operating deficits will always emerge. In fact, the optimistic prognosis that concludes the 1903 *New York Times* article proved wrong. The growth of orchestra's revenues from concert performances, recordings, and broadcasting continues to lag behind the growth of performance expenses. And orchestras have had variable success in offsetting their operating deficits with the resources of guarantors.

Understanding the economic choices facing symphony orchestras requires an understanding of why they cannot evolve as self-supporting organizations. This chapter first reviews the history of how U.S. symphony orchestras rapidly moved from self-supporting status to permanent operating deficits. Then follows a discussion of why self-supporting status is an elusive goal.

The Evolution of Symphony Organizations

Many of the earliest symphony orchestras in the United States were organized as musicians' cooperatives. After acceptance into an orchestra, players paid an initiation fee and an annual charge, chose their conductor, hired rehearsal and performance venues, and accepted a share of the net proceeds as their compensation. As residual claimants, however, they bore most of the economic risk of early musical ventures and had to divide their time between artistic and management activities. Some musicians mitigated the risk by giving preference to outside paid performances over symphony rehearsals. The cooperative structure of some early symphonies also gave musicians a property right in their positions, which proved a barrier to changing personnel to upgrade orchestra quality (Caves 2000). Orchestras clearly required a different organizational form if they were to improve performance quality. By the late 19th century, most symphony orchestras no longer earned a surplus that could be divided among the musician-owners. As the *New York Times* quote reminds us, operating deficits became a way of life.

Several major orchestras eventually acquired individual "angels" or small groups of committed donors who pledged funds to cover the ubiquitous operating deficits. The New York Philharmonic, founded in 1842, initially lacked such support and was unable to operate as a full-time resident orchestra. The Boston Symphony Orchestra, founded in 1881, enjoyed the support of a single wealthy individual. The Chicago Symphony Orchestra, founded 10 years later, relied on the members of an orchestral association who pledged funds for the orchestra's operation. With this support, major symphonies were able to expand in size, to lengthen seasons, and to guarantee musicians a weekly salary for the duration of the season. Those who pledged the funds also took over or arranged for the management of symphony activities, and musicians were able to focus on their art.[1] While donors expected no monetary return on their contributions, many were surprised by the persistent growth of operating deficits (Hart 1973).

Shifting from labor cooperatives to professional management no doubt improved artistic quality, but contrary to the hope expressed at the end of the *New York Times* excerpt, revenues earned from performances continued to fall short of performance expenses, eventually exceeding the resources of even wealthy individuals. Individual angels gave way to small groups of committed wealthy guarantors who covered performance deficits. As deficits continued to grow, however, the function of symphony boards expanded from giving money to also raising money so that orchestras could survive. Yet by 1940, a wide-ranging study of the industry could state that "in spite of their vitality, growth in numbers, and the volume of their attendance, all symphony orchestras are facing serious financial problems and their future rests on an unstable basis. Receipts from tickets have never been enough to balance the costs. . . . All, therefore, have had to resort to various kinds of deficit financing. . . . Endowments are becoming more difficult to build up and the income therefrom has been found uncertain when most needed in depressions. Annual maintenance fund drives are finding fewer large donors and are reaching out for more contributors of small sums. Subsidies have been little tried in this country and involve many problems" (Grant and Hettinger 1940). This same study reports that by the late 1930s, the three most successful major symphony orchestras earned "only an average of 85 percent of their total budgets, while . . . the whole group averages abut 60 per cent" (Grant and Hettinger 1940, p. 21). By the early 21st century, these operating results would be viewed with great envy by most orchestras.

Twenty-six years later, a landmark study of the performing arts opened with these words, which parallel the opening paragraphs of this book: "In the performing arts, crisis is apparently a way of life. One reads constantly of disappointing seasons, of disastrous rises in cost, of emergency fund drives and desperate pleas to foundations for assistance. While some performing organizations have improved their financial position, there always seem to be others in difficulties" (Baumol and Bowen 1966).

If symphony orchestra operating deficits are not news, what accounts for them? What explains the *persistence* of the problem of generating surpluses for symphony orchestras and other performing arts?

The Cost Disease and Its Critics

In their influential study, William Baumol and William Bowen (1966) identified a "cost disease" as the root of persistent operating deficits in the
performing arts and other activities with comparatively low productivity
growth. If pay in these activities increases at roughly the same rate as pay in
high-productivity growth sectors, costs per unit of product or service must
increase in activities with low productivity growth. The mechanics of the
cost disease merit careful attention.

Labor productivity is simply output divided by labor input—output
per employee or output per hour of work. At the time that Baumol and
Bowen were writing, productivity growth was most rapid in the "goods-
producing" sector (manufacturing and mining industries) and slowest in
the service sector, including the performing arts. If both pay and output
per employee in the goods-producing sector increase at 3 percent each year,
labor costs per unit of output remain constant. Higher pay is exactly offset
by the additional units produced, and there is no labor cost pressure on
prices. But if pay increases at 3 percent per year in an industry with *no* productivity growth, labor costs per unit of output will increase at 3 percent
per year, creating pressure to cover the increased costs with higher prices.
Or, to take an intermediate case, if productivity in the low-productivity-
growth industry increases at 1 percent annually (rather than zero), pay increases of 3 percent will produce unit labor cost increases of 2 percent per
year, with somewhat less upward pressure on prices. This arithmetic is the
essence of the infamous cost disease. Although one still hears claims that
the cost disease does not exist or has been "repealed," in fact the disease
cannot be repealed without repealing the laws of arithmetic.

The relevance of the cost disease to the performing arts is readily
apparent. Activities in which the relationship between labor inputs and
outputs cannot be extensively altered by technical changes have the highest potential for cost disease. Symphony orchestras and other performing
arts provide prime examples. Composers of classical music and the authors
of plays largely determine the number of musicians or actors required for
their works, and that number rarely changes over time. Indeed, in the performing arts, a performer's presentation often *is* the real product—there is
no way to separate output (a performance) from labor input. The performance ("output") and the performer ("labor input") are one and the same.

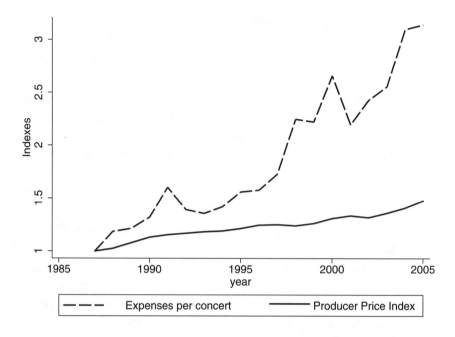

Figure 2.1. Symphony Expenses and Producer Prices, 1987–2005
Source: League of American Orchestras, U.S. Bureau of Labor Statistics

So low productivity growth in the performing arts is not anybody's "fault"; it is inherent in the nature of performance.

The consequences of relatively low productivity growth are clear: performance expenses will rise relentlessly as long as pay in the performing arts grows at about the same rate as pay elsewhere in the economy—as it must if the performing arts sector is to retain its employees. Year in and year out, the costs of presenting symphony (and opera and theater) performances will grow relative to the costs of producing products in high productivity-growth industries. In fact, this has happened. Figure 2.1 compares the evolution of the median performance expense per concert of 32 large symphony orchestras with costs in the goods-producing sector—the prices of finished goods as they leave the factory. Between 1987 and 2005, performance expense per concert increased over 300 percent, while the cost of finished goods increased much less (148 percent). Unless performance revenues increase ever more rapidly, an orchestra's operating deficit—the gap between performance expenses and performance revenues—will increase.

There are only two ways to escape the unpleasant implications of the cost disease. Either the underlying facts can change, so that the arithmetic of the cost disease changes in ways that "cure" the disease; or the consequences of the incurable disease can be offset by other factors.

Curing the disease requires a change in either of two key facts. Either differences in productivity growth between the performing arts and other industries must diminish, or employees in performing arts industries must accept pay increases that lag further and further behind the pay increases received in jobs outside the performing arts sector. Neither of these events has occurred, and in the first decade of the 21st century, neither seems imminent. In the words of Baumol and Bowen (1966, p. 164): "Whereas the amount of labor necessary to produce a typical manufactured product has constantly declined since the beginning of the industrial revolution, it requires about as many minutes for Richard II to tell his 'sad stories of the death of kings' as it did on the stage of the Globe Theatre. Human ingenuity has devised ways to reduce the labor necessary to produce an automobile, but no one has yet succeeded in decreasing the human effort expended at a live performance of a 45-minute Schubert quartet much below a total of three man-hours."

Casual observers sometimes confuse recent productivity developments in the broad services sector with developments in the performing arts. Since 1995, productivity in much of the service sector has increased as rapidly as in the goods-producing sector, leading some authors to proclaim "the end of the cost disease" (Triplett and Bosworth 2003). The source of this historic surge in service productivity is believed to be heavy investments in new information technology in *some* service industries. The performing arts, however, have been an exception to this productivity surge: they have much more limited opportunities to apply the new technologies that are believed to be the source of the productivity surge elsewhere. Indeed, the studies that proclaim the end of the cost disease do not even include data on the performing arts in their analysis of the service sector. Instead, they examine the experience of distinctively different service industries, such as financial services, transportation services, telecommunications, public utilities, and personal services, in which new technologies have indeed played an important role in advancing productivity. But productivity growth remains slower in orchestras and other performing arts.

The cost disease also has not been cured by lagging pay growth in symphony orchestras. Instead, pay in symphony orchestras has grown at least as rapidly as in the rest of the economy. (Details are provided in chapter 6.) In short, while the cost disease may have been cured in those service industries that were able to raise productivity growth through the application of information technology, the cure did not extend to symphony orchestras and other performing arts.

Can Higher Performance Revenues Offset the Cost Disease?

Even when the cost disease cannot be cured, other economic developments might increase performance revenues rapidly enough to offset the consequences of the disease. With the costs of presenting live performances rising more rapidly than costs in the rest of the economy, one would expect the price of live concert performances to increase more rapidly than other prices as orchestras tried to pass on increasing costs into prices. Up to a point, raising ticket prices may raise concert revenues, but at the cost of discouraging some attendance (see chapter 5). Moreover, to the extent that rising ticket prices discourage attendance, they are also likely to change the composition of concert audiences—thinning the ranks of low- and middle-income classical music lovers. Smaller audiences also may have artistic consequences; many performing artists believe that larger audiences tend to stimulate superior artistic performances.

Will increases in income offset the effects of rising ticket prices on attendance? After all, real incomes in every economy rise with the growth in average productivity. General productivity growth effectively increases purchasing power so that over time a society can afford to spend more on concerts as well as all other goods and services. When real (adjusted for inflation) family income increases, patronage of the arts may increase to the extent that families are better able to afford the higher prices for tickets to live performances. The additional patronage possible with higher incomes might offset losses in attendance attributable to increases in relative ticket prices. This argument has its limits. Attending a live performance requires both cash and time. Only cash budgets expand with growing real incomes. Time constraints are inherently rigid and limit attendance that higher income might otherwise permit. Moreover, higher real incomes raise the value of time. As the opportunity cost of attending live performances increases with higher incomes, attendance could decrease.

Can the cost disease be overcome by presenting concerts in larger venues? Larger concert halls only produce larger revenues per performance if more people are willing to buy tickets. As will become apparent in chapter 5, however, few U.S. orchestras fill their concert halls, and the average orchestra sells tickets for only 70 percent of its seats. Even if there are more patrons to fill the seats, there is a more subtle limitation to the capacity-expansion strategy: the cost disease has a continual cumulative effect on an orchestra's financial balance. To cope with the disease, the number of seats would have to continually expand (and be filled).

Can television, compact discs, and other mass media cure the cost disease by permitting broader exposure per performance? Unfortunately, some mass media mechanisms are also subject to the cost disease. Mass media incur two types of costs: performance costs and distribution costs. Performance costs are subject to the cost disease—a symphony performance on television incurs about the same costs as a live performance in a concert hall. In neither venue does the labor requirement of the performance decline over time. In contrast, distribution costs may be reduced by technical innovations. As distribution costs are reduced, however, they become an increasingly smaller fraction of total costs. The performance costs, which are subject to cost disease no matter where the performance occurs, come to dominate the total costs. Because the high-tech input is subject to continual innovation, it constitutes a diminishing share of total costs over time.

Theoretically, there is a possible exception. CD, video, and other media performances that can be replayed "as many times as one desires for as many additional persons who care to listen or watch, without any additional performance inputs, may be able to offset the consequences of the cost disease of the original recording if audience size per recording rises cumulatively *at a sufficiently rapid rate*." (Baumol and Baumol 1984, emphasis added). In fact, there has been a dramatic decline in the sales of sound recordings. The Recording Industry Association of America reports that the 2008 value of U.S. shipments of sound recordings was only 58 percent of the value of 1999 shipments. While the 2008 figure surely reflects some impact from the Great Recession, shipments declined throughout the nine-year period, with the exception of a brief uptick in 2004. The news was even worse for classical music recordings, whose share of sound-recording shipments declined from 3.5 percent in 1999 to 1.9 percent in 2008. The value of 2008 shipments of classical recordings was only 32 percent of the 1999 value (Recording Industry Association of America).

Whatever the original hopes for mass media, it is clear that income from broadcasting and recording has played a negligible role in offsetting the relentless performance deficits experienced by orchestras. Many orchestras today have *no* broadcasting and recording income. In 1987 only half of the 63 orchestras studied for this book received broadcasting and recording income. A decade later only 28 orchestras reported such income. Recall that each of these musical organizations has been one of the top 50 orchestras in the United States for at least two years since 1987. The proportion of *all* orchestras without income from mass media is much larger, since the 30 percent of the industry not included in this study are all smaller orchestras that are less likely to receive broadcast and recording opportunities. (In recent years, the League of American Orchestras has not published separate data on broadcast and recording income, but there is no reason to believe that there have been significant changes.)

For the median orchestra with access to mass media in 1987, broadcasting and recording income constituted a mere 0.9 percent of total revenue (2 percent of performance revenue). A decade later this source of income accounted for 0.4 percent of total revenue and 1.2 percent of performance revenue. The percentage ranged from almost zero to just over 6 percent of performance revenue. The evidence that broadcast and recording revenue constitute a small and declining fraction of symphony orchestra income parallels the findings of an earlier Ford Foundation study of symphony orchestras in the 1960s and 1970s (Ford Foundation 1974).

Even these numbers overstate the impact of mass media on orchestra financial balance, because orchestras incur costs for their broadcast and recording activities. On an annual basis, the broadcast and recording income of some orchestras actually falls short of the associated expenses, thereby worsening the performance income gap. In 1987 only 12 of the 31 orchestras with broadcast and recording activities reported revenues that exceeded the costs of these activities. A decade later the situation was even worse: only 5 of the 27 orchestras with such activities reported a surplus on broadcasting and recording. Of course, the income accruing from a particular recording session will be spread over time, so annual figures may not provide an accurate comparison of the benefits and costs of recordings made in a particular year. (Indeed, a few orchestras report broadcast and recording expenses but no offsetting income in some years—presumably reflecting recording activity that has not yet been released.) For about a dozen orchestras, however, broadcast and recording revenues failed to cover expenses throughout 1987–97. At the other extreme, only 15 orchestras averaged a positive net gain from their broadcast and recording activities between 1987 and 1997.

Structural Deficits

All in all, it seems unlikely that performance revenues will increase sufficiently to offset the increasing performance expenses of orchestras. When
performance revenues fall short of performance expenses in a fully employed economy, an orchestra faces what is known as a *structural deficit*.
The disquieting implication of the cost disease arithmetic is that orchestras
will be saddled with ever-growing structural deficits. The evolution of a
structural deficit boils down to a single empirical question: do performance
revenues cover an increasing or decreasing fraction of an orchestra's performance expenses over time? If the incurable cost disease has been offset,
structural deficits will decline as performance revenues cover an increasing
proportion of performance expenses. But if the cost disease has not been
neutralized, performance revenues will cover an ever-diminishing fraction
of performance expenses, and structural deficits will increase. Resolving
this question is of enormous importance for discussions of symphony orchestra policy: if the cost disease cannot be offset, symphony orchestras
will face increasing structural deficits.

Unfortunately, the evidence indicates that the cost disease operated
throughout the 20th century and remains alive and well in the early 21st
century. One may begin with historical observations on the financing of
symphony organizations. As previously mentioned, during a comparatively
brief period in the late 19th century some symphony orchestras were able
to survive as labor cooperatives: performance revenues of those orchestras
actually exceeded their performance expenses sufficiently to provide an ac-
ceptable income for the orchestra musician-owners. The progress of the
cost disease quickly diminished net performance income to levels that were
too small to sustain the allegiance of musicians, however. To survive, orchestras needed to supplement performance revenues sufficiently to provide
musicians with pay increases commensurate with pay growth elsewhere in
the economy. Initially, individual donors made the financial commitments
required to permit orchestras to survive, but as performance revenues covered a declining fraction of performance expenses over time, the resources
and efforts of such angels and their friends gave way to more broadly
based fundraising operations. Second, successive studies of orchestra finances have documented a steady decline in the fraction of performance
expenses covered by performance revenues. While the 1940 study noted
with despair that performance revenues covered "only" 60 percent of their

budgets (Grant and Hettinger 1940), this study finds that, by the 1990–91 concert season, performance revenues averaged 46 percent of performance expenses before declining further to 41 percent in the 2005–6 season. Finally, we present even stronger statistical evidence of the presence of a cost disease in the next chapter.

In short, the revenues collected from concert ticket sales, broadcasting, and recordings have fallen short of the expenses of presenting orchestra concerts for over a century. If the facts were otherwise, we might observe private, profit-seeking orchestras that attracted the funds of investors, many of whom might have no more than a passing interest in music. Financial returns alone would be enough for them to invest. Instead, we find that U.S. symphony orchestras must organize as not-for-profit entities and supplement their revenues from performances with various types of nonperformance income in order to achieve even a financially fragile economic existence. Indeed, this is a key implication of the cost disease: organizations in performing arts, education, and other afflicted sectors must seek other sources of income to offset their ever-increasing structural deficits.

The Need for Nonperformance Income

How do symphony orchestras achieve the financial balance needed to survive in their environment of ongoing, ever-increasing structural deficits? In brief, financial balance requires raising sufficient *nonperformance income* to cover the gap between performance revenues and expenses. Private philanthropy, government subsidies, and investment income (mainly from the orchestra's endowment) constitute the three principal sources of nonperformance income for U.S. orchestras. As not-for-profit organizations, symphonies may receive tax-deductible private contributions from individuals, businesses, and foundations as well as grants from all levels of government. Not-for-profit status may raise the confidence of prospective donors that their funds will be used to pursue the organization's central mission (Hansmann 1996). To obtain some contributions and subsidies, however, orchestras must incur fundraising costs that could be avoided if performance revenues covered operating expenditures.

While nonperformance income can provide economic salvation for symphony orchestras and many other nonprofit institutions, there is a catch. Even with access to nonperformance income, many orchestras continue to lead the precarious economic existence outlined in chapter 1, because there is no guarantee that the various sources of nonperformance income—private philanthropy, government subsidies, and investment income—will exactly cover the structural performance deficit in any particular year. Nor is there a guarantee that nonperformance income will grow rapidly enough over time to offset the growing deficit that is a consequence of the cost disease. This point is of key importance. The implication of the cost disease arithmetic and the century-long evidence of increasing structural deficits is that the nonperformance income provided by private donors, government, and investment earnings must increase indefinitely. Nonperformance income that is sufficient to cover this year's performance deficit will generally be inadequate to cover next year's deficit. Donors should not be surprised when, having stretched to help a symphony meet a financial crisis in one year, they are expected to stretch even further in subsequent years. Diligent orchestras may shrink a performance deficit by devising strategies and policies to raise performance revenues or reduce performance expenses, but without ongoing annual improvements, their need for ever-increasing amounts of nonperformance income will continue indefinitely.

A Model of Symphony Orchestra Finances

The discussion in this chapter is compactly summarized by a simple model of symphony orchestra finances (fig. 2.2). Read from left to right, orchestras

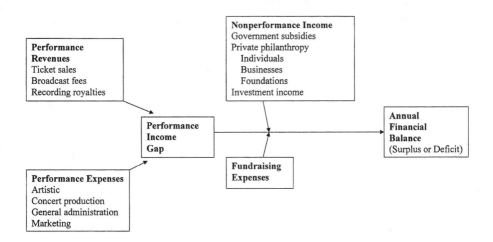

Figure 2.2. Symphony Orchestra Finances

earn performance revenues from their concert ticket sales, broadcasts, and royalties from recordings (discussed further in chapters 4 and 5). Their revenues invariably fall short of their performance expenses for artistic personnel (chapter 6), concert production, general administration, and marketing, yielding a significant operating deficit. The simple arithmetic of the cost disease explains why the operating deficit grows over time.

The performance income gap may be offset in whole or in part by three types of nonperformance income received by orchestras: government subsidies (discussed further in chapter 7), private philanthropy (chapter 8), and investment (endowment) income (chapter 9). To obtain government subsidies and contributions from individuals, businesses, and foundations, however, orchestras must incur fundraising costs that could be avoided if performance revenues exceeded operating expenditures. If philanthropy, government support, and investment income more than offset the performance income gap, the orchestra has an overall financial surplus for the year; if nonperformance income falls short of the gap, there is an overall financial deficit.

The flow of funds outlined in figure 2.2 permits one to "account" for changes in the performance income gap or the annual surplus or deficit. It provides a guide to organizing information on how these financial outcomes changed without providing insights on why the changes occurred. This behavioral question—why various revenues and expenses change in ways that strengthen or weaken an orchestra's financial balance—constitutes the central theme in the rest of this book. The first task, addressed in the next chapter, is to separate the consequences of the cost disease from changes in the general state of the economy.

CHAPTER 3

Cost Disease or Business Cycles?

From Baltimore to Detroit to Pasadena, venerable performing arts institutions are laying off performers, cutting programming, canceling seasons and doing without new sets and live music. Some are closing down completely. Those on the brink face the difficult task of soliciting money from loyal donors who might be facing bankruptcy or unemployment themselves. (Flaccus 2009)

This Associated Press dispatch, bearing the headline "Recession Closes 10% of U.S. Arts Organizations," signals how recessions undermine the economic security of symphony orchestras and other arts organizations. As personal and business incomes fall in the face of layoffs, rising unemployment, reduced work hours, and declining sales, orchestras suffer losses in both performance and nonperformance income. Sales of concert tickets and recorded music wax and wane with variations in personal incomes. And just when orchestras require more nonperformance income to pay their bills, orchestra patrons lack the resources to provide it. Of course, when real incomes subsequently recover during economic expansions, the balance between symphony revenues and expenses improves.

These *cyclical* impacts on symphony budgets—reflecting the impact of business cycles—are quite different from the structural impacts discussed in the previous chapter. Cyclical impacts are reversible; what an orchestra loses during a decline in general business conditions, it generally regains when business conditions improve. The structural impacts on symphony budgets discussed in chapter 2 generally are not reversible. Instead, they are cumulative and produce a need for ever-increasing amounts of nonperformance income. One may think of a structural deficit as the deficit that exists under normal business conditions—when the economy is running at full employment.

Distinguishing carefully between cyclical and structural influences on orchestra finances facilitates diagnoses of the long-term health of symphonies and their policy choices. The first part of this chapter clarifies the respective effects of cycle and trend on the finances of U.S. symphonies and finds that both influences are present. The second part of the chapter considers *why* recessions have such a devastating effect on orchestra finances. The key question is why orchestra revenues fall more rapidly than orchestra expenses in the face of deteriorating business conditions. We are able to compare the responsiveness of different revenues and expenses to changing economic conditions. The chapter concludes with a discussion of the policy choices for orchestras facing both cyclical and structural challenges to their budgets. To the extent that deficits are cyclical, symphonies can view their financial problems as transitory, as long as the government takes prompt countercyclical action with its monetary and fiscal policy tools. To the extent that economic challenges are structural—deficits that persist and worsen even when the economy is operating at full employment—more fundamental changes in orchestra policies are required.

Separating Cyclical and Structural Influences

Fluctuations in general business conditions can obscure underlying trends in revenues and expenses, leading to misinterpretations of the long-term economic health of symphony orchestras. Economic declines, such as followed the September 11, 2001, tragedy and later the collapse of parts of the U.S. financial sector beginning in 2007, produce both excessively optimistic and excessively pessimistic assessments of the economic security of orchestras. Optimists maintain that the financial difficulties are mainly cyclical—a temporary but reversible problem stemming from poor economic conditions. Some may encourage the view that the cost disease does not exist; orchestras only have to address cyclical economic challenges. Pessimists may misinterpret the economic challenges produced by a recession as an increasingly adverse trend in orchestra finances, understating the influence of cyclical conditions.

The analysis in this section confirms that *both* cyclical and structural factors influence symphony deficits. Recessions increase and business expansions reduce the financial distress of orchestras. At the same time, improved economic conditions do not signal that an orchestra's financial challenges are past history. The elimination of the distress associated with a recession still leaves the long-term ongoing financial challenges posed by the cost disease.

These conclusions are not apparent from looking at only one or two years of data. But when both influences are present, statistical analysis of data for a large number of years and orchestras can reveal the respective influence of cycle and trend on performance deficits. Many of the findings reported in this book emerged from multiple regression analyses—a widely used statistical technique that enables one to discover the role of a single influence, say the trend, after controlling for the influence of other factors (such as general economic conditions) in the analysis.

The regression analysis of data for 63 orchestras from 1987–2005 finds both statistically significant cyclical and trend influences on the average orchestra's finances.[1] The results first confirm the importance of cyclical influences (measured by the unemployment rate for the area in which each orchestra is located) on the financial balance of symphony orchestras. On average, a 1 percentage point increase in the local unemployment rate is associated with a .7 percentage point fall in the proportion of performance expense covered by performance revenue—a measure of an orchestra's performance deficit that we shall refer to as the *performance income ratio*. This finding signals an important difference in the responsiveness of performance revenues and performance expenses to changes in business conditions, which can be seen in the next two lines of table 3.1. Performance expenses are much less responsive than revenues to changing business

TABLE 3.1   CYCLE AND TREND BEHAVIOR OF SYMPHONY DEFICITS

	The Effect of	
Dependant Variable	One Percentage Point Increase in Unemployment Rate	One Additional Year
Performance income ratio*	−0.7	−0.2
Performance revenue	−3.8%	1.9%
Performance expense	−1.2%	2.7%

Source: Appendix to chapter 3.

Performance revenues and expenses are in year 2000 dollars.

* The fraction of performance expenses covered by performance revenues.

conditions. For each percentage point increase in the unemployment rate between 1987 and 2005, real (adjusted for inflation) performance revenues declined by almost 4 percent, while real performance expenses declined by only 1.2 percent.

The analysis also finds a statistically significant *trend* deterioration in the performance income ratio (table 3.1, line 1). Year in and year out, after holding the influence of business cycles constant, the percent of performance budgets covered by performance revenues declined by 0.2. That is, each decade the ratio of performance revenue to expenses declined by about 2 percentage points. This is an important, if unwelcome, finding: after controlling for the effects of business conditions, we find that a structural deficit not only exists, but steadily worsens over time. Notwithstanding the many efforts of orchestras to raise performance revenues by developing broader portfolios of concerts (including pops, summer, and family performances), by increasing national and international concert tours, by expanding broadcasting and recording activities, and by educational work in schools, performance revenues cover a decreasing share of performance expenses. Put differently, the implication first discussed in chapter 2—that orchestras can only achieve financial balance by raising ever-increasing amounts of nonperformance income—survives even after considering the impact of general economic conditions on symphony finances. Small wonder that decades-old studies of symphony orchestras reported performance income ratios of 60 percent, while 45 percent is closer to the modern average.

In short, each time business conditions return to normal, orchestras find themselves in a somewhat worse financial condition than they were prior to the economic downturn; their performance revenues cover a smaller fraction of performance expenses. Even if orchestras were able to adjust successfully to the cyclical "weather," the long-run economic "climate" discussed in chapter 2 produces ever-increasing operating deficits. The long-term economic challenges facing symphony orchestras cannot be obscured, denied, or explained away by invoking the consequences of poor business conditions.

Recessions, Revenues, and Expenses

Symphony orchestra performance income ratios decline during recessions because performance revenues are more responsive to business conditions than performance expenses. (Indeed, if expenses declined more rapidly than revenues, an orchestra would actually *reduce* its performance deficit during a recession.) The statistical findings reported in table 3.1 document this asymmetry. As a result, orchestras, like for-profit businesses, face increasingly dire operating deficits as economic conditions worsen.

We also see in table 3.1 that, after adjusting for the effects of general economic conditions, real performance revenues increased 1.9 percent per year more rapidly than inflation between 1987 and 2005. But during the same period, the trend increase in real performance expenses (that is, non-fundraising expenses) was even more rapid—about 2.7 percent per year for the average orchestra. Because the base level of performance expenses exceeded revenues for all orchestras during this period, the difference in the dollar increases in revenues and expenditures was even more dramatic. In terms of dollars, the trend increase in real performance expenses for this group of orchestras was three times larger than the trend increase in real performance income.

The experience of individual orchestras varies considerably around the averages reported in table 3.1. For most of the 63 orchestras in the sample, the trend increase in real performance expenses has exceeded the trend increase in real performance income. As a result, the majority of orchestras have experienced a long-term worsening of their performance income ratio, even after controlling for the perturbations introduced by changes in general economic conditions that are beyond the control of the symphony community.

Business Conditions and Expenses

Orchestra expenses decline less rapidly than revenues during recessions because of decisions made by symphony management or the constraints under which they work. In considering why overall expenses are comparatively unresponsive, it may be helpful to examine the responsiveness of specific expense categories. This section examines the sensitivity of various orchestra expenses to economic conditions and the long-term trend in each expense after holding cyclical influences constant.

The cycle-trend analysis of specific expenses is reported in table 3.2. We see in line 3, for example, that artistic expenditures, which mainly include the compensation of musicians, conductors, and guest artists, average 50 percent of total orchestra expenses, and that a 1 percent increase in the

TABLE 3.2   CYCLE AND TREND BEHAVIOR OF SYMPHONY EXPENSES

Expense Category	Share of Total Expenses	The Effect of	
		One Percentage Point Increase in Unemployment Rate	One Additional Year
Total	100	−1.1%	2.7%
Performance	95	−1.2%	2.7%
Artistic	50	No effect	2.1%
Concert production	16	−1.3%	5.5%
General administration	10	−1.8%	2.4%
Marketing	11	−2.8%	4.2%
Fundraising	5	No effect	4.1%

Source: Appendix to chapter 3.

Notes: All expenses in year 2000 dollars.

"No effect" = no statistically significant effect.

local unemployment rate is not significantly associated with artistic expenditures. In other words, these expenditures are not sensitive to changes in general business conditions. There is also a statistically significant upward time trend in artistic expenditures (column 3). After controlling for the effects of economic conditions, artistic expenditures increase by 2.1 percent per year for the average orchestra. The rest of table 3.2 may be interpreted accordingly.

Artistic costs and fundraising costs (which account for 5 percent of total expenses) are largely responsible for the fact that orchestra expenses are less responsive than orchestra revenues to changing economic conditions. These are the only expense categories that are *not* significantly related to business conditions. Since the data that have been analyzed reflect the effect of any efforts that symphony organizations have made to contain expenses, one may surmise that it is more difficult to reduce these expenses than the costs of concert production, general administration, and marketing in the face of deteriorating economic conditions.

The table also clarifies the main sources of the trend growth of orchestra expenses. All categories of orchestra expenses grew more rapidly than inflation between 1987 and 2005. (The right-hand column reports the annual growth rate.) After holding the effects of general economic conditions constant, concert production, marketing, and fundraising expenses grew most rapidly. At 2.1 and 2.4 percent per year, respectively, artistic and general administration costs grew least rapidly.

Business Conditions and Revenues

The preceding analysis established that symphony orchestras in the United States face a growing structural deficit, exacerbated at times by the effects of recessions. Orchestras try to acquire nonperformance income to maintain overall financial balance, but there is no guarantee that the amounts raised will be sufficient to cover performance deficits. Clearly, an orchestra's need for supplementary income is greatest in recessions, when performance revenues decline more rapidly than expenses. Unfortunately, as the Associated Press dispatch that began this chapter implied, nonperformance income is not always available when orchestras need it most.

Regression analyses of the cycle and trend behavior of specific sources of orchestra revenue indicate that each percentage point increase in the local unemployment rate is associated with a 1.5 percent reduction in nonperformance income (table 3.3, line 3). This outcome reflects underlying cyclical variations in government support, private philanthropy, and investment income. Government support, constituting the smallest share of nonperformance income, is three times more sensitive to economic conditions than private support. While each component of private support taken alone was not reliably related to general economic conditions between 1987 and 2005, aggregate private support was sensitive to business conditions. Investment income is also highly sensitive to cyclical conditions. The twin declines in performance and nonperformance income leave orchestras with little choice but to turn to endowment reserves to meet the financial challenges of recessions.

Contributed support has played a more constructive role in meeting the long-term financial challenge, however. After holding the cyclical influences on symphony revenues constant, statistically significant trends result in all categories of real performance and nonperformance income except government support (table 3.3, column 3). Each year, the performance revenue of U.S. orchestras on average increases about 1.9 percent faster than inflation. The trend increase in real nonperformance income is even larger: 3.5 percent per year more than inflation. Underlying this increase are sharply divergent trends in private and government support. For the

TABLE 3.3   CYCLE AND TREND BEHAVIOR OF SYMPHONY REVENUES

		The Effect of		
Revenue Category	Share of Total Income	One Percentage Point Increase in Unemployment Rate	One Additional Year	Post-2000
Total income	100	−1.5%	3.5%	0.1%
Performance revenue	30	−3.8%	1.9%	No effect
Nonperformance income	70	−1.5%	3.5%	0.2%
Public support	5	−4.2%	−4.4%	0.1%
Private support	42	−1.1%	4.4%	No effect
Individual	22	No effect	4.8%	0.1%
Business	6	No effect	1.7%	−0.01%
Foundation	9	No effect	8.7%	−0.2%
Investment inc.	13	−8.6%	5.5%	0.5%

Source: Appendix to Chapter 3.
Notes: Revenues in year 2000 dollars.
"No effect" = no statistically significant effect.

average orchestra in this sample, real government support failed to keep up with inflation, diminishing by 4.4 percent per year, after controlling for the effects of economic conditions. More than counterbalancing this decline was a trend increase in private support. After controlling for the effects of economic conditions, all sources of private support have increased more rapidly than inflation over time. The trend increase has been most rapid for foundations (about 8.7 percent per year). The growth of donations from individuals accounted for a much larger volume of support, however, because of their large share (50 percent) of total private support.

A Post-2000 Effect?

Estimates of how orchestra revenues change during economic cycles and how they evolve over time can guide our understanding of the impact of current economic events on orchestras. Consider the economic recession that greeted the 21st century and was exacerbated by the September 11, 2001, tragedy. Increasing unemployment accompanied this deteriorating economic situation, and the preceding analysis would predict that symphony revenues would initially decline before improving as the economy recovered. The analysis would also predict that, following the economic recovery, orchestras would be left with larger performance deficits given the trend decline in the ratio of performance revenues to expenses. This in essence is what happened.

An alternative view, sometimes expressed by parties that wish to maintain the status quo in orchestra policies, holds that the events of the early 21st century produced an unusually large decline in revenues in response to growing unemployment. This view further holds that economic recovery would restore the revenues, so that no fundamental changes in orchestra policies would be needed to restore financial balance.

The orchestra data used in this study permit a careful examination of this alternative view. Several statistical tests were conducted to determine whether a "post-2000" effect on orchestra revenues could be identified. These tests indicate that the cyclical change in orchestra revenues in the early 21st century was no different than in earlier recessions. The analyses also examined the possibility that the trends in various orchestra revenues changed after 2000. The right-hand column of table 3.3 reports the results of those tests. No evidence of a post-2000 decline in the trends in performance revenues or private support emerges from the analysis. On average, these revenues continued to increase at the rates reported in column 3 of the table. Contrary to the alternative view, there is evidence of small but statistically significant *increases* in the trends for government support and investment income.

This brings us to the bottom line: the role of cyclical and trend factors in the evolution of the overall financial balance of symphony orchestras in the United States. Since both performance deficits and contributed support are cyclically sensitive, recessions worsen but economic expansions improve the overall surplus/deficit position of the average orchestra. In short, the financial burdens that recessions place on orchestras reflect the impact on both performance *and* nonperformance revenues and expenses. Recessions aggravate the financial balance of symphony orchestras to an important extent by depressing private contributions and investment income when they are needed most to offset growing performance deficits.

Each year between 1987 and 2005, the trend increase in combined performance and nonperformance revenue modestly exceeded the trend increase in total expenses. As a result, there was a small but statistically significant trend improvement in the overall financial balance of the average symphony in the sample. In interpreting this gentle trend toward surplus, however, consider the following factors: (1) A trend toward surplus is different from a surplus. Most of the 63 orchestras continued to run an overall deficit at the end of the sample period. (2) To the extent that the trend toward surplus reflects excessive draws of investment income from endowments, it masks a serious long-run financial challenge to orchestras (see chapter 9). (3) The effects of small adverse cyclical changes can overwhelm the positive trend. The statistical results indicate that the financial consequences of a one-half of a percentage point increase in the unemployment rate would completely counter the trend toward surplus in any year. The practical importance of this point for orchestra finances became all too apparent during the Great Recession that ended the first decade of the 21st century.

Adjusting to the Weather and Adjusting to the Climate

This chapter began by noting that financial challenges rooted in business cycles have very different policy implications for symphony orchestras than financial challenges rooted in long-term, structural factors. The former present no fundamental challenge to an orchestra's policy status quo—only a need to adapt the basic business model to the ebb and flow of general economic conditions. In contrast, structural financial challenges require fundamental alterations in an orchestra's basic business model to counter the ongoing effects of the cost disease, changing tastes for live performance of classical music, or both. With such differences in policy implications, understanding the root cause of an orchestra's financial difficulties becomes crucial.

As it happens, the data submitted by orchestras themselves indicate that U.S. symphony orchestras face *both* cyclical and structural (trend) financial challenges. One cannot deny the existence of a long-term financial challenge by claiming that current difficulties are only cyclical and will take care of themselves. The evidence is quite clear on that. Instead, orchestras need policies to address both the short-term cyclical weather and the long-term climate defined by the cost disease. Here are some examples.

Adjusting to the Weather

Forecasting changes in the weather. Symphony orchestras cannot by themselves reverse economic cycles, but with sufficient advance warning those orchestras that are financially and operationally nimble may be able to take actions to mitigate the impact of cyclical changes. There are leading indicators of economic activity that provide advance warning of changes in business conditions. For almost 50 years, the Conference Board's Composite Indexes of Leading Economic Indicators (http://www.conference-board .org/data/bci.cfm) has, on average, predicted the onset of recessions about 11 months in advance and the onset of recoveries about seven months in advance. Leading economic indicators can provide the orchestra industry with information that assists forward planning to address the variations in the performance income gap and contributed support that accompany cyclical fluctuations.

Saving for a rainy day. Orchestras may build surpluses when economic conditions are good, creating the reserves that may be used to achieve financial balance when business conditions are poor. Building and managing endowments, an important part of this approach, are discussed in chapter 9.

Reducing the cyclical sensitivity of financial balance. The cyclical variation in performance deficits results from the combination of flexible revenues and less flexible costs. Insulating symphony orchestras from the effects of business cycles requires less flexible revenues, more flexible expenses, or both. If costs were more responsive or revenues were less responsive to general business conditions, financial balance would be less dependent on the cyclical weather. There may be little that orchestras can do about the expenditure decisions of potential patrons and donors during recessions, but they can determine how and why different expenses vary with business conditions.

Adjusting to the Climate

Addressing a structural deficit requires rethinking an organization's underlying business model—a potentially more threatening process than meeting cyclical challenges. Combating structural deficits often requires a hard look at the nature and composition of expenses, the interactions among expenses and revenues, and the relationship between these fiscal measures and the financial strategies that support and advance the organization's mission.

Historically, orchestras have introduced many changes in their business models to offset structural deficits. Most symphonies have moved beyond the old labor cooperative model by identifying wealthy angels, expanding the size of boards of trustees, broadening their subscription base, instituting public fund drives, building endowments, introducing domestic and foreign orchestra tours, taking advantage of broadcast and recording opportunities, targeting different tastes through a variety of concert series (regular season, pops, summer, and so on), and expanding educational work in school systems. Some of these activities can produce immediate gains for orchestras. Others, such as educational work, seek a long-term payoff by building future audiences.

One must recognize, however, that the effects of these activities on the financial position of orchestras are already embedded in the data analyzed for this chapter. The long-term trends reported in this chapter have emerged despite the wide-ranging audience-building activities that symphonies have adopted to date. The structural problem facing orchestras would have been even worse without those policies. Continual policy innovations that variously raise performance and nonperformance revenues and reduce expenses are necessary to counter the ongoing growth of structural deficits.

The rest of this book tries to explain the behavior of orchestra revenues and costs in ways that illuminate how orchestra policies might achieve structural change while maintaining artistic goals. In particular, it explores how the various orchestra revenues and expenses are linked to three potential influences: policy decisions of symphony orchestras, economic characteristics of local markets, and competition from other performing arts organizations.

The influence of orchestra policy decisions and the effectiveness with which those decisions are implemented is perhaps most obvious. Less obvious is the role of local market characteristics. The market areas in which symphony orchestras operate in the United States vary enormously in population, income, wealth, and other attributes that influence the potential for concert and nonperformance income, and hence the artistic and nonartistic expenses that orchestras can support. Moreover, the economic capacity of local markets changes over time. Symphonies must live within the means provided by a community's economic base and accommodate their operations to changes in that base. Perhaps least obvious is the role of competition among performing arts organizations. Irrespective of their financial wealth, everyone faces the same fixed time budget. Time spent attending an opera or ballet performance cannot be spent enjoying a symphony orchestra concert. Consumers must make choices not only about *whether* they patronize the arts, but also *which* performing arts they patronize. To an extent, the financial strength of any performing arts organization may depend on the policies of other (competing) arts organizations.

CHAPTER 4

Snapshots of Symphony Orchestra Finances

While it should now be clear why orchestras cannot survive as profit-seeking organizations, we cannot understand the varied economic success of nonprofit symphony orchestras without learning more about where their money comes from and how it is spent. That is the task of this chapter, which describes the flows of revenues and expenses for orchestras in the United States and provides clues about how these economic flows may differ for orchestras in other countries. The chapter leads to identification of three broad strategies available to orchestras in their quest for financial balance.

The Revenues of Symphony Orchestras

All the highly visible ways in which symphony orchestras earn income yield less than half the funds that they need to survive. Between 1987 and 2005, performance revenue dropped from 48 percent to a mere 37 percent of the average symphony's income. During this period, private philanthropy and investment income grew sufficiently rapidly to counter the growing operating deficits of orchestras and declining government support. Private contributions from individuals, businesses, and foundations, which grew to 70 percent of nonperformance income (45 percent of total income) by 2005, have been the key source of external support for orchestras (fig. 4.1).

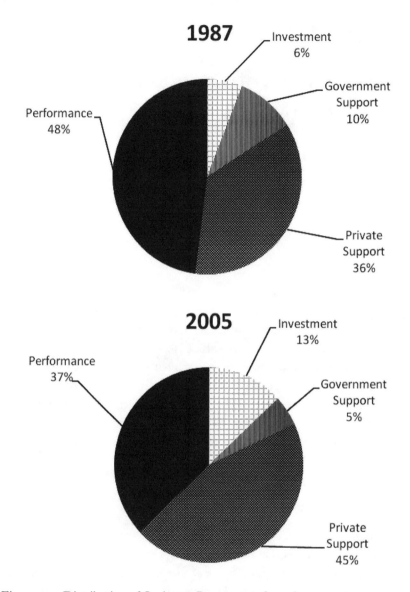

Figure 4.1. Distribution of Orchestra Revenues, 1987 and 2005
Source: League of American Orchestras

Symphony orchestras earn most of their performance revenues from a variety of concerts offered to their communities, from broadcasts, and from the sales of recordings. Virtually all orchestras perform regular season concerts, which offer both subscription tickets for a series of concerts and single tickets for individual concerts. These regular season concerts provide the largest single component of performance income, averaging about 36 percent in the early years of the 21st century. Most orchestras also offer other types of concerts targeted at particular audiences or tastes. Most common are pops concerts and summer concerts, which respectively average 24 and 8 percent of annual performance revenues. Educational concerts in area schools introduce many students to the orchestral literature and may help to build future audiences. Modern concert audiences are disproportionately composed of people who participated in some form of musical performance during their youth. Orchestras also may offer chamber orchestra concerts or accompany choral, ballet, or opera performances.

A minority of orchestras supplement the income received from local concerts by taking domestic or foreign concert tours. In an average year between 1987 and 2005, 15 of the 63 sample orchestras performed concerts elsewhere in their home state, 18 toured other states, and 11 earned income from foreign concert tours. Orchestras that tour nationally often tour other countries as well, but there is little correlation between giving additional in-state concerts and conducting domestic and foreign tours. Only the more renowned orchestras appear to have consistent domestic and foreign touring opportunities. Whatever the prestige associated with concert tours, the income that orchestras receive from those tours constitutes a small percentage of performance revenue—usually in the low to medium single digits. The income earned from domestic and foreign touring (adjusted for inflation) has increased over time, but the share of tour revenues in performance income has declined slightly. One might add that tours impose incremental costs. If these costs are not covered by tour ticket sales or special donations, orchestras may pay a price for the prestige of touring.

Some of the more renowned orchestras may supplement their concert income by broadcasting and recording. As noted in chapter 2, however, fewer than half of the 63 orchestras receive such income, and it averaged just over 1 percent of their performance income by the early 21st century. Over time the share of broadcasting and recording income in U.S. orchestra revenues has declined. The opportunities for expanding income from recordings seem limited now, as more and more classical music recording activity shifts to Europe.

A minority of orchestras own the concert halls in which they perform. Economists stress that they do not avoid rental expenses by owning the hall, however. For each performance, they incur an opportunity cost equal

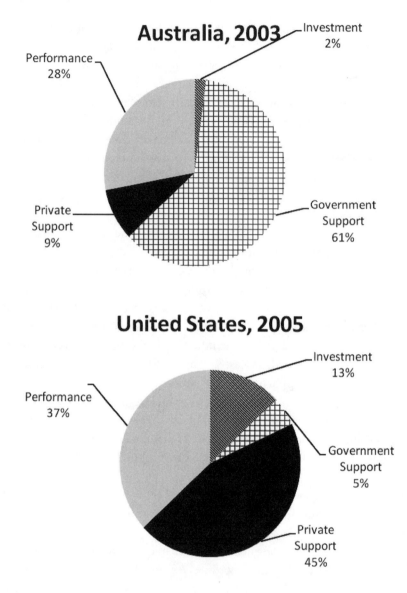

Figure 4.2. Orchestra Revenues, Australia and the United States
Source: Australia, Orchestras Review (2005) and League of American Orchestras

to the amount they could have earned by renting the hall to another organization rather than using it themselves. When an orchestra does rent its hall to another organization, it earns revenues. For the minority of orchestras reporting such rental earnings, the share of earned income is in the low single digits.

TABLE 4.1   DISTRIBUTION OF REVENUES, U.S. ORCHESTRAS, 2005

Revenue Source	Mean	Minimum	Maximum
Performance revenue	37%	18%	74%
Private support	45%	18%	66%
Government subsidies	5%	0.2%	28%
Investment income	13%	−2%	36%

Source: League of American Orchestras, Orchestra Statistical Reports (OSR).

The respective roles of the public and private sectors in funding symphony orchestras are quite different outside the United States. Contrast the revenue sources of Australian and U.S. orchestras reported in figure 4.2, for example. Government subsidies, a small and declining resource for U.S. orchestras, provide over 60 percent of the annual revenues of major Australian orchestras. Almost as arresting are the facts that private contributions to Australian orchestras are comparatively small, and investment income barely exists. Moreover, Australian orchestras receive just a little over a quarter of their income from performance revenues—mainly ticket revenues from private patrons. Clearly the United States and Australia follow radically different approaches to funding their orchestras. (Figure 4.2 is but a preview of a broader discussion in chapter 10, where we shall see that the Australian approach is closer to the norm for supporting orchestras in other countries.) Direct subsidies, of course, are not the only way in which governments offer support to the arts. Readers are urged to suspend judgment on this issue until chapter 7.

Individual U.S. orchestras do not follow a common financial model. Their performance revenues range from 18 to 74 percent of total revenues; the share of government subsidies ranges from 0.2 to 28 percent, and private support can be as low as 18 percent for some orchestras and as high as 66 percent for others (see table 4.1). In chapter 10 we shall see that even the smallest reliance on private support by a U.S. orchestra greatly exceeds the share of donations in the revenues of foreign orchestras.

The Expenses of Symphony Orchestras

The audience at a fine symphony concert might be surprised to learn that no more than half the costs of the concert are payments to the musicians, conductor, and guest soloist(s) that they observe on the stage. Artistic costs

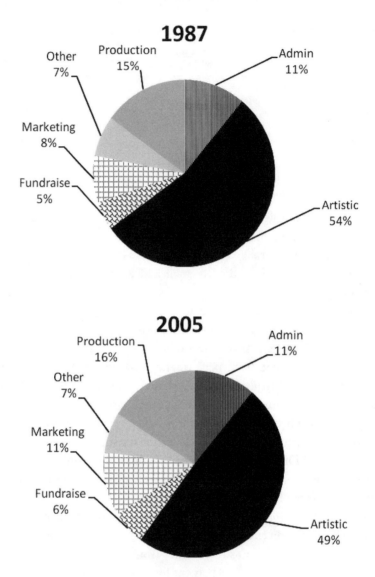

Figure 4.3. Distribution of Orchestra Expenses, 1987 and 2005
Source: League of American Orchestras

remain the primary expense of orchestras, but their share of the annual budget has slowly diminished (fig. 4.3). The cost of musicians dominates artistic costs. While there are claims that the escalating salaries of superstar conductors and concert soloists drive cost pressures in symphony orchestras, these claims seem exaggerated. Conductors' pay averaged 6 percent of artistic personnel costs each year between 1992 and 2001, the years for which such data are available. Between 1987 and 2005, payments to guest soloists and guest conductors averaged between 14 and 16 percent of artistic personnel costs (i.e., roughly 7 to 8 percent of total orchestra costs), with no clear trend. In short, the remarkable salaries received by extremely talented artists sometimes attract notorious publicity, but they represent a modest and rather constant fraction of the artistic costs incurred by orchestras.

Concert production costs include expenses for the rental of a concert hall; stagehands; operation of a ticket office; the purchase, rental, or commissioning of the orchestra's music; musical instrument maintenance, tuning, and (during tours) cartage; and salaries and benefits for production personnel. These expenses remained a fairly constant share of orchestra expenses between 1987 and 2005. Orchestras also incur a variety of general administrative expenses, including legal and accounting fees, rental of office space, utilities, insurance, and, of course, salaries and benefits for administrative personnel. The share of these expenses has also remained constant.

Orchestras also incur marketing expenses in their efforts to sell tickets and to build and retain audiences. These expenditures fund an increasingly diverse array of direct mail, print, and broadcast advertising, the identification of distinct audience segments through research into classical music tastes, and the design of novel concert and pricing packages. As orchestras try to combat declining attendance trends (in ways discussed more fully in the next chapter), marketing expenses have slowly increased as a fraction of total performance expenses. The fundraising activities that orchestras mount to increase nonperformance income claim a small but increasing fraction of orchestra budgets.

The structure of orchestra expenses can also differ elsewhere in the world. Orchestras that can rely on government support do not need to spend money on major fundraising campaigns, and they may be less worried about attracting audiences. It is not surprising, therefore, that fundraising and marketing costs are lower in Australia than the United States. At the same time, there is a huge difference in the share of artistic costs, possibly because regular public subsidies erode resistance to wage demands by musicians (see fig. 4.4).

Further evidence that U.S. orchestras do not follow a common financial model emerges from the wide variation in the cost structures of indi-

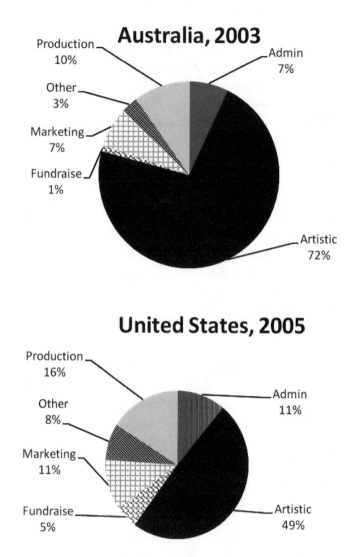

Figure 4.4. Orchestra Expenses, Australia and the United States
Source: Australia, Orchestras Review (2005) and League of American Orchestras

vidual orchestras (table 4.2). Artistic costs range from a quarter to two-thirds of annual expenses, while administrative costs range from 5 percent to over half of costs. The remarkable differences in cost structures raise the question of best practices in the orchestra industry. Despite differences in their concert portfolios, most orchestras perform a similar set of activities. If they were in more direct competition with each other, one might

TABLE 4.2   DISTRIBUTION OF EXPENSES, U.S. ORCHESTRAS, 2005

Expense Source	Mean	Minimum	Maximum
Artistic	49%	25%	67%
Production	16%	6%	26%
Administration	11%	5%	53%
Marketing	11%	4%	21%
Fundraising	6%	1%	12%

Source: League of American Orchestras, OSR.

expect superior practices to be widely emulated, generating more similar revenue and expense structures. The wide variation that exists may signal a tendency to address economic challenges by seeking new sources of non-performance income rather than identifying and adopting best practices that might reduce performance deficits.

Three Strategies for Meeting Economic Challenges

This brief review of where a symphony orchestra's money comes from and how it is spent clarifies the three broad strategies available to addressing their economic challenges. Orchestras may work to increase the growth of performance revenues, reduce the growth of performance expenses, and/or increase the growth of nonperformance income. Each of these broad strategies implies specific activities. Subsequent chapters illuminate the possibilities and pitfalls associated with each strategy, and why different orchestras might choose different strategy combinations.

Growing performance income is largely a matter of building new audiences for symphonic music, the topic of the next chapter. Reducing the growth of expenses—no doubt the least welcome of the strategies in any organization—forces attention on the evolution of artistic costs, the largest category of expenses (chapter 6), and incremental expenditures on marketing (chapter 5) and fundraising activities (chapter 8). Increasing nonperformance revenues more rapidly offers the most eclectic possibilities from seeking government funds (chapter 7), attracting private donations from individuals, companies, and foundations (chapter 8), or generating more investment income by improving the management of orchestra endowments (chapter 9).

CHAPTER 5

The Search for Symphony Audiences

Raising performance revenues is largely a matter of building and retaining audiences and pricing tickets to increase revenues, the topics of this chapter. These goals must be easier to state than to achieve, since the evidence in chapter 3 showed that performance revenues have fallen further and further behind performance expenses over time. This chapter shows how the policies of orchestras, the economic characteristics of local communities, and competition from other performing arts all play a role in the search for larger audiences.

Who Attends Symphony Orchestra Concerts?

Much of what we know about performing arts audiences in the United States comes from surveys conducted by the National Endowment for the Arts (NEA) since 1982 of the "arts participation" of the U.S. population. In these surveys, the proportion of the adult population reporting that they attended at least one performance of various art forms in the past year increased with education and income. Almost 60 percent of the audience for classical music (symphony, chamber, or choral music performance), but only 27 percent of the general population, had at least a college degree in 2008. Likewise, 72 percent of the classical music audience, but only 52 percent of the general population, had incomes over $50,000. The frequency of concert attendance also increased with education and income (NEA 2009).

Whites are more likely to attend a classical concert than other racial/ethnic groups, and women are more likely to attend than men (although

TABLE 5.1   CLASSICAL MUSIC CONCERT ATTENDANCE, 1982–2008

	1982	1992	2002	2008
Percentage of adults[1]	13.0%	12.5%	11.6%	9.3%
Millions of adults[1]	21.3	23.2	23.8	20.9
Number of attendances	n.a	60.3	72.8	60.4
Attendances per adult	n.a.	2.6	3.1	2.9

Source: NEA (2009), figures 3–7 and 3–8.

[1]Percentage or number of adults attending at least one classical music concert during the past year.

n.a. = not available.

men attend more frequently). Differences in education, income, and other socioeconomic characteristics explain only some of the differences in attendance between ethnic groups (DiMaggio and Ostrower 1992). The remaining differences presumably reflect ethnically based differences in taste or access to classical music.

In some respects, these attendance patterns seem like good news for symphony orchestras, since both the proportion of the population with a college degree and the level of real income have increased over time. From these facts, it would seem that the fraction of the population attending classical music concerts should have grown. But the surveys tell us that it has not. In fact, the NEA surveys record a distinct decline in the public's overall participation in classical music. After declining quite slowly for 20 years following the first survey in 1982, the percentage of adults who say they attended at least one classical music performance a year dropped precipitously between 2002 and 2008 (table 5.1, line 1). Of course, the U.S. population increased over this period, so the size of the concert audience could have increased. But the second line of table 5.1 shows a decline of almost 2.9 million people attending at least one classical concert annually between 2002 and 2008. Some concertgoers attend multiple concerts each year, but we see that both the number of attendances and the number of attendances per person have fallen since 2002 (table 5.1, lines 3 and 4).

The 2002–8 decline cannot be attributed to a weakening economy—the national unemployment rate was identical in each year. Despite changes in the income and education of the American population, and despite the increasingly sophisticated marketing strategies developed and implemented by symphony orchestras, audience size has not kept pace with population increases during the late 20th and early 21st century.

With declining attendance despite increasing education, income, and population, a smaller proportion of each new cohort of college graduates must attend concerts. Analyses of NEA surveys confirm that the proportion of college-educated people attending classical concerts declined substantially between 1982 and 2008 (DiMaggio and Mukhtar 2004; League of American Orchestras 2009). Reduced participation by each new cohort generates another frequently noted trend: concert audiences are aging more rapidly than the general population. Since 1982 the proportion of classical music audiences over the age of 45 years has increased from 40 percent to 59 percent, while the proportion of the U.S. adult population in that age group has increased from 42 percent to 51 percent (Peterson, Hull, and Kern 1998; League of American Orchestras 2009).

These developments are not unique to U.S. orchestras. Many foreign orchestras report similar trends, as will become apparent in chapter 10. Even within the United States, symphony orchestras are not the only art form losing their audiences; the NEA surveys reveal similar trends in other performing arts. By 2008 the number of adults attending at least one opera, ballet, or jazz performance during the year was lower than in 1992. Of all the performing arts, only musical plays had increased attendance (NEA 2009). Recognizing that the experience of orchestras may be part of a much broader social phenomenon may facilitate diagnosis of the problem and should caution against the view that orchestra policies alone may reverse this unwelcome development. A problem that affects the entire performing arts industry calls for a broader perspective on solutions. We return to this theme at the end of the chapter.

Concerts and Attendance

Offering more concerts may seem like an obvious, if somewhat mechanical, approach to building audiences. The experience of U.S. symphony orchestras since 1987 illustrates the limitation of this approach. Symphony orchestra activity increased in the late 20th century. In 1987 the number of concerts per season by the median orchestra in the sample was 175. Subsequently, most orchestras added more concerts to their schedules, with larger symphonies expanding their concert schedules the most. Between the 1987 and 2003 concert seasons, the median number of concerts of all types rose about 11 percent to 197 per year, before falling to 179 concerts in the 2005–6 season. The mix of concerts played by U.S. symphony orchestras changed modestly as the total increased, with the share of regular season, summer, and on-tour concerts declining and the share of pops and educational concerts increasing.

Despite the increasing number of concerts, however, concert attendance declined. Median annual attendance at U.S. symphony orchestra concerts was about 218,000 in 1987. After declining during the first half of the 1990s, it recovered to about 215,000 in 2000, before falling during the recession that began the new century to about 192,000 in 2005.[1] By that year the median annual concert attendance for these symphonies was only 88 percent of its 1987 level.

Interpretations of changing concert attendance often confuse short-term cyclical impacts with long-term trends. Concert attendance generally rises in good times and falls in bad times as the income and employment of concert patrons changes. Such cyclical fluctuations in attendance are the major source of the cyclical sensitivity of performance revenues noted in chapter 3. But cyclical variations in concert attendance reflect different influences than long-term trends. Efforts to counter fluctuating attendance therefore require knowledge of the exact roles of cycle and trend. Since cyclical and trend influences on concert attendance operate concurrently, it takes a statistical analysis to identify their separate influences.

A statistical analysis of our sample of 63 U.S. symphony orchestras confirms the importance of both cycle and trend changes in concert attendance. A one percentage point increase in the local unemployment rate (say, from 5 to 6 percent) is associated with a 4 percent decrease in annual concert attendance for the average orchestra (and conversely during expansions). After holding the cyclical impact constant, the analysis also reveals a statistically significant trend decrease in average annual attendance of about 2 percent per year.[2] Clearly, more factors than changing general business conditions were at work in the 1987–2005 decrease in concert attendance. Some of the trend increase in performance deficits identified in chapter 3 reflects a trend decline in concert patronage. Orchestras seeking higher performance revenues must reverse that trend.

Making matters worse, an adverse change in the composition of ticket sales accompanied declining concert attendance. Sales of subscription tickets for a season of concerts—a mainstay of orchestra finances since the 18th century—fell relative to sales of tickets for single concerts. In 1991 the median orchestra sold five subscription tickets for every single ticket for both regular and pops concerts. By 1997 it sold only three subscription tickets for every single ticket sold for regular concerts. For pops concerts, the ratio declined from 5 to 3.5 subscription tickets per single ticket.

More is at stake than the loss of patrons who are most likely to have a long-term commitment to orchestras. Single ticket prices generally exceed subscription ticket prices, but two factors offset this positive effect on performance revenue. The cost of marketing and selling a single ticket is also higher, and subscribers are a more reliable source of philanthropic donations to orchestras than purchasers of single tickets.

Attendance per Concert

The combination of increasing concerts and declining total attendance produced a precipitous decline in attendance per concert at the end of the 20th century (fig. 5.1). The decline was broad-based, ranging from the regular season concerts that historically have attracted the most dedicated patrons to the educational concerts designed to build future audiences.

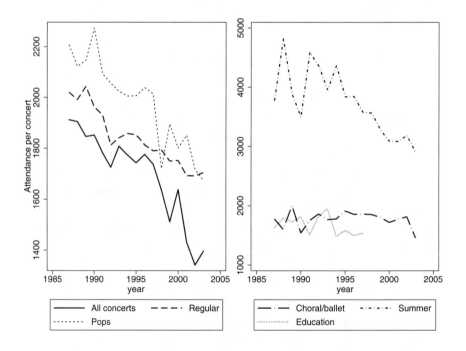

Figure 5.1. Attendance per Concert, 1987–2003
Source: League of American Orchestras

After adjusting for the effects of cyclical fluctuations, overall attendance per concert declined by 2.8 percent per year. The annual decline was about 1.5 percent at regular season and pops concerts and about half that rate at choral concerts. No type of concert experienced a trend increase in attendance per concert.

The eventual shortcomings of trying to build audiences and revenues by adding concerts are now apparent. Orchestras offer more concerts in an effort to increase concert attendance and performance revenue. *Total* concert attendance does increase with the number of concerts performed, but each additional concert yields a smaller increase in attendance and hence revenues. There is a further problem. Even though many costs incurred by symphony orchestras are fixed annually, the incremental costs of adding another concert are usually far from zero. Eventually, the diminishing attendance gains yield so little incremental revenue that additional concerts will worsen performance deficits.

Here is an alternative perspective from the analysis. Each year trend factors reduce attendance by about 2 percent. Each additional concert restores only a small fraction of that loss. The average orchestra would have to incur the costs of adding 13 concerts per year to its schedule in order to counter one year's trend decline in attendance. Because of the diminishing effects of concerts on attendance, orchestras with the largest concert schedules would have to add even more concerts annually to overcome the trend decline in attendance. And at some point the diminishing revenues do not justify the costs that are incurred.

Influences on Attendance per Concert

If we are to understand why performance revenues do not keep pace with performance expenses, we must determine why attendance per concert fell during the late 20th century. A simple supply-and-demand model facilitates understanding. Symphony orchestras supply concert performances. The capacity of the hall sets the number of seats for each performance, but the capacity is rarely reached by most U.S. orchestras. The demand for each performance determines how many of the seats are actually filed.

Explaining changes in attendance per concert becomes a question of discovering what influences the demand for performances. The key underlying fact is that attending any performance entails significant commitments of money and time. While real income generally increases over time, relaxing the financial constraints faced by potential concert patrons, time budgets remain fixed and constitute a significant deterrent. A 1997 study of how people spent their time found that "attendance at museums, concerts and other cultural events . . . translates to an average of 5 minutes a week or just over 4 hours a year of arts participation per capita" (Robinson and Godbey 1997, p. 174). Of course, this average includes the behavior of people who never attend concerts along with that of regular concert patrons, but it makes the point that time constraints force consumers to choose among arts performances and between attending any arts performance and other uses of their time.

Orchestra Policies: Ticket Price Levels

The ticket prices set for admission to a concert constitute a potentially powerful influence on attendance and performance revenues. The answers to two questions define the link between ticket pricing and performance revenues: How sensitive is concert attendance to the average ticket price? What is the structure of ticket prices for different seats that will maximize symphony revenues?

Between 1987 and 1997, the prices of subscription tickets to regular season and pops concerts increased more rapidly than indices of all consumer prices and of the prices of movies, theater, and sports events (fig. 5.2).[3] Raising relative prices does not guarantee higher revenues, however, because higher prices may make movies, sports events, and other activities more attractive uses of leisure time. Virtually all products and services face a tradeoff between the price charged and the quantity sold. Raising prices invariably reduces sales.

Nevertheless, if a ticket price increase is proportionately greater than the reduction in tickets sold, performance revenues will increase. The key empirical question is whether ticket sales are sufficiently inelastic in response to ticket price increases to produce a revenue increase. In general, the sales response will be least sensitive to price changes when there are few related products or services that the consumer can shift to in the face of a price increase. In the case of symphony orchestra performances, a perfect substitute would be the same program performed by another orchestra of comparable quality on the same night in a nearby venue—an unlikely event. Other cultural experiences, however, can provide near substitutes. In cities with a relatively large number of alternative cultural experiences,

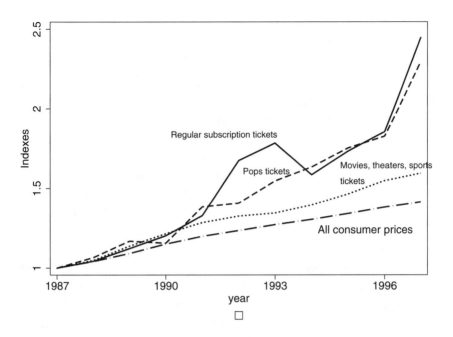

Figure 5.2. Concert Ticket Prices and Consumer Prices, 1987–97
Source: League of American Orchestras and U.S. Bureau of Labor Statistics

ticket sales may be more sensitive to ticket pricing than in cities with few cultural alternatives. Higher ticket prices may also encourage potential patrons to spend their leisure time in activities outside the arts.

The pricing of concert tickets is further complicated by the fact that concert patrons—particularly subscribers—are among the most reliable contributors of nonperformance income to orchestras. Indeed, symphony orchestras and other cultural organizations often encourage "voluntary" annual, lump-sum donations by subscribers in order to maintain or improve the quality of their seats. Any loss of subscribers from higher ticket prices may reduce private donations to an orchestra. Put differently, in pricing tickets, orchestras must consider the effects on *total* revenue—not just the impact on performance revenue discussed in the prior paragraph. The fact that concert patrons are also reliable sources of contributions argues for ticket prices that are below the level that maximizes performance revenue (Rosen and Rosenfield 1997; Caves 2000).

A statistical analysis of variations in attendance per concert between 1987 and 2005 confirmed the importance of the ticket pricing policies of symphony orchestras.[4] Attendance at both regular season and pops concerts is inversely related to the ticket prices charged for those events. Higher ticket prices are associated with lower attendance and vice versa. The fact that symphony patrons can turn to alternative uses of their leisure time as the price of symphony tickets rises helps to explain declining attendance. The increasing relative prices of symphony concerts so visible in figure 5.2 discourage some attendance.

Nonetheless, ticket price increases still raised performance revenue, because the relationship between ticket prices and attendance is inelastic. The loss in performance revenues from diminished attendance does not completely offset the gain in revenues from charging a higher price to the people who do attend. For regular season concerts, for example, a 10 percent increase in the average ticket price is associated with a 5 percent decline in attendance per concert. Attendance at pops concerts is somewhat less responsive to differences in price: a 10 percent increase in the average price of a pops concert ticket is associated with a 2.5 to 3 percent decline in attendance. These results are in line with estimates of the price sensitivity of concert attendance in earlier studies (Seaman 2005).

Orchestra Policies: Ticket Price Structures

Carefully designed ticket-price structures can also raise a symphony orchestra's performance revenues. Ticket prices vary with the type of concert offered by an orchestra, for example. Regular concerts command the most expensive tickets, followed by pops concerts, summer concerts, family concerts, and chamber or ensemble concerts. For any concert, the demand for seats in a concert hall varies with their visual and acoustical qualities. Much less visible are differences in what individual patrons are willing to pay for a given quality of seat. In pricing seats, most orchestras traditionally have assumed that demand is highest for seats closest to the orchestra and diminishes as distance from the orchestra increases. Accordingly, ticket prices are highest for seats close to the stage and decline with distance from the stage. (Prices may also vary by day of week and time of day.)

Orchestras that take the trouble to investigate demand patterns may reach different conclusions, however. Recently the Chicago Symphony Orchestra discovered that the strongest subscriber demand was for seats in the center of their main floor, and demand decreased for seats that were further from the center in any direction. With this information the orchestra management raised revenues by increasing the number of price categories from 13 to 20, raising the highest prices, and lowering the lowest prices (Ravanas 2008).

Economists label efforts to charge different prices to different classes of patrons "price discrimination" strategies. The key idea behind such policies is to maximize revenues by charging patrons according to their "willingness to pay."[5] Early in the 20th century, the Boston Symphony Orchestra practiced the ultimate form of price discrimination for the best seats in the house: every autumn the orchestra auctioned each of these seats off to the highest bidder. By requiring wealthy patrons to bid against each other for cherished seats, the orchestra greatly increased its performance revenue and at that time was purportedly the one U.S. orchestra whose performance revenues covered its expenses. Notice that the auction turned private information—a patron's maximum willingness to pay for a seat— into a public bid. Moreover, "there [was] a large portion of the symphony hall in Boston that [was] kept for the music lovers who [could] afford only 25 cents or 50 cents" (Aldrich 1903). The pricing policies of some early orchestras made attendance by a broad range of the population feasible.

When patrons can be charged according to their personal willingness to pay, ticket price variation normally increases, and the extent of price variation may be taken as an indicator of the degree of price discrimination. A study of the pricing of popular music concert tickets in the United States between 1992 and 2005 found that greater ticket price variation could increase concert revenue by as much as 5 percent (Courty and Pagliero 2009). By the metric of ticket price variation, many U.S. orchestras appear to possess unexploited opportunities to increase performance revenues by altering ticket price structures. Consider the range of ticket prices charged by 23 large U.S. orchestras during the 2004–5 concert season. For regular concerts, the highest ticket prices charged by individual orchestras ranged from 3 to 16 times their lowest ticket prices. For pops concerts, the range of high ticket prices was from 2.2 to 14.4 times the price of the cheapest ticket, depending on the orchestra. Orchestras with the most limited ticket price variation have the most to gain from altering their price structures.

Orchestra Policies: Marketing Activities

Once ticket prices are established, an orchestra's marketing activities may increase the number of tickets sold at each price. The varied marketing activities that orchestras have developed to increase attendance per concert were noted in the previous chapter. But do marketing campaigns really build symphony audiences? Casual empiricism suggests that marketing expenditures by orchestras may have been unproductive: as the share of marketing expenses in orchestra budgets has increased since the late 1980s, attendance per concert has decreased. As it happens, this correlation says more about the dangers of casual empiricism than the effectiveness of marketing activities. Since many factors influence concert attendance choices, the impact of marketing activities cannot be identified without holding the effects of other influences on attendance constant. Even if attendance and marketing expenses remain inversely correlated in a more comprehensive analysis, we cannot tell whether marketing activities are unproductive or that orchestras with poor attendance are deciding to spend more on marketing. Simple comparisons cannot sort out causality.

If marketing activities and attendance per concert are correlated, orchestras may also benefit from knowing whether the effects of marketing activities change with the level of marketing expenditures. When the best marketing opportunities are exploited first, incremental marketing expenditures may be subject to diminishing returns, yielding smaller increases in attendance per concert. On the other hand, when there are economies of scale in marketing activities, additional expenditures may produce successively larger attendance gains. In each of these cases, past experience would provide a poor guide to the impact of incremental marketing expenses on attendance.

Contrary to casual empiricism, when other influences are held constant, attendance per regular season concert increases with marketing expenditures. Marketing activities also encounter diminishing returns, however. Incremental increases in marketing expenditures produce successively smaller gains in attendance per concert. This phenomenon may be connected to the declining ratio of subscriptions to single ticket sales. The phone and mail expenses incurred to acquire subscription renewals are lower than the media advertising expenditures used to target the growing number of single-ticket purchasers. Past marketing results tend to provide overly optimistic predictions of the effects of incremental marketing expenditures.

How should one interpret the phenomenon of diminishing returns for marketing expenditures by orchestras? The strongest clue comes from surveys of the reasons for not attending symphony concerts. Many survey respondents mention time constraints as a key factor limiting their concert attendance. Incremental marketing activities cannot relieve the time constraints that prevent even those who are attracted to symphonic music from attending concerts. Instead, the potential for marketing is in developing new audiences, but even here marketing efforts will encounter the growing list of activities, including competition from other performing arts, that compete for the limited leisure time of potential concertgoers.

Orchestra Quality

Holding all other influences on attendance constant, high-quality orchestras may attract larger audiences than low-quality orchestras. With a reliable measure of the artistic quality of orchestras, one might even explore links between attendance and quality. But how is one to measure orchestra quality in a way that commands widespread agreement?

Expert opinion provides one approach. But which or what kind of expert? Prominent music critics, musicologists, and music historians might be candidates, but each might weight the diverse aspects of quality differently, yielding different rankings of orchestras. Moreover, all orchestras have stronger and weaker periods as personnel and conductors change; rankings are likely to lack consistency over time. Any ranking by expert opinion is bound to be contentious and affected by the personal idiosyncrasies of the rater(s).

Gramophone, a British magazine devoted to recorded classical music, published a ranking of the 20 best orchestras in December 2008, based on a survey of music critics around the world. The Concertgebouw Orchestra in Amsterdam received the top ranking, followed by the Berlin Philharmonic, Vienna Philharmonic, and London Symphony Orchestra. The Chicago Symphony Orchestra, which placed number five in the survey, was the top U.S. orchestra according to the participating critics. *Gramophone*'s top 20 also included the following U.S. orchestras: Cleveland (7), Los Angeles (8), Boston (11), New York Philharmonic (12) , San Francisco (13), and the Metropolitan Opera Orchestra (18). Many classical musical aficionados disagreed with the ranking of U.S. orchestras, but even if there were agreement, *Gramophone*'s list ranks only 7 of the orchestras in our sample.

Opportunities for broadcasting and recording provide another indicator of quality. Since recording companies and broadcasters seek profits, these opportunities should be positively correlated with orchestra quality as perceived by consumers. (Of course, consumer opinion may itself be influenced to some degree by music critics or other perceived experts.) Unfortunately, less than half of the orchestras in the study sample reported income from broadcasting or recording, so the majority of these orchestras could not be ranked by this criterion. Even orchestras that do record and broadcast report highly variable annual income from these activities.

The mobility of orchestra musicians provides a third possible indicator of quality, but in this case quality as perceived by working musicians rather than critics or general listeners. Patterns of job changing during musicians' careers clarify which orchestras are most favored as destinations and which are most likely to experience departures. Unfortunately, it would take a major study using musicians' resumes or pension records held by the American Federation of Musicians to implement this approach. Such a study could also illuminate many other aspects of musicians' careers, including movement into nonorchestral activities.

This brief review has clarified the difficulties encountered by efforts to define orchestra quality. Rankings will surely differ with the different perspectives of critics, the general listening public, and orchestra musicians. Tastes and the weighting of different elements of musical quality will also vary within each of these groups. Most challenging of all, for the majority of orchestras there is no information readily available for any of these measures, preventing further analysis of the role of orchestra quality.

Economic Capacity of the Community

The potential audience for symphony concerts also may vary with the economic and demographic characteristics of the markets in which orchestras operate. Some orchestras exist in the country's largest and wealthiest metropolitan areas, while others are based in cities of modest size and means. This study's statistical analysis of how concert attendance varies between symphonies and over time for individual symphonies included variables for population, real per capita income, and the unemployment rate in each area in which a sample symphony orchestra was located. Population captures the potential size of an audience, while real income and unemployment signal the economic capacity of the population to attend concerts and support a local orchestra.

The key local characteristic that emerged from the statistical analysis is population size. Orchestras in areas with larger populations experience higher attendance per concert; within an area, attendance per concert rises as population increases and declines as people move out of an area. Detroit, Philadelphia, and other cities have encountered increasing difficulties in supporting their orchestras as the population of their city centers has declined. In contrast, attendance per concert is not significantly related to either the real per capita income or the unemployment rate of an area.

Competition with Operas

Limitations on the time and money of potential patrons may place performing arts organizations in competition with each other. How performing arts organizations compete for audiences facing these constraints and the consequences of such competition for the financial balance of arts organizations has received little study in the past.

Ticket pricing policies and marketing activities that attract new patrons to an opera, dance, or theater performance may do so at the expense of attendance at concerts by the local symphony orchestra. Conversely, pricing and marketing activities by orchestras may cut into attendance at other performing arts. This kind of competition can affect the financial balance of all performing arts organizations. Higher marketing expenses by arts organizations seeking to increase attendance may be countered by other arts organizations in order to prevent a loss of attendance. If an opera increases its marketing effort to fill its hall, a nearby symphony orchestra may have to increase advertising and marketing expenditures to prevent an erosion of patronage. At its worst, the outcome could be an escalating war of marketing expenditures whose only purpose is to prevent a loss of market share. The escalating expenditures may be purely defensive, producing no net gain in attendance for either organization.

One cannot rule out a more appealing alternative hypothesis, however: self-interested pricing and marketing activities by any arts organization will raise general interest in and attendance at all performing arts. Ultimately, the nature and effects of competition between different performing arts organizations must be settled by an analysis of actual experience. The database developed for this study permitted an analysis of competition between orchestras and local opera companies for classical music audiences.

The statistical tests revealed evidence of a statistically significant but quantitatively small relationship between opera ticket prices and regular season symphony attendance (and conversely) in some analyses. Higher season ticket prices charged by a local opera company are associated with higher symphony attendance. The effect is symmetric. If the price of a season ticket for a local opera falls relative to the price of symphony tickets, symphony attendance per concert will decline. Note that the relative price of an opera ticket could fall either because the opera reduces its price relative to the symphony ticket price or because the symphony raises its ticket price relative to the price of opera tickets. (No statistically significant relationship emerged in the analysis between the price of single opera tickets and regular season symphony attendance, or between the price of any opera tickets and pops concert attendance.)

The direct relationship between opera ticket prices and regular season symphony concert attendance in some analyses confirms the intuition that these two performing arts are to some degree substitutes: when the relative price of opera tickets increases, some opera patrons reduce their opera attendance and increase their symphony attendance (and conversely). Nevertheless, this effect is quantitatively small and not always reliable: if an opera doubled its ticket prices (relative to symphony ticket prices), attendance per concert at the local symphony would at most increase by 3 percent.

The statistical analysis did not reveal further significant impacts of opera companies on attendance at a symphony's regular season concerts in the same market area. In particular, neither the presence of an opera company in the market area nor the level of marketing expenditures by that opera company had a reliable impact on attendance at those concerts during the time period studied. No aspect of a local opera's operations, including its ticket pricing, had a significant impact on attendance at pops concerts.

Performance scheduling can influence competition between performing arts. In some communities, the symphony and opera performances occur at different times of year, an arrangement that not only reduces direct competition for patrons between the two performing arts, but also permits musicians to play in both orchestras.

Broadcasts and Recording

We should not leave the topic of arts competition without raising the intriguing question of whether some symphony orchestras effectively compete with themselves when they broadcast their concerts or make and sell sound recordings. These activities raise all of the issues posed by the presence of competing performing arts organizations. Do live broadcasts and recordings of the symphony repertoire substitute for live performances or raise the demand for them?

Throughout most of the history of classical music in the United States, symphony orchestras seem to have assumed that broadcasts and recordings stimulated the demand for live performances. From the vantage point of the early 20th century, Grant and Hettinger (1940, p. 21) commented that "there is considerable evidence that these media have created wider interest in symphonic music and have contributed to the growth in the number of symphony orchestras and the size of their audiences." By today's standards, early sound reproduction was mediocre, however, and exposure to symphonic music on radio and, later, television may have built demand for the superior quality of live performances.

Over the decades, the quality of sound recordings increased immensely, and their relative price has declined, raising the possibility that recorded music no longer raises the demand for and may even substitute for concert attendance. NEA surveys again provide some evidence on the use of potential substitutes for live performances in the late 20th century. While a larger proportion of the population listens to broadcast and recorded classical music than attends concerts, the use of these alternatives has declined since 1992 (table 5.2). This decline coincides with the rise of the Internet as a source of recorded and broadcast music—an option not anticipated in the original design of these surveys. Notwithstanding the dramatic improvements in the quality of broadcast and recorded sound since the early 1980s, the survey data do not support the hypothesis that performing arts attendance has stabilized because people have allocated more time listening to broadcast and recorded performances.

Changing Tastes for Classical Music

The previous sections have considered how changing economic constraints might have influenced classical concert attendance, even if tastes for classical music remained unchanged in the population. We now consider the possibility that some of the downtrend in attendance also reflects a declining attraction to classical music in the U.S. population.

The NEA surveys ask adults whether they "like" various types of music. According to these surveys, about twice as many people like classical music as actually attend classical concerts. That is, recordings and broadcasts alone must account for the exposure of some respondents to classical music. More important for the question of preferences, the percentage of adults who report liking classical music has declined steadily since 1992 and by 2008 was below the 1982 level. This information contributes to an

TABLE 5.2   PERFORMING ARTS BROADCASTING AND RECORDING
(PERCENTAGE OF U.S. ADULTS)

	1982	1992	2002
Watch on TV, Video, or DVD			
Classical music	25	26	18
Opera	12	12	6
Jazz	18	22	16
Musical theater	21	17	12
Nonmusical theater	26	18	9
Dance	—	20	13
Museums	23	34	25
Listen to on the radio			
Classical music	20	31	24
Opera	7	9	6
Jazz	18	28	24
Musical theater	4	4	2
Nonmusical theater	4	3	2
Listen to recordings			
Classical music	22	24	19
Opera	8	7	6
Jazz	20	21	17
Musical theater	9	6	4

Source: NEA (2004), pp. 55–58.

understanding of the trend decline, since cyclical influences on the evolution of tastes seem unlikely. Once again, classical music is not special. While some types of music (classic rock and country and western) are more popular than others (opera and bluegrass), virtually all varieties of music have declined in public favor since 1992 (NEA 2009).

This trend is easier to report than to explain. The trend does coincide with the increasing demographic heterogeneity of the U.S. population, particularly in the cities that typically support orchestras. In the words of one observer: "The ethnic groups that do not trace their roots to Europe will increasingly affect the definition of national cultural values. The traditional value system associated with classical music concerts is not universal, but derived from a European cultural heritage. The style of concert performances may not appeal to members of ethnic groups" (Kolb 2001, p. 20). The distinctly smaller proportion of ethnic minorities attending classical music concerts in the United States is consistent with this view. There is a certain irony in this development, since earlier generations of immigrants stimulated the formation of early U.S. orchestras in the 19th century.

The early orchestras adopted the ensemble forms and music familiar to the European immigrants of their day. Can programming that features more compositions from new immigrant countries of origin raise attendance at contemporary symphony concerts? The prospects seem limited, because most of these countries do not have a national tradition of composing for symphonic ensembles. Consider a few examples. In 2008 the Vietnam National Symphony Orchestra presented 29 programs (some in multiple concerts)—about 100 compositions. Anyone searching the programs for examples of Vietnamese music that might be played by U.S. orchestras in cities with significant Vietnamese communities would be disappointed. Only two of the compositions were by Vietnamese composers, and one was a new commission. The remaining programming consisted of standard European classical music.

In 19th- and early 20th-century China, Christian missionaries brought gifts of Western musical instruments, provided lessons on their performance, and offered examples of Western music in their churches. Ultimately, symphonic ensembles formed and performed Western classical music, but traditional Chinese music did not fit comfortably within Western harmonic traditions and instrumentation (Melvin and Cai 2004). Similarly, Japanese composers did not start composing for the symphony orchestra—an unfamiliar musical form—until 1912, and there were few orchestral works by Japanese composers in 1927, when the first stable Japanese orchestra formed. Most Japanese orchestral works have been composed since 1945 (Kurabayashi and Matsuda 1988).

In short, the fact that non-European countries have musical traditions that do not favor symphonic presentation appears to limit the prospects of filling orchestra halls with new immigrant groups. Exposure to Western classical music may eventually lead to non-Western symphonic compositions. But the process is slow, and the symphonic literature from non-Western cultures remains slim. Paradoxically, the successful performance of Western symphonic music is a prominent goal for aspiring musicians in many non-Western cultures, but the attraction of the public at large to Western classical music remains underdeveloped.

Other students of classical music offer a broader hypothesis: classical music has lost adherents because (unlike other arts) it has failed to keep up with the cultural changes of the late 20th and early 21st century. In this view, declining attendance may reflect both concert content—particularly the heavy emphasis on music from the Baroque, Classical, and Romantic periods—and the formality with which the music is presented. Simply programming more 20th-century music is not necessarily a solution, for some observers argue that modern composers are less interested in connecting with or pleasing audiences than in past periods. Concert attendance has a "social purpose" that arguably existed in earlier periods (Sandow 2007). As noted earlier, however, all performing arts have lost adherents—including those that purportedly have kept up with cultural changes.

The Limits of Audience-Building Policies

This chapter has focused on orchestra policies that influence how many people attend orchestra concerts and how much they will pay for their concert tickets. Now is the time to point out inherent limitations in the strategy of increasing performance revenues to achieve financial balance. Orchestras must live with the luck of where they are located, and we have seen in this chapter that the size and demographic mix of a community's population is one influence on the size of concert audiences. (We shall see in chapter 8 how the local economic base also influences the scale of private philanthropy.) Given the time and money constraints faced by all potential concert patrons, orchestra attendance also depends to a degree on competition for audiences from other performing arts. Some audience gains by a local opera or ballet company may come at the expense of a symphony's audience size. Before leaving this topic, however, we should recognize two other significant limitations on the ability of orchestra organizations to achieve economic balance by raising performance revenues.

Social Patterns of Time Use

As previously discussed, the declining attendance for symphony concerts is typical of virtually all performing arts, so that the root causes of the decrease may have little to do with orchestras per se. This point can be carried much further, for adult participation in many traditional leisure activities outside the performing arts has also declined since at least 1992 (table 5.3).

TABLE 5.3   PERCENT OF ADULTS PARTICIPATING IN NONARTS
LEISURE ACTIVITIES

	1982	1992	2002	2008
Movies	63.0	59.0	60.0	53.3
Sporting events	48.0	37.0	35.0	30.6
Exercise	51.0	60.0	55.1	52.9
Playing sports	39.0	39.0	30.4	26.3
Outdoor activities	36.0	34.0	30.9	28.2
Gardening	60.0	55.0	47.3	41.6
Volunteer/charity	28.0	33.0	29.0	32.0

Source: NEA (2009).

Reinforcing these survey results are several eclectic but intriguing facts: sales of fishing and hunting licenses have declined as new generations of young people find other uses for their time. Like orchestras, hunting outfitters now find that most of their clients are in their 50s and older (Yost 2010). Golf memberships have also declined. According to the National Golf Foundation, "about 10.2 percent of Americans age 6 and above played at least one round in 2008, compared with 12.1 percent in 1990" (Futterman and Blockman 2010). Motion picture attendance peaked in 2002, and by 2008 was 86 percent of that peak. Public television viewing has declined, although the audience for noncommercial radio has increased (Kushner and Cohen 2010). (Radio offers less distraction from other activities than watching television.)

In short, the decline in attendance at classical music concerts (and other arts performances) may reflect broad social shifts in the use of leisure time that have little to do with orchestra policies (or policies of the performing arts industry in general). These patterns are all the more puzzling because they are occurring during a period in which leisure time has increased.

Surveys of how people spend their time record an overall increase in the amount of leisure time of over 5 hours per week since 1965 for the average U.S. adult (Aguiar and Hurst 2006). More educated people—the traditional supporters of the arts—experienced comparatively small increases in leisure, however.

It has been easier to record these trends than to explain how time formerly spent on these diverse activities has been reallocated. New generations face an ever-growing variety of personal entertainment options not available to prior generations—video games, YouTube clips, social networking activities, and the like. Although not yet fully understood, these diverse indications of a broad shift in the use of leisure time suggest that, to an important extent, building audiences and performance revenue may be beyond the reach of orchestra policies.

Will Filling the Concert Hall Achieve Financial Balance?

Key to the strategies for building audiences and performance revenues is an assumption that filling the concert hall will achieve financial balance. But even if the various pricing and marketing policies discussed in this chapter worked like a charm and filled the hall, would performance revenues in fact cover performance expenses?

There is no question that seats are available. For most U.S. symphony orchestras in this study, attendance at regular season concerts was well below the seating capacity of their performance venues. Attendance at regular season concerts averaged between 65 and 76 percent of seating capacity between 1987 and 2006. These averages conceal considerable variation, with only five orchestras regularly at over 90 percent of capacity, while others barely filled half their seats. The percentage of seats filled varied with business conditions, but statistical analyses also uncovered a small but statistically significant downward trend in the fraction of seats that were filled. Holding other influences constant, the proportion of available seats filled by concert patrons declined by about 0.4 percentage points per year. (After controlling for cyclical effects, only two orchestras had positive trends in the fraction of capacity filled.) If the trend continues, the percentage of regular season seats sold will decline by about four percentage points (for example, from 70 percent to 66 percent) every 10 years for the average orchestra.[6]

How much better off would orchestras have been if they had been able to fill every seat at every regular-season concert? A 1970 profile of the Cleveland Orchestra noted that "in an average week, there are two concerts, which means a total of forty-one hundred and eight tickets sold, at an average of five dollars a ticket. The orchestra thus takes in twenty thousand dollars, but there are a hundred and six players, and the average weekly salary is three hundred and ten dollars—a weekly payroll of thirty-three thousand dollars. The payroll alone, then, is thirteen thousand dollars more than the box-office receipts, and there are conductors' and soloists' fees, staff wages, the cost of the hall's upkeep, and so on. 'Before the orchestra plays a note, we are thirty thousand dollars a week in the red,' says . . . its general manager" (Wechsberg 1970).

Thirty years later, little had changed. On average, the 63 orchestras in this study filled about 71 percent of their regular-season seats between the 1987 and 2003 concert seasons, although the fraction filled was lower at the end of the period than at the beginning. Under the strong assumption that vacant seats can be filled for the same prices charged for occupied seats, one can estimate each orchestra's potential concert income from a full house for every performance. The procedure undoubtedly produces an overestimate of the revenues from a full house, because it is unlikely that a full house would be achieved without reducing some ticket prices. If an orchestra could sell the empty seats at current prices, the concert hall should already be sold out.

The performance deficits of orchestras can be recomputed using the estimate of hypothetical concert income with a full house. This procedure also overestimates the deficit reduction because it ignores additional costs incurred to fill the vacant seats. Applying these very optimistic assumptions about ticket pricing and costs, selling out each concert performance would eliminate about 45 percent of performance deficits on average, with considerable variation among individual symphonies. Only a few orchestras might eliminate the performance income gap by filling every seat. In short, even if every seat were filled, the vast majority of U.S. symphony orchestras still would face significant performance deficits.

Conclusions

This chapter has focused on orchestra policies that influence how many people attend orchestra concerts and how much they pay for their concert tickets. This strategy for achieving economic balance receives the most attention within the orchestra industry. These are the main findings: (1) As orchestras added concerts in the late 20th and early 21st centuries, attendance per concert declined for virtually all types of concerts. (2) Ticket pricing policies have an important influence on performance revenues. Because the demand for symphony performances is only moderately sensitive to ticket price, higher ticket prices will raise performance revenues, even though they discourage some attendance. A full evaluation of the effect of higher ticket prices should consider the effect of lower attendance on philanthropic contributions, an issue that could not be addressed with the data available for this study. (3) In some analyses, there is a statistically significant but quantitatively small competitive interaction between symphony orchestras and operas. Changes in the relative price of symphony and opera tickets in the same area are associated with small changes in relative attendance. Data limitations currently preclude extending the analysis of performing arts competition.

A clear message from this chapter is that a strategy limited to raising performance income will not restore economic balance for most orchestras. Successful audience-building activities reduce performance deficits, but even filling the concert hall—an ambitious goal for an industry usually selling 70 percent of its capacity—would not eliminate deficits at most orchestras. Moreover, the economic capacities of local communities and broad social changes in the use of leisure time place inherent limitations on audience building by orchestras and other performing arts groups.

Less frequently mentioned in discussions of eliminating orchestra deficits is the more conflictual strategy of slowing the growth of orchestra expenses. This chapter included evidence that some expenses could be carried too far. While marketing activities tend to raise attendance per concert, they are subject to diminishing returns. Beyond some level, marketing expenditures may not generate enough additional attendance and performance revenue to pay for themselves. Somewhat lower expenditures would then leave the orchestra in a stronger financial position. We carry the analysis of expenses forward into the next chapter on the largest element in an orchestra's budget—artistic costs—and still later in the discussion of fundraising activities in chapter 8.

CHAPTER 6

Artistic and Nonartistic Costs

Most people who attend a symphony orchestra concert do not realize that the musicians, guest soloists, and conductors who deliver the performance account for little more than half of the orchestra's expenses. Nor do they realize that the share of artistic costs in orchestra budgets slowly declined in the late 20th century. But because artistic costs remain the largest component of symphony expenses, even small increases can have a notable impact on the overall financial balance of orchestras.

Symphony patrons also might be surprised at the variation in pay among an orchestra's musicians. A violinist in one major symphony orchestra could receive as little as $106,000 or as much as $407,000 per year in 2005, for example. In most major U.S. orchestras the most highly paid violinist receives over three times the pay of the lowest-paid violinist. Why do musicians playing the same instrument and performing identical musical parts in a single orchestra receive different pay? Concertgoers are more likely to have read of superstar salaries for a short list of high-profile conductors and guest soloists and wondered why these artists receive much higher salaries than orchestra musicians.

Standard labor market analysis illuminates some of these issues by clarifying the basic setting of the labor markets for artistic personnel. But a complete understanding of pay variations and other working conditions in orchestras requires recognition of the importance of labor market institutions, because orchestras constitute one of the last highly unionized sectors in the United States. Examining the interplay of labor market and institutional forces helps us understand both the level and structure of symphony musicians' pay and resolves a puzzle that emerged earlier in the book: why artistic expenses are so slow to adjust to changes in general economic conditions and to the financial balance of orchestras.

The Symphony Musicians' Labor Market

The development of a musician's art begins with advanced training on one or more instruments in a specialized music school or university music department. The instrumental performance ability and knowledge of orchestral literature developed at these institutions is a general skill that can in principle be applied at any symphony orchestra. As a general skill, the cost of training is borne by the musician. Nonetheless, the supply of aspiring symphony musicians is huge relative to the demand for their services: between July 2005 and June 2006, for example, music schools in the United States graduated 3,671 students who majored in performance on a symphonic instrument (NASM 2006). Even this figure understates the new supply of potential symphony orchestra musicians, as it does not count performance graduates from music departments in colleges and universities. While some graduates may move directly into symphony orchestra positions, most teach and accept a variety of other performance opportunities while waiting for vacancies for their instrument to arise in symphony orchestras.

The annual number of vacancies is very small—about two to four per year at top orchestras—relative to the annual number of music performance graduates. A fact sheet on orchestras reported that "during the 2003 calendar year there were 159 openings for musicians in [52 major] orchestras."[1] Since 1964, vacant positions at top orchestras have been listed in the *International Musician* (published by the American Federation of Musicians), and each vacancy can produce hundreds of applicants—both new graduates in performance and established musicians at other orchestras.

Michael Grebanier, the principal cellist with the San Francisco Symphony Orchestra, provided a revealing picture of how competition for symphony positions has increased in recent decades: "This is an extremely difficult profession to succeed in. There are so many musicians and conservatories; it's gotten more and more crowded, with the same number of opportunities. When I became principal cello of the Pittsburgh Symphony, I was one of four people invited to audition. By the time I auditioned here [San Francisco] in 1976, there might have been 100 people who applied for the job. Now, we might have 300 people—who all went to school, who have qualifications, who have experience and are good. The odds have really changed." (San Francisco Symphony 2008, p. 38A.)

Symphony orchestras use audition procedures to select from among the generally trained applicants for vacant positions. The design of audition procedures influences the extent to which merit triumphs over favoritism in the selection of musicians. Until recent decades, the sometimes arbitrary tastes of a symphony's music director (conductor) were the dominant factor in selection. Nowadays, most applicants participate in as many as three rounds of auditions before a committee that includes current members of the orchestra. Generally, the music director participates only in the final round, in which the committee must select from a small group of applicants who are judged well qualified to perform with the orchestra.

In an effort to minimize the role of gender, race, or preferences for the students of current symphony musicians (or their teachers) in hiring musicians, almost all orchestras conduct "blind" auditions: a screen permits the audition committee to hear but not see applicants. The authors of one study concluded that the adoption of blind audition processes explained as much as a third of the increase in the proportion of female musicians in the top U.S. symphony orchestras between 1960 and the mid-1990s. Much as in universities, successful applicants receive tenure after a probationary period and a tenure review. "The basis for termination is limited and rarely used" (Goldin and Rouse 2000, p. 722). The many unsuccessful applicants for scarce orchestra vacancies move into positions as freelance musicians, private teachers, and educators. A significant fraction eventually abandons musical performance as their primary source of income.

Once hired by an orchestra, musicians tend to have long tenures— often 20 to 40 years, given the paucity of new positions available at other orchestras. During that tenure, a musician develops skills specific to that orchestra (for example, accommodating personal performance style to the style of the orchestra's particular mix of musicians and the regular conductor) via rehearsals and performances. The gradual development of such ensemble-specific skills provides the basis for wage differentials based on seniority (discussed later in this chapter). Seltzer (1989, pp. 187–88) provides a revealing portrait of the work of symphony musicians:

> For members of major orchestras, their commitment to the orchestra means seven or eight services (either rehearsals or concerts) per

week with special provisions for unusual situations and out-of-town engagements. Since each service is usually two and one half hours in length, a work week of twenty-some hours might sound quite easy to the uninitiated. It isn't. Because major orchestra players are at the top of their profession, they are expected to produce music at that level every rehearsal and concert, every week . . . despite some inadequate conductors and with occasional physical or mental stress. . . . Performers are expected to know the symphonic (or operatic) literature well enough that programs can be presented with a minimum of rehearsal even with guest conductors and unknown soloists.

In this setting, even accomplished classical musicians face significant labor market risks. Until recent decades, symphony musicians did not have full-year positions and resorted to working multiple jobs (for example, teaching and chamber music performance) to increase their annual income. The genuine threat of orchestra bankruptcy also limits the employment security of U.S. symphony musicians. Moreover, a labor market in which supply consistently exceeds the demand by a huge margin places ongoing downward pressure on compensation.

Collective Representation of Symphony Musicians

In the face of such challenges, symphony musicians sought collective representation almost from the moment that their early labor cooperatives gave way to professionally managed organizations. The American Federation of Musicians (AFM) was founded in 1896, but the historical relationship between the AFM and symphony orchestra musicians has been decidedly uneasy. Labor unions are political organizations, and orchestra musicians constituted a distinct minority of the AFM membership. Most early members of the AFM played theater, dance, or parade music, and the political and bargaining agenda of the union reflected their economic interests— reducing competition from foreign musicians, military bands, and traveling musicians. Later, as the advent of sound movies and electronic recording techniques reduced the demand for theater musicians and live music, the union's attention shifted to techniques for capturing some of the gains from the use of new technologies for nonsymphonic musicians.

Collective bargaining authority rested with AFM local unions, in which symphony musicians were always a minority. Local union officials would negotiate symphony labor contracts, which were ratified by the local union executive board. Symphony musicians often did not participate in either the negotiation or ratification processes. "Nonsymphonic musicians provided the major source of funding for the AFM, as well as the votes for union officers and initiatives. Union leaders were primarily concerned with the majority of their membership and had little knowledge of or interest in the symphonic musician. Board presidents and administrators of American symphony orchestras made contract and wage agreements with the local union officials behind closed doors. . . . Local union officers were unfamiliar with the working conditions that comprised professional orchestra life. They often listened with considerable sympathy to the pleas of financial hardship that boards and managers put forth" (Ayer 2005, pp. 31–32). Given this environment, it seems unlikely that collective bargaining provided significant upward pressure on the wages and working conditions of symphony musicians during the first 70 to 75 years of the American Federation of Musicians.

Frustrated with the failure of the AFM to address their needs, symphony musicians from several locals met and formed the International Conference of Symphony and Orchestra Musicians (ICSOM) in 1962. The immediate reaction of the AFM was to accuse ICSOM of "dual unionism." In 1969, however, the AFM agreed to formally affiliate ICSOM within its structure.[2] ICSOM members—the musicians in 52 member orchestras with budget sizes of $5 million and higher—hire their own legal counsel and conduct their own local negotiations. In 1984 musicians in smaller orchestras formed a similar organization, the Regional Orchestra Players Association (ROPA) and received a similar affiliation with the AFM. The AFM also established a Symphonic Services Division to provide technical services to symphony musicians.

At the time that these organizations formed, symphony orchestra musicians had a long list of concerns (Seltzer 1989, p. 99). Their objectives included:

- representation by symphony musicians in negotiations with symphony management;
- the right to ratify proposed collective bargaining agreements;
- improved job security, including more transparent hiring (auditions) and dismissal procedures;
- a guaranteed work year;

- health and hospitalization insurance; and
- a pension plan.

Orchestra musicians also had concerns about their treatment while on tour and the availability of strike funds to provide benefits to musicians in the event of a work stoppage.

Collective bargaining negotiations occur between local orchestra musicians and orchestra management. Currently the national organizations (ICSOM, ROPA, and the Symphonic Services Division of the AFM) provide negotiation assistance and information on other settlements in the industry to unions involved in these local negotiations. Local bargaining objectives typically dominate negotiations, but negotiators provided by the national organizations often emphasize pay comparisons with orchestras in other cities as a criterion for local wage settlements.

Bargaining Role of Symphony Management

Symphony musicians bargain with orchestra managers and boards of trustees. The management side of the collective bargaining relationship has a remarkable degree of autonomy. Nonprofit organizations do not have owners or shareholders whose interests the board is required to represent and to whom the board is accountable. Trustees are not even legally obligated to pursue the objectives of donors, although the membership of most boards includes some large donors. Boards are rarely subject to election, and takeovers are not a disciplining factor. Except at times of dire financial emergencies, these features of symphony orchestra governance are unlikely to provoke the strength of resistance to union demands normally found in the private sector.

The nonprofit status of orchestras accords certain advantages in countering their operating deficits. Management's efforts to raise nonperformance income are assisted by the favorable tax treatment of donations and the fact that not-for-profit status may raise prospective donors' confidence that their funds will be used to pursue the organization's central mission (Hansmann 1996).

Such access to nonperformance revenue can create ambiguity about the true budget constraints faced by symphony orchestras, however. Labor representatives may view an orchestra's budget constraint as "soft" or "elastic," given the access of symphonies to private contributions, government support, investment income, and endowment draws. If contributed support is viewed as continually responsive to fundraising activities, labor may adopt wage objectives that exceed what they would seek if facing a less ambiguous budget constraint. In this scenario, union wage demands will drive the level of fundraising activity as orchestras seek sufficient nonperformance income to cover wage demands and other cost increases. In fact, donors sometimes step forward with special contributions to "save the season" during periods of financial distress, not realizing that their well-meaning efforts to bail an orchestra out of a financial emergency may create a kind of moral hazard that raises future pressures on orchestra budgets. By removing the risks associated with high wage demands, donors inadvertently may encourage higher future pay demands.

In the for-profit sector, the scope for moral hazard in collective bargaining is much smaller, because absent a credible possibility of a government bailout, business firms lack access to significant nonoperating income. Negotiators must live with and adjust their behavior to the operating bottom line—the balance between operating income and expenses. When faced with a hard budget constraint, unions are more likely to consider concessions when faced with adverse financial outcomes. Collective bargaining in the auto and steel industries during the late 20th century offered many such examples.

Alternatively, the prior level of philanthropy and government support may influence wage demands. In this scenario, wage increases will absorb increases in nonperformance income, undermining its contribution to long-term financial stability. (See the discussion of endowments in chapter 9.) These two scenarios each stress the crucial role of nonperformance income in determining wage settlements but disagree over the lead actor.

Several factors create an inelastic demand for the services of symphony musicians. Most orchestras have local monopoly power, since most communities can support only one orchestra. Consumers either accept the higher ticket prices that follow wage increases or shift their consumption to other performing arts. The small cross-elasticities of demand between orchestras and operas, reported in chapter 5, imply that symphony patrons tend to accept the price increases. In contrast to goods-producing industries, orchestras have few opportunities to reduce expenses by altering production methods. The number of musicians and the mix of instruments used by an orchestra are determined by symphonic composers and can only be altered by limiting the range of music that an orchestra performs. (The music of the Baroque and early Classical periods generally requires fewer musicians than the music of the late Romantic period and the twentieth century, for example.)

The Ford Foundation Program

In 1965, midway between the formation of ICSOM in 1962 and the AFM's formal recognition of ICSOM's role in representing symphony musicians within the union structure in 1969, the Ford Foundation announced a program of major support for symphony orchestras. The coincidence of this grant with the formation and recognition of ICSOM greatly complicates efforts to assign responsibility for subsequent collective bargaining outcomes in the late 1960s and 1970s. The foundation's program, which emerged during a period of increasing symphony concert attendance, provided about $85 million (over $450 million in year 2000 dollars) to 61 orchestras in an effort to secure three related objectives. The primary objective was to improve the economic lot of musicians. The foundation was quite forthright that orchestra musicians were "one of the most underpaid professional groups in American society" and believed that enabling more musicians to devote their primary energies to symphony work would raise the artistic quality of American orchestras (Ford Foundation 1966).

Increasing audiences through longer seasons and a more diversified portfolio of concerts constituted a second objective and supported the first objective by providing more work for musicians. (Prior to the Ford Foundation program, only two orchestras provided musicians with 52 weeks of employment, and most symphonies had concert seasons running less than six months.) Finally, the foundation hoped to attract more young people to orchestra careers by increasing the income and prestige of the players. It is not clear that the foundation appreciated the tension created by a program that would increase both the demand for and supply of musicians.

To implement these objectives, the Ford Foundation designated three-quarters of its fund for endowments and required the orchestras receiving these funds to match them at least dollar-for-dollar within five years. In addition, special "developmental funds" were provided to 25 orchestras with the shortest concert seasons and the weakest financial resources. These funds could be used to match outside salary offers to musicians that an orchestra wished to retain, thus encouraging superior musicians to reduce their multiple job holding and specialize in symphony work.

The Ford Foundation program effectively reduced the bargaining resistance of symphony management. Even disregarding the inherent advantages that a union may have in bargaining with not-for-profit organizations and the specific advantages in bargaining with symphony management, the new program loosened budget constraints. Although the foundation's intention was to encourage a revolution in long-term orchestra strategies, there was considerable pressure from the union side to capture the largesse in immediate wage gains, which musicians (supported by the foundation's very public analysis of the industry) viewed as long overdue.

Musicians' Pay and Working Conditions

In the wake of these institutional developments, virtually all symphony musicians are now covered by collective agreements that determine their pay, the pay structure of their orchestras, and a variety of work rules governing the frequency and intensity of their work. The content of these negotiated agreements clarifies why musicians playing the same instrument and part in an orchestra may receive significantly different salaries. There is also considerable pay inequality between orchestras, and we shall try to understand why different contracts provide such different levels of pay for musicians.

Symphony Musicians' Pay

In the face of the downward pressures on symphony pay from the increasing supply of classical musicians, collective bargaining agreements in the industry typically establish a minimum weekly salary for all musicians in an orchestra and certain supplements that raise the pay of some individual musicians above the minimum. In 2005 the median minimum weekly negotiated salary among 44 large orchestras was $1,125, with a range from $585 to $2,190 across individual orchestras.[3]

The agreements also establish a pay structure for musicians by providing for "seniority" and "over-scale" payments, which account for much of the variation in pay between members of an orchestra. The ensemble-specific skills developed while playing with a particular orchestra provide a basis for pay differentials based on seniority. A violinist who spent most of his professional career with the renowned Cleveland Orchestra illuminated the nature of those skills: "I never tried to analyze how . . . [the conductor

George] Szell slowly turns his right hand down for a slow, soft entrance and we all come in together a certain fraction of a second later. . . . When you think of a hundred and six players doing it, with absolute precision, it staggers the imagination. Yet I don't think it's a matter of intuition; . . . it is the result of hard work and playing together for years. . . . Young players who join the orchestra have a lot to learn. . . . but in most cases the new player's reflexes get faster, and he acquires the exact timing that our orchestra is known for. He learns to play phrases rather than single notes. He learns to watch the conductor instinctively before approaching a change of tempo, a *ritardando* or *accelerando*. He watches the conductor's beat *and* his eyes." (Quoted in Wechsberg 1970)

Virtually all orchestras provide seniority increments to the minimum salary, but the exact formulas used to determine seniority pay vary. In a typical arrangement, musicians accrue an additional increment to their weekly salary per year of service, but the seniority pay is only adjusted in five-year intervals. For example, a collective agreement may provide for musicians to receive a weekly salary increment of $10 per year of service, but orchestra musicians will not be paid a seniority increment until they have been with the orchestra for five years. After five years, the increment is "earned" and $50 per week in seniority pay will be added to the contractual minimum salary. Seniority accrual will continue, and musicians completing 10 years with the symphony will then receive an additional $50 increment, for a total of $100 per week in seniority pay. The majority of symphony collective bargaining agreements set a limit to the number of years over which seniority increments can accrue. Seniority arrangements help to raise average salaries above minimum salaries. An orchestra fact sheet reported that in 2003 "the average seniority pay for an ICSOM musician with 20 years seniority was 5% above minimum scale," and ranged from 1.3 percent to 15.5 percent.[4]

Over-scale pay produces much larger compensation differences between some orchestra musicians. It consists of salary payments above the minimum scale and seniority increments to compensate musicians with titled positions (for example, "first chair" or "principal") for their more prominent roles and musical leadership responsibilities. Every orchestra has a strict hierarchy of authority among musicians. At the pinnacle is the orchestra's music director (conductor). Next is the first-chair violinist or concertmaster. A former symphony musician described some of the extra duties of a concertmaster, perhaps slighting their musical leadership responsibilities:

> When the conductor enters, or when he asks the orchestra to stand for a bow, everyone in the orchestra watches the concertmaster. When the concertmaster stands, we stand. When he sits, we sit. When the applause is dying down at the end of a concert, we look at the concert-master. When he walks off, we walk off. The concertmaster's job also includes, and I kid you not, taking over as conductor in case the con-ductor drops dead in the middle of the show. . . . Another immuta-ble custom of orchestral pecking orders: if the concertmaster's violin breaks in the middle of a concert, it is the solemn duty of the second chair violinist to hand their violin over to the concertmaster to play until the broken violin can be fixed. This is the case even when you're talking about the second chair violinist having to hand over (to some-one that they may not like all that much) a violin that cost well over $100,000 and hasn't been paid for yet. (Locke 2005, pp. 47–48)[5]

> Section leaders, the "first-chair" or "principal" players for each instru-mental section, are next in line of authority and responsibility. Mu-sicians in each section are expected to defer to the section leader on issues of performance style. (Within string sections the principal also establishes the "bowings" on the music, so that all bows move in the same direction at the same time.) The hierarchy continues, with each player being assigned a rank. The ranking below principal players may not provide a basis for over-scale payments, but it implies quality dis-tinctions and has practical performance implications. When sharing a music stand, the lower ranked person always turns pages for the higher ranked person. (Locke 2005, p. 48)

In larger orchestras, over-scale payments for first-chair and some other musicians are negotiated individually with orchestra management. Collec-tive bargaining agreements for smaller orchestras tend to specify an over-scale percentage for key players. Agreements also often provide extra pay for "doubling"—playing more than one instrument during a performance, as when a clarinetist also plays passages on a bass clarinet or E-flat clarinet. In a relatively recent development in the largest orchestras, each musician who does not have an individually negotiated contract receives a standard

TABLE 6.1 ANNUAL SALARIES AS MULTIPLES OF MUSICIANS' MINIMUM SCALE, 2005

Large-Budget Orchestras

	Boston	Chicago	Los Angeles	New York	Philadelphia	San Francisco
Conductor	14.0	8.3	11.9	24.9	14.0	15.3
Concertmaster	3.1	2.3	3.1	3.8	2.0	3.5
Next highest–paid musician	2.0	2.0	1.9	2.7	2.1	1.7
Average musician salary	1.2	1.2	1.2	1.5	1.3	1.1
Minimum musician salary	1.0	1.0	1.0	1.0	1.0	1.0
Orchestra manager	3.6	3.7	7.9	5.3	2.6	3.3
Development director	1.9	1.6	1.9	4.0	1.6	1.7

Small–Budget Orchestras

	Alabama	Fort Wayne	Knoxville	Memphis	Virginia
Conductor	n.a.	6.7	4.7	5.0	5.9
Concertmaster	2.5	n.a.	n.a.	n.a.	n.a.
Next highest–paid musician	2.0	n.a.	n.a.	n.a.	n.a.
Average musician salary	1.1	1.1	1.0	1.1	1.3
Minimum musician salary	1.0	1.0	1.0	1.0	1.0
Orchestra manager	3.2	5.4	3.6	4.3	4.1
Development director	1.9	n.a.	2.4	n.a.	2.7

Sources: www.guidestar.org, Senza Sordino.

n.a. = not available.

amount of over-scale pay—effectively an increase in their minimum scale salary. For some key players, individual negotiations may establish salaries well above contractual requirements. In 2005, for example, the compensation of concertmasters at the top five orchestras ranged from $245,390 to $406,920.[6]

Table 6.1 summarizes the structure of artistic pay within six large-budget and five small-budget symphony orchestras in 2005. The minimum weekly scale wage for musicians, which does not vary much among the large-budget orchestras, is set equal to 1.0, permitting the other salaries in each orchestra to be expressed as multiples of the minimum scale. We see that the concertmasters in these orchestras earn from two to almost four times the pay of musicians receiving minimum scale.

After the concertmaster, the next most highly paid musician is invariably another first-chair musician. There is no convention among orchestras or within an orchestra over time regarding which section leader receives this distinction. In 2005 the next most highly paid musicians in three of the high-budget orchestras happened to be the principal cellist, but in the remaining orchestras it was the principal oboist or the principal trumpet player. Five years earlier, the next most highly paid musician in each orchestra was the principal player of a different section. The table shows that these musicians generally negotiate a salary that is about double the minimum scale. Salaries are generally lower in orchestras with smaller budgets. Although these orchestras report less information on the salaries of concertmasters and other relatively high-paid musicians in their tax returns, we see in the bottom panel of table 6.1 that the artistic salary structure is less dispersed.

Perhaps the biggest difference between orchestras with relatively large and relatively small budgets is in the pay of the conductor. In the large-budget orchestras, conductors receive between eight and 24 times the annual pay provided by minimum scale, while in small-budget orchestras the differential is a more modest five to seven times minimum scale. Differences in pay per service are even larger, as most conductors only spend a fraction of the season with their "home" orchestra. When they are conducting elsewhere, the home orchestra must hire and compensate guest conductors. In part, these pay differences reflect the different labor markets for symphony musicians and conductors. Markets for conductors do not seem to be characterized by the huge supply relative to demand that one observes in the market for symphony musicians.[7] A small number of conductors achieve international superstar status, resting on evidence that they have a gift for achieving superior interpretations of the orchestral literature and perhaps for adventurous programming.

Nonartistic Personnel

At the beginning of the 21st century, the concert programs of major symphony orchestras would list around 100 musicians and an even larger number of administrative staff. The fundraising and development staff would approach three dozen people. Marketing and communications would account for another two dozen employees. Other staff would be engaged in managing concert production, finance, domestic and international touring, and orchestra personnel. Much less is known about their pay. Nonetheless, orchestra tax returns normally provide information on the compensation of the highest paid staff members.

Table 6.1 also includes information on the annual salaries in 2005 of the orchestra manager (often known by other titles) and director of development. Roughly speaking, orchestra managers receive about four times the annual salary of musicians receiving minimum scale, while development and fundraising directors receive about half the orchestra manager's salary. The skills required for these jobs are quite different from the skills required of musicians, and these nonartistic personnel operate in quite different labor markets than musicians. Many of the skills applied in the management of symphony orchestras could be applied in other not-for-profit organizations.

Musicians' Pay Growth and the Cost Disease

An important aspect of the cost disease facing orchestras and other performing arts is the assumption that costs will increase more rapidly than productivity, as the pay of orchestra personnel follows pay increases elsewhere in the economy (see chapter 2). Writing in the mid-1960s, Baumol and Bowen (1966, p. 209) observed that "performer incomes have been rising at a rate faster than that of the price level, but still have not kept up with incomes elsewhere in the economy, and . . . salary payments have constituted a declining portion of overall costs of performance in recent years."

By the end of the 20th century, the situation in orchestras was quite different. Since 1987 the minimum weekly salary increases for orchestra

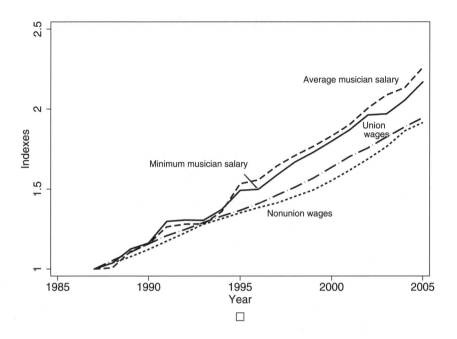

Figure 6.1. Musicians' Salaries and Union and Nonunion Wages, 1987–2005
Source: League of American Orchestras, *Senza Sordino*, U.S. Bureau of Labor Statistics 2007

musicians negotiated by management and labor for the orchestras in our sample averaged about 4.2 percent per year. After including the effects of seniority and over-scale payments, average weekly musicians' salaries increased at about 4.5 percent per year. In comparison, the annual pay increases of other union and nonunion employees in the United States averaged about 3.6 percent over this period (fig. 6.1), as did the pay increases for service workers (fig. 6.2). Pay increases for orchestra musicians also exceeded the pay gains of university teachers and health workers, who also work in sectors that have low productivity gains but face much stronger demand (Flanagan 2010). In short, the pay of orchestra musicians not only kept up with pay increases elsewhere in the economy, as suggested by the cost disease argument; their pay also increased more rapidly than the pay of most other groups of workers in the United States in the late 20th and early 21st century.

During the same time period, conductors' salaries increased even more rapidly than musicians' pay. Conductors are typically represented by artis-

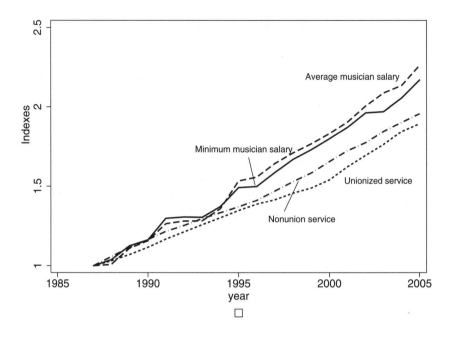

Figure 6.2. Orchestra Salaries and Service Workers' Pay, 1987–2005
Source: League of American Orchestras, *Senza Sordino*, U.S. Bureau of Labor Statistics 2007

tic management agencies, and their salaries are determined by individual negotiations between the agency (on behalf of the conductor) and symphony management. Between 1997 and 2001, the salary of an orchestra's regular conductor averaged about 5 percent of artistic costs and roughly 3 percent of total expenses. For individual orchestras, the conductor's salary ranged from much less than 1 percent to about 8 percent of total expenses during this period.

Symphony concerts usually include a performance of at least one composition featuring a guest instrumental or vocal soloist. Such soloists frequently enjoy international reputations and, like conductors, employ artist management companies to negotiate fees and other details of their appearances. Fees for guest soloists and guest conductors vary widely but average about 15 percent of artistic costs and roughly 8 percent of total expenses annually. For individual orchestras, these fees range from as little as 3 percent to as much as 14 percent of total expenses.

Few contemporary orchestras appear to ask whether guest soloists increase ticket sales sufficiently to pay for themselves. Would an orchestra's artistic reputation and financial security suffer from using soloists from within the orchestra (as some symphonies do) or from offering concerts without a featured soloist? There appears to be no evidence on these questions nowadays. But over a century ago, the trustees of the Pittsburgh Symphony Orchestra were asking the right questions: "In Pittsburgh the Trustees have been experimenting with high-price soloists this season, and have found that the home audiences really want the orchestra and not the soloists, which is in itself an encouraging feature, although it has cost a little money to ascertain the fact. With a few exceptions, the high-priced soloists failed to draw into the house as much additional money as had to be spent on them" (Aldrich 1903).

By the 21st century, musicians' salaries compared favorably with the salaries of other white-collar professionals. Table 6.2 records the 2005 average weekly earnings for full-year employees in various white-collar occupations. "Musicians and composers"—an occupational category that includes but is not limited to symphony musicians—earned more and worked fewer

TABLE 6.2   EARNINGS AND HOURS OF SELECTED PROFESSIONALS, JUNE 2005

Occupation	Hourly Earnings	Weekly Hours	Weekly Earnings
White collar	$24.03	39.5	$949.18
Professional	32.89	39.0	1,282.71
University teachers	43.69	39.2	1,712.65
Music, art, drama	38.79	38.5	1,416.42
Other teachers	32.06	36.8	1,179.81
Lawyers	50.89	41.5	2,111.94
Other professionals	25.48	39.6	1,018.81
Musicians and composers	38.84	37.3	1,448.73
Actors and directors	33.13	40.5	1,341.76
Orchestra musicians (2003)			
Minimum salary			1,341.00
Average salary			1,587.00

Source: U.S. Bureau of Labor Statistics 2006b, table 2-1; League of American Orchestras.

Notes: Data are for full-time workers. Weekly earnings = hourly earnings multiplied by weekly hours.

hours than the average white-collar and professional worker, although much of the time that musicians spend practicing to maintain their skills is off-the-job and hence not recorded in official statistics. Still, given the evidence of extreme excess supply of orchestra musicians and the attractive nonmonetary aspects of most musicians' work, the comparatively high salaries stand out. As will become apparent in chapter 10, the salaries also stand out when compared to the pay of orchestra musicians abroad.

Nonmonetary Working Conditions

Collective bargaining agreements covering symphony orchestra musicians also define certain nonmonetary working conditions. Most agreements specify hiring and firing procedures along with the number and duration of "services" (concerts or rehearsals) each week. Agreements for orchestras that tour may specify a maximum number of services per tour or per tour week, the length of rest periods between the end of a tour and the next home service, and details pertaining to the treatment of musicians and their instruments during the tour.

Collective agreements also specify procedures for auditioning and hiring orchestra musicians. By increasing the involvement of current orchestra musicians in the process, contractual hiring procedures may have increased the role of merit in hiring and contributed to the increasing proportion of women and nonwhite musicians in major symphony orchestras. The median share of women among orchestra musicians increased modestly from about 37 percent in 1987 to over 40 percent in 2005. Over the same period the median share of minority group musicians rose from under 5 percent to about 12.5 percent.

From Variable to Fixed Artistic Costs

Since 1970, collective bargaining agreements signed by symphony musicians and management have gone a long way toward transforming the compensation of musicians from a variable to a fixed cost. At one time orchestra musicians were mainly hired on a "per-service" basis, which offers the greatest flexibility in labor costs to management and the greatest income insecurity to musicians. Today collective bargaining agreements usually specify the number of "regular" musicians in the orchestra. These musicians are entitled to various benefits specified in the contract. Depending on the number of regular musicians, orchestras may hire additional musicians on a per-service basis, either regularly or for performances of music requiring an unusually large orchestra.

The guaranteed number of annual weeks of employment for symphony musicians also increased. In the early 1960s only two orchestras guaranteed 52 weeks of employment. By the mid-1990s musicians in 40 percent of the ICSOM orchestras received a full-year employment contract. Over the next 10 years the guaranteed weeks of employment increased for musicians at other orchestras, although the number of orchestras offering a 52-week guarantee remained unchanged.

With these developments in the work year came a shift from pay per service to pay per week. Weekly pay combined with a guaranteed number of weeks per year eliminated musicians' uncertainty about their minimum annual salary. Collective bargaining agreements also limit the number of services per week. The most common provision sets an average maximum of eight services per week and limits the number of weeks in which the average can be exceeded.

The transformation of musicians' pay into a fixed cost has been furthered by the development of Electronic Media Guarantee (EMG) payments. For those orchestras that have an EMG, the collective bargaining agreement specifies a guaranteed amount against which electronic media work at union scales can be charged. Examples of electronic media work include television broadcasts, CD or DVD recordings, and National Public Radio broadcasts. When an agreement includes an EMG, it must be paid to the orchestra's musicians even if the electronic media activities do not occur. Effectively, it is a salary supplement. In the 2003–4 concert season, agreements for 18 out of 51 ICSOM orchestras provided EMG payments, which ranged from $553 to $6,760 with an (unweighted) average payment of just under $2,300. For individual orchestras, the EMG raises the minimum annual salary from 2 to 8 percent.

Most private-sector collective bargaining agreements in the United States specify the wage requirements of the contract but allow employers considerable discretion in setting employment levels. Contracts are likely to state how economic opportunity will be allocated (for example, by seniority), while letting employers choose employment levels. In contrast, labor agreements with symphony orchestras effectively fix *both* the price and quantity aspects of the bargain. Orchestra management may acquiesce with some regulation of employment levels, because the symphonic music literature largely determines the labor input. Neither the number nor the portfolio of instrumentalists employed by an orchestra may be altered in response to wage costs without circumscribing the music that the orchestra may perform.

Contractual guarantees regarding the length of the work year are more constraining, notwithstanding the employment security that they provide to symphony musicians. In the short run, work-year guarantees restrict the ability of symphony orchestras to reduce expenses in the face of declining revenues. Reduced flexibility of labor costs contributes to significant cyclical variation in the performance income gap. In the long run, work-year commitments encourage the growth of concerts in the face of declining attendance per concert and total attendance. Together, these provisions also insulate insider musicians from the vast number of qualified outsiders seeking symphonic positions.

These contractual provisions emerged in the wake of the Ford Foundation grants to U.S. symphony orchestras during a period of rising demand for symphony performances (the late 1960s and 1970s). But many of the collective bargaining provisions underpinning improvements in the financial and employment security of musicians have limited the ability of orchestras to adjust artistic costs in response to the financial pressures that emerge during periods of declining concert attendance. How suitable are provisions agreed to by both management and labor during good times for adjusting labor costs during cyclical or other sources of economic adversity?

Musicians' Wages and Financial Balance

Orchestra management and musicians usually approach collective bargaining negotiations with conflicting interests. Management seeks an agreement consistent with financial balance for the orchestra. Sometimes this is a matter of maintaining an existing balance. Often it is a matter of reaching an agreement that eliminates a deficit and restores balance, for none of the orchestras in this study have consistently avoided annual deficits. Much of the conflict rests on the fact that the incomes of symphony musicians constitute the major costs of maintaining an orchestra.

Orchestra musicians often seek to match the pay of musicians at orchestras of similar prominence. For them, equity criteria generally outweigh an orchestra's ability to pay, and equity with a more highly paid group of symphony musicians is the objective. During collective bargaining negotiations at the Cleveland Orchestra in January 2010, for example, a union spokesman stated that Cleveland's symphony musicians could not permit their salaries to fall further behind salaries at other orchestras. The consequence, he claimed, would be that "our musicians are going to leave for greener pastures" (Wakin 2010). At the time, musicians at six other U.S. orchestras (Boston, Chicago, New York Philharmonic, Philadelphia, Los Angeles, and San Francisco) received higher salaries. Each of these orchestras differed in their access to ticket revenues, private contributions, and endowment income—the revenue side of ability to pay.

If differences in total real compensation emerged between orchestras, there would be an incentive for musicians to move when more highly compensated positions became available at other orchestras. Lost in the rhetoric of collective bargaining disputes, however, is the fact that the monetary salaries determined in negotiations are not the total real compensation of an orchestra position. The cost of living varies significantly between cities, for example, and real salaries vary accordingly. Musicians who receive identical nominal salaries from different orchestras will find that their real salaries— their purchasing power—vary inversely with differences in the cost of living. (In the Cleveland Orchestra example, residents of Cleveland enjoy a lower cost of living than residents of New York, Boston, Los Angeles, San Francisco, and several other American cities with major orchestras.)

There is another way in which total real compensation is broader than the salaries determined in collective bargaining. Workers also weigh the nonmonetary characteristics of jobs when deciding where to work. Most workers find jobs with a risk of injury or death less attractive than riskless jobs. Most teachers prefer to work in schools with bright, hard-working students and adequate supplies of books and other classroom materials. People with musical talent would rather play classical music than work on an assembly line. And so forth. These tastes and distastes for various nonmonetary conditions of work produce a subtle but distinct effect on salaries. Since the writings of Adam Smith, almost 250 years ago, economists have recognized that salaries tend to vary systematically with nonmonetary characteristics of jobs in competitive labor markets. If most workers find risky jobs unattractive, the many applicants for safe jobs will force down salaries in those jobs. Part of the overall compensation of workers in safe jobs is the nonmonetary benefit of a safe work environment. Employers with risky jobs will have to pay higher salaries if they are to attract workers away from safe jobs. The salary premium effectively compensates workers for the nonmonetary cost of bearing extra risk (and provides incentives for employers to reduce the risk associated with their jobs). Labor market competition will produce a difference in money salaries between safe and risky jobs, but total monetary plus nonmonetary compensation will be identical. Salary differentials offset or compensate for differences in the value of nonmonetary working conditions.

Nonmonetary compensation influences the market for symphony musicians in two ways. First, it explains the overwhelming supply of aspiring symphony musicians. Attracted by the prospect of a career performing music they love, the flow of well-trained musicians continues to grow. The growing supply places ongoing downward pressure on wages. That pressure is resisted in collective bargaining, which usually prevents salaries from falling to their competitive level. The fact that the monetary rewards for symphony musicians have increased relative to the pay in most other occupations in recent decades makes symphony employment doubly attractive, further increasing the supply of classical musicians. But by raising labor costs, the pay increases also reduce the number of positions available for the growing number of aspiring musicians.

Nonmonetary working conditions also influence the attractiveness of positions in different orchestras. The caliber of the music director, the ability of other musicians, and the characteristics of the city in which an orchestra is located all influence the choice of employment. Where these factors are relatively attractive, a competitive market would produce lower salaries and conversely. Only when nonmonetary working conditions are identical across a group of symphony orchestras would equal salaries produce equality in compensation. When equal salaries are imposed by collective bargaining, orchestras with favorable nonmonetary conditions will effectively provide higher compensation to their musicians than orchestras with less favorable conditions.

Salary Determination for Symphony Musicians

In the face of the conflicting objectives of symphony management and symphony musicians, how sensitive are musicians' wages to the financial balance of symphony orchestras? A statistical analysis of the wage and financial balance data from our sample of orchestras from the 1987–88 through the 2005–6 concert seasons addressed this question. The overall financial balance of orchestras was separated into the performance deficit (difference between performance revenues and expenses) and the contributed support from private and government sources—both as a percentage of performance expenses. This approach permitted an examination of whether musicians' salaries are equally responsive to changes in performance deficits and to changes in contributions or government subsidies. The measures of financial balance were often lagged one year to capture the idea that financial conditions in the recent past influence current negotiations.[8]

The statistical analysis found that symphony musicians' salaries did not vary reliably with the overall financial balance of orchestras (performance and nonperformance revenues minus performance and nonperformance expenses). Instead, there was a reliable positive relationship between the level of current and past private contributions to orchestras and musicians' salaries (Flanagan 2010). Effectively, higher wages tend to undermine efforts to offset performance deficits with increased private support. The availability of private support may create significant ambiguity about the true economic constraints faced by an orchestra. It is clear from the record of symphony orchestra bankruptcies since the late 1980s that wage settlements that ignore measures of an organization's economic strength can have serious consequences.

Orchestra Bankruptcies

Situations of extreme financial distress, such as the bankruptcies of symphony orchestras, may provide an even sharper perspective on how collective bargaining policies respond to adverse economic conditions.[9] Since 1989, a dozen significant U.S. symphony orchestras ceased operations for some period. Some orchestras eventually reopened, often with a different name. Others closed permanently.[10]

Available data permit a review of changes in collectively bargained wages and weeks of work before and (for orchestras that reorganized) after the cessation of operations. The central question is whether these data reveal evidence of collective bargaining concessions in the face of financial crises. For symphony orchestras that eventually resumed operations after a bankruptcy, the data also permit an evaluation of the impact of symphony closures on musicians.

Prior to cessation of operations, minimum musicians' salaries fell in only one of the orchestras (one year before the shutdown) and were frozen in two others (also for the year preceding the shutdown). Wages continued to increase in the remaining orchestras. Declines in *relative* wages were somewhat more common, occurring in about half of the orchestras in this sample of distressed organizations. (The relative pay of an orchestra's musicians is the ratio of their minimum salary to the average minimum salary paid by a group of 32 orchestras.) Declining relative wages did not prevent closures, but they raised the odds that a symphony would eventually reopen. Permanent closures invariably occurred in orchestras in which the musicians' relative wages did not fall in response to the financial distress that preceded bankruptcy. Finally, there was little evidence of concessions in guaranteed weeks of work preceding shutdowns. Only two orchestras seem to have gained such concessions (in the year preceding their shutdown). Both of these orchestras eventually reorganized and reopened.

The consequences of the closures for symphony musicians were severe. Half of the closures were permanent; temporary closures lasted from two to five years. In about half of the orchestras, musicians' minimum salaries were lower when the orchestra reopened than they had been before suspension of operations. Some orchestras that paid higher salaries after reopening eventually experienced salary declines. Compared to wages in benchmark orchestras, the wages of musicians in reorganized orchestras were lower, and the relative wages often continued to decline for several years after reorganization. The annual concert season (guaranteed weeks of work) was shorter in virtually all orchestras that reopened.

Given the nature of symphony orchestra operations and the collective bargaining agreements that regulate musicians' work life, collective bargaining's muted and lagging response to financial distress is difficult to explain. In unionized goods-producing industries, where job security is to a large degree dependent on seniority, resistance to pay concessions in the face of economic challenges is easier to understand. Layoffs generally affect the least senior workers. Because high-seniority workers are not at risk, they are likely to resist concessions in the face of economic adversity. Only when economic challenges threaten job security of the median union member are pay and other concessions likely to be considered seriously. This scenario does not describe the work environment of a symphony orchestra, where seniority influences pay but not the allocation of most employment opportunities. The delayed and incomplete adjustments to financial difficulties may reflect musicians' belief that emergency philanthropic appeals will produce the funding to ride out another financial crisis.

Orchestra Survivals

Not all orchestras experience the endgame scenario. In the face of economic adversity, musicians in some surviving orchestras have supported concessions that significantly eased the financial stress of an orchestra during a recession. In April 2009, for example, musicians at the Atlanta Symphony Orchestra, then the sixth largest symphony in the United States, modified their four-year collective bargaining agreement to accept compensation reductions of 5 percent for the remainder of their current season as well as the following season. Previously, the orchestra had announced pay cuts of 5 percent for nonartistic staff employees, 6 percent for vice presidents, a minimum of 10 percent per year for the CEO, and, in successive years, 7 percent and 14 percent cuts for the music director (Atlanta Symphony Orchestra 2009). The musicians also agreed to leave a minimum of two unfilled positions open, while the orchestra agreed to freeze unfilled administrative staff positions and require administrative staff to take several mandatory unpaid furlough days during the 2009–10 concert season.

In a similar adjustment to the severe recession that began in 2008, Chicago Symphony Orchestra musicians joined a general cost-cutting plan implemented by the orchestra's management. In October 2008 orchestra management initiated a staff salary and hiring freeze and announced reductions in performance fees for guest soloists and conductors in an effort to reduce expenditures by 25 percent and 50 percent during the 2008–9 and 2009–10 concert seasons, respectively. In May 2009 the musicians agreed to a 2.5 percent salary reduction and donated an extra rehearsal and performance in the 2009–10 and 2010–11 seasons to perform concerts that would benefit orchestra revenues.

An important lesson of these episodes is that modifications of a collective bargaining agreement are easier to achieve in the face of economic adversity when an orchestra's nonmusician personnel accept economic sacrifices first. But such actions do not guarantee reciprocity. Efforts by orchestras in several other cities to adjust to their diminished financial circumstances in the wake of the Great Recession were met with strikes by their musicians, canceled concerts, and even bankruptcies.

Successor Orchestras

Some orchestras have reorganized following bankruptcies, albeit with reduced economic circumstances and sometimes unusual governance arrangements. One of the more interesting stories concerns the demise of the New Orleans Symphony in 1990 and its subsequent reorganization as the Louisiana Philharmonic Orchestra (LPO) in 1991.

A majority of the musicians from the failed symphony established the LPO as a musician-owned cooperative, which by 2007 consisted of 66 members playing a 36-week season of about 90 performances per year. Under this arrangement, musicians are the residual claimants—their salaries depend on the income that remains after paying orchestra expenses. Each year orchestra musicians vote on their own compensation, which averages about half the pay in comparable orchestras in similar markets with similar seasons. In short, their pay is considerably below the level of the failed New Orleans Symphony.

The musicians also establish the orchestra's size; choose the music director; work cooperatively with the music director and artistic administrator in programming; have the majority vote on all musician audition, tenure, and disciplinary matters; and set their own work rules without any formal collective bargaining. Each year the musicians record their choices and present their "collective bargaining agreement" to the AFM local for signature. By 2006 the LPO had a 15-person professional staff—well below the staff size of comparable orchestras.

Formal governance arrangements have evolved over time. Orchestra musicians elect all but two members of the board of trustees, and board membership was 100 percent musicians through the first four seasons. Later the board was evenly split between musicians and community members, but retained a musician as president. Still later the organization adopted a two-president model—a musician president for the orchestra and a community president for the board. Eventually the composition of the board changed to one-third musicians and two-thirds community.

Conclusions

The dominating feature of the labor market for symphony musicians is the huge supply of well-trained classical musicians seeking employment. The supply responds to both pay and the distinctive nonfinancial rewards that accompany opportunities for artistic expression. The huge supply relative to demand puts a downward pressure on artistic pay.

Downward market pressures on the financial rewards have been countered by collective bargaining negotiations, producing agreements signed by both symphony managements and the musicians' union. The content of these collective agreements reflects the inherent bargaining weakness of a not-for-profit organization as much as the bargaining strength of labor unions. Unions lack the ability to alter the main challenge to the working conditions of symphony musicians—the growing supply of new classical musicians. In fact they may exacerbate the problem. Ironically, the collective agreements that improve pay, employment stability, and other nonmonetary working conditions for employed symphony musicians also attract more musicians to symphony jobs, even though the odds of finding a position continue to diminish.

We can now understand that the cyclical insensitivity of artistic costs identified earlier in the book flows from special institutional rules. In the face of a recession, most organizations can mitigate employment costs by reducing the amount of employment or the pay of employees. Symphony collective bargaining agreements reduce the economic insecurity faced by employed symphony musicians by specifying both the wage and the labor input. The agreements now go beyond the constraints imposed by repertoire, specifying the number of regular musicians, annual weeks of work, number of services per week, and so on.

With the labor input more or less fixed, collective bargaining focuses on wage determination, but there is little incentive to shape wages to standard measures of organizational performance. Since the late 1980s the wages of symphony musicians have increased more rapidly than the wages of most other workers. The pay increases of symphony musicians in this study's sample were even greater than those assumed in the cost-disease argument discussed in chapter 2. Moreover, the pay increases were not strongly correlated with the financial performance of orchestras. Instead, musicians' wages were strongly correlated with private donations to orchestras. The large number of orchestra bankruptcies over the past 20 years demonstrates that a wage policy that ignores measures of an organization's economic strength will have serious consequences for both musicians and music lovers. Without some moderation in the growth of artistic and other expenses, these consequences can only be avoided by attracting ever-increasing flows of nonperformance income. The next three chapters examine the prospects for this strategy, beginning with an analysis of government support in chapter 7.

CHAPTER 7

Government Support of Orchestras

The relentless advance of costs has made it increasingly difficult for wealthy individuals to cover the growing operating deficits of symphony orchestras. In response, orchestras have attempted to adjust to the diminishing role of wealthy angels. First, they gradually developed fundraising operations that sought a much broader base of private support. The revenue modern orchestras now receive from their private fundraising activities will receive attention in the next chapter and in chapter 9, which addresses building and managing endowments.

Symphony orchestras and other performing arts organizations have also increasingly sought government support for their activities, but there has been far more resistance to public expenditures for the arts in the United States than abroad. In fact the evolution of nonperformance income for orchestras in the United States differs sharply from that in most other countries, where government subsidies account for most outside support. Proposals to balance the budgets of U.S. arts organizations through government subsidies have produced long and ultimately unresolved academic and political debates about whether there is a case for ongoing government support for the arts. The extensive literature produced by these debates will not be reviewed here; interested readers should consult Baumol and Bowen 1966 (chap. 16), Peacock 1993, Frey 2000, and the many references therein.

More than finances are at stake when arts organizations turn to governments for support. How that support is delivered and whether it is delivered at all may have profound effects on how art is defined, what works are performed, and the nature and distribution of creative activity. This chapter examines the role of federal, state, and local governments in the financing of U.S. symphony orchestras and the broader implications of the U.S. approach to public support of the arts. Chapter 10 covers the strikingly different role of government support of orchestras in most foreign countries.

Direct Government Support for Orchestras

Most symphony orchestras in the United States now receive some direct monetary support from federal, state, or local governments, but this was not always so. Prior to the 1960s, most subsidies for orchestras and other performing arts came from local governments that donated land for the construction of concert halls, built civic auditoriums that could be used for concerts, or provided property tax exemptions. But the resources of local governments are necessarily limited. Indeed, some government activities can be subject themselves to the cost disease that confronts orchestras and other performing arts (Baumol 1967). When arts organizations seek government support, they are turning to other institutions that face the problem of coping with growing structural budget deficits.

While some federal government support for musical organizations can be traced to the establishment of the U.S. Marine Band in 1790, most proposals to broaden public support for the arts over the next 150 years died in congressional committees. The historical absence of state and federal support in the United States reflected a laissez-faire culture and a widespread belief that the scope of government should be kept as small as possible. The following observation nicely captures the prevailing sentiment prior to the 1930s: "A government that did not subsidize agriculture or housing, provide unemployment insurance to workers, or offer a subsistence income to the poorest of its poor was not going to be asked to subsidize operas, symphony concerts, or ballets." (Heilbrun and Gray 2001, p. 251)

While some federal support for artists emerged during the Great Depression, those programs were designed to provide relief to unemployed symphony musicians for the duration of the economic emergency rather than to provide ongoing support for the arts. Most prominently, the Federal Music Project provided nationwide relief to musicians by establishing and supporting orchestras, other musical performance ensembles, and music teaching centers (Grant and Hettinger 1940, chap. 8).

Ongoing federal support for symphony orchestras and other arts had to await the creation of the National Endowment for the Arts (NEA) in

1965. Even then, there was deep suspicion and significant political resistance to the notion of centralized allocation of artistic support. To address this concern, the legislation establishing the NEA required the agency to distribute some funds to states that established arts agencies and appropriated matching funds. At the time only five states had official arts agencies, but the NEA legislation encouraged the rapid establishment of such organizations in all states by awarding up to 20 percent of its program funds to qualifying state and regional arts organizations (NEA 2007, p. 6).

By the late 1980s, the funds spent by the 50 state arts organizations exceeded federal funding for the arts, which peaked in real terms in 1979. Initially states tended to allocate most funds to symphony orchestras, opera companies, ballet companies, art museums, and other institutions presenting traditional "great art" largely rooted in European artistic traditions. Underlying this priority was the challengeable view that private market mechanisms would not produce great art. (See the discussion of this view in chapter 10.) With time, state agencies encountered criticisms that their philosophy was too restrictive to appeal to the increasingly multicultural society in the United States. Political decision making argued for providing broad support, which required broader concepts of supportable art. State agencies responded by developing more inclusive definitions of art and by decentralizing more funding decisions to the growing number of local arts agencies. Together these agencies met the political challenge by awarding many small grants to a wider array of arts organizations—an approach that reduced the support available for symphony orchestras and other large traditional arts organizations. Some larger arts organizations responded by seeking specific line-item budget support from state legislatures.

Between the growth of subsidies to the arts by state and local governments and the fact that much federal support is channeled through state and local agencies, decision making over the allocation of public funds for the arts has been considerably decentralized since the mid-1960s. By statute, block grants to state and local agencies now constitute 40 percent of the NEA budget.

Funding Decisions by Government Arts Agencies

Since the late 1980s, Congress has diminished the amount of direct federal support for the arts and altered the methods by which federal support is distributed. These developments have further decreased the federal funds available to symphony orchestras. When some members of Congress regarded the work of a few NEA-supported visual artists as obscene in the early 1990s, the agency encountered a difficult period in which its continued existence was in doubt.[1] The agency's budget peaked at just under $176 million in fiscal year 1992. Between the 1995 and 1996 fiscal years, Congress cut the NEA budget from $162 to $99 million, forcing a 47 percent reduction in the NEA staff. By fiscal year 2006, the nominal budget had returned to $124 million—43 percent of the peak NEA budget in real terms.

The following quote from an NEA chair trying to adjust agency policies to congressional assaults on arts budgets captures how the choice between public or private arts funding can influence the freedom to pursue specific acts of artistic expression (Alexander 2000, p. 274): "I thought I knew how to make the Endowment bulletproof. As long as we gave blanket grants for an entire season of an organization's work without knowing exactly where the money was to be used, Congress, which called this buying 'a pig in a poke,' would be after us indefinitely. If, however, we gave to an organization for a specific work in progress, or for presentation or conservation of that work, it would be clear where the money went. Organizations would then be able to present what they wished during the rest of their season [financed by foundations and philanthropists] and not have the feds on their back." The implication that private philanthropy arrives without strings attached is perhaps too strong. As will become apparent in the next two chapters, private contributions may be tied to specific purposes or performances. But private donations generally carry fewer restrictions.

Congress insisted on revised and more restrictive procedures for distributing federal funds for the arts. Although none of the political controversy pertained to NEA support for symphony orchestras, a standard set of operating procedures applies to proposals for support for all performing and fine arts. NEA support now goes to *organizations*, not individuals, except in the case of literature and recognition of jazz masters.[2] Peer review panels assess the artistic merit of proposals from arts organizations. The use of outside peer review removes judgments of artistic merit from a government bureaucracy. To combat the risk that outside peer review presents opportunities for capture by a particular set of tastes, NEA panels include term limits, practice geographical and ethnic diversity, and do not permit panel members to screen proposals from current or former employers.

Decisions about how much federal funding should be awarded to each successful proposal are left to the National Council for the Arts and the chair of the NEA. Congress limits NEA support to a maximum of 50 percent of the cost of any proposal. The requirement that NEA grant recipients cofinance the projects may have reassured members of Congress that federal support did not undermine incentives to seek private support. The ability to attract matching funds also signaled that federally funded projects had some community appeal.

At this point, the political objectives of Congress and of government bureaucrats trump the evaluation of artistic merit to an important degree. In the words of the NEA:

> NEA support for state arts agencies is allocated through a combination of competitive awards and funding that is *distributed equally to each state and on a per-capita basis* [emphasis added]. In FY2006, approximately 91 percent of the Arts Endowment's contribution to the states was driven by a formula—whether funding the states in equal proportions, or based on state population—and the remaining 9 percent was awarded competitively (NEA 2007, p. 7).

Importantly for our concerns about how orchestras may cover their performance deficits, 1996 legislation eliminated NEA grants for operating support. If the NEA cannot provide operating support, it is unlikely to narrow the performance deficits of orchestras materially. To the extent that NEA grants are awarded for new projects, orchestras and other arts organizations must incur new costs in order to qualify for NEA support. Grants from other levels of government and private philanthropy must be relied upon to close the gap between performance revenues and expenses.

The procedures of state and local arts agencies differ most from the NEA on this issue. While most state agencies favor gifts to organizations and usually include cofinancing arrangements, they also provide operating support. In fact, it appears to be the largest category of state aid to arts organizations generally. Many of the approximately 4,000 local (city and county) arts agencies also include operating support in their portfolio of activities. As a result, state and local aid offers the prospect of slowing the growth of the performance deficits of orchestras and other arts organizations.

The outcome of this turbulent political history is a complex and highly decentralized system of allocating public subsidies for the arts. Funding decisions are also highly dispersed. If proposals fail at one agency, there are other agencies that an arts organization may approach for support. The decentralized approach limits the influence of arts elites and is more responsive to the diversity of public tastes, but it is not without its costs.

Considerable public money never reaches artists because it is spent on the bureaucracy of arts agencies. In this environment, moreover, arts organizations must develop active but costly fundraising operations in order to attract sufficient funds.

Public Subsidies and Symphony Finances

How did the outcome of these funding decisions influence symphony orchestra finances at the end of the 20th century? We have just seen two reasons why legislative appropriations for the arts provide a poor guide to the government support of any particular art form. Appropriations are not necessarily divided equally among the various arts, so changes in arts appropriations may not signal similar changes in support for any art form. Furthermore, the arts bureaucracies—staffs and advisers of federal, state, and local arts agencies—may capture a significant amount of an appropriation to fund the application, evaluation, and oversight processes that accompany government support.

The correlation between changes in NEA budgets and federal support received by individual orchestras therefore ranges widely. For the period covered by this study, the correlation between the NEA budget and the federal support received by orchestras in the study sample ranged between $-.50$ and $+.94$. For some orchestras there was a strong positive correlation between federal support actually received and the size of the NEA budget. Counterintuitively, there are also orchestras for which federal government support was inversely related to the size of the NEA budget or not significantly related at all. Understanding the influence of government on the financial stability of orchestras requires focus on the money actually received, not the money appropriated.

With three levels of government decision making, each subject to diverse political and artistic considerations, it makes little sense to maintain the fiction of a single level of "public" support. In fact, in any given year there is no significant correlation between the levels of support provided by the three levels of government. Clearly, comparisons of support by level of government will facilitate interpretations of trends in overall public support.

In the face of the growing need for nonperformance income, real direct subsidies from all levels of government combined declined at about 3.6 percent per year between 1987 and 2005 for the average orchestra, after

TABLE 7.1   TRENDS IN GOVERNMENT SUPPORT FOR SYMPHONY ORCHESTRAS, 1987–2005 (ANNUAL PERCENT CHANGE)

	Nominal	Real
Government (all levels)	−1.4%	−3.6%
Federal	−7.1%	−9.1%
State	−1.4%	−3.6%
Local	2.9%	0.7%

Source: Appendix to chapter 7.

holding cyclical influences constant. Two developments dominated falling public support to orchestras (table 7.1): declining federal support (over 9 percent per year in real terms) following the troubled political history of the NEA, and a much smaller drop (3.6 percent) in state support. More than inflation is at work in these trends. Nominal federal and state support also declined. Inflation may have diminished the purchasing power of public subsidies, but federal and state governments also appropriated smaller and smaller nominal amounts for symphony orchestras and other performing arts. In contrast, nominal support from local governments increased, but at a rate (2.9 percent) that barely stayed ahead of inflation. Subsidies from local governments constituted an increasing share of public support received by symphony orchestras (fig. 7.1). But the rising share of local government support reflects declines in federal and state support more than increases in local support.

Not all orchestras receive support from all levels of government. In 1987, 58 of the 63 orchestras reported government support. Forty-seven (81 percent) of these orchestras received some support from all three levels of government. Two received no federal support, three received no state support, and eight received no local support. By 2005 the patterns of government support had shifted substantially. Only 22 (45 percent) of the 49 orchestras that reported receiving government support received funds from all three levels of government. Fourteen received no federal support, eight received no state support, and ten received no local support.

To some extent, patterns of government support vary by orchestra size. About half of the orchestras analyzed had budgets exceeding $9 million in 1999. The federal share of government support was distinctly larger (and the local share distinctly smaller) for these large orchestras than for

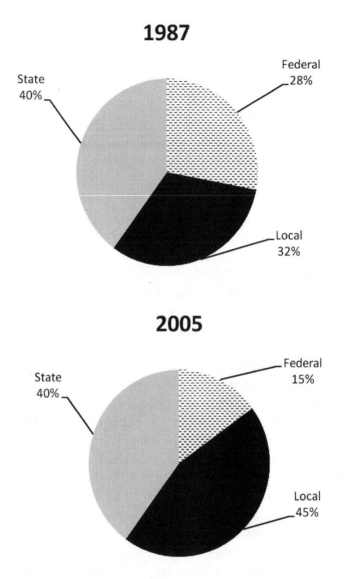

Figure 7.1. Distribution of Government Support for Orchestras, 1987 and 2005
Source: League of American Orchestras

orchestras with smaller budgets. The state share of government support was about the same for each group of orchestras. Between 1987 and 2005, the smaller orchestras experienced much larger declines in federal support. By 2005 federal funds accounted for less than 7 percent of government support to small orchestras (but 20 percent of the support to large orchestras).

In short, trends in government support have exacerbated the long-term financial challenges faced by U.S. symphony orchestras by diminishing as the need for nonperformance income increased. Making matters worse, annual changes in government support worsen the short-term challenges posed by recessions. Overall government support is cyclically sensitive, diminishing in recessions when orchestras need it most. Changes in the flow of state and local funds to orchestras drive the cyclical sensitivity; in contrast, federal support to orchestras is not reliably correlated with changes in general economic conditions.[3] The difference in the cyclical patterns of support may reflect the fact that, unlike the federal government, state and local governments are required to balance their budgets annually, and support of the arts may be viewed as a highly discretionary budget item.

How Is Public Support to Orchestras Distributed?

Given the tensions between artistic merit, economic balance, and broad political objectives in allocating government support to orchestras, what do the data reveal about how public funds are in fact distributed? There are several possibilities. First, government support to symphony orchestras may vary with their financial need—the size of their performance deficit. The ban on using NEA funds to provide operating support implies that the relationship between operating deficits and federal government support would be weak at best. But support from state and local government sources may be less restricted. If financial balance is a factor in allocating public funds, government support should be directly related to the size of an orchestra's deficit.

There is a danger, discussed further in chapter 10, that allocating support on the basis of financial need will create moral hazard. Organizations that can count on a government bailout when they encounter serious deficits may become less diligent in avoiding deficits. When this occurs, support remains positively correlated with orchestra need, but with reversed causality. With moral hazard, government support encourages rather than responds to higher deficits.

Second, government funds may be allocated to reward perceived success, but how are the perceptions formed? Orchestra budget size is easy to observe and may reflect elements of artistic success such as long seasons, an active touring schedule, commissions of new symphonic compositions, and so on. Allocating funds on this basis reinforces past successes but may exacerbate resource and artistic differences between orchestras. A related budget issue concerns the effectiveness of fundraising expenditures in attracting public funds to orchestras.

Finally, since states and localities vary in their ability to support orchestras, government support might be allocated to narrow inherent geographical inequalities in economic capacity. If this motivation is important, government support should be *inversely* related to an area's income and population. As the NEA case illustrates, however, political support may only be available for arts funding that is distributed between states on an equal per capita basis. If equalization of per capita payments is a strong motivation, funds received by orchestras will be positively related to an area's population.

A statistical analysis clarifies how each of these diverse factors was associated with the support from each level of government between 1987 and 2005. The analysis reveals how that support varied with the income and population of each orchestra's community, the orchestra's financial need as signaled by its performance income ratio (fraction of performance expenses covered by performance revenues), the orchestra's budget size, and development expenditures. (All monetary variables were adjusted for inflation.)

The results of the statistical analysis confirm some hypotheses but challenge others (table 7.2). The real income of an orchestra's community is unrelated to the total amount of government support received by an orchestra, but this outcome reflects a balance of two conflicting forces. High-income areas received more local but less federal support on average. Put differently, direct federal government support tended to offset differences in community economic strength, while local support tended to reflect and reinforce differences in local ability to pay. Local and federal support increased with the population of a community, consistent with an emphasis on per capita subsidies. State government support was not reliably related to either of these measures of community economic strength.

Only state support was reliably responsive to the economic condition of individual orchestras, with proportionately more support reaching orchestras with worse or deteriorating performance deficits. At the same time, large-budget orchestras received more support from all levels of government than small-budget orchestras. The analysis separated the fundraising budget from the rest of the orchestra's budget in order to assess the effect of fundraising activities on the level of public support received. The statistical results reported in table 7.2 may strike some readers as odd. After holding

TABLE 7.2 DETERMINANTS OF GOVERNMENT SUPPORT, 1987–2005

Level of Government	The Effect of One Percent Increase in				The Effect of One Point Increase in		The Effect of One Additional Year
	Real Income	Population	Budget	Fundraising Expense	Performance Income Ratio[a]	Unemployment Rate	
Local	1.5%	.3%	.3%	No effect	No effect	No effect	−3.2%
State	No effect	No effect	.6%	No effect	−1.0%	−6.2%	−5.1%
Federal	−1.2%	.2%	.8%	No effect	No effect	No effect	−10.1%
All levels	No effect	.1%	.4%	.2%	−.6%	−3.6%	−5.5%

Source: Table A7.2 in appendix to chapter 7.

Notes: All monetary variables in year 2000 dollars.

"No effect" = no statistically significant effect.

[a] Fraction of performance expenses covered by performance revenues.

the influence of the other variables on government support constant, there was no statistically significant relationship between an orchestra's fundraising expenditures and the amount of support that it received from any level of government. Yet total support received from all levels of government combined had a small but statistically reliable correlation with an orchestra's fundraising expenses. Since fundraising efforts are normally targeted at specific levels of government, this result is probably most sensibly viewed as an anomaly of data aggregation.

Federal support places more, although not exclusive, weight on broader economic conditions. The net effect of the distribution of federal support, however, is to create greater inequality in the financial resources of symphony orchestras. Finally, no significant relationship exists between local support and any of the potential influences. The lack of a significant statistical result is consistent with the claim that local resources are distributed widely and in small amounts in order to build and maintain a political base.

Does Government Support Displace Private Support?

The full effect of government support for symphony orchestras depends on how that support influences private contributions. If government support for orchestras discourages private support from individuals, businesses, and foundations, nonperformance income will increase by less than the amount of government subsidies. If potential supporters of orchestras believe that their inclination to contribute has been fulfilled by tax-financed government subsidies, government expenditures on orchestras would displace or crowd out private donations. On the other hand, government support of orchestras might "validate" them in the eyes of the public and attract more private donations. Moreover, requirements that government funds be matched by private funds could increase private donations to symphony orchestras and other performing arts. In the end, the displacement issue is a question that must be settled by an appeal to data.

The economics literature now contains several studies testing for displacement effects from government support of nonprofit organizations. The evidence is mixed, with studies of some organizations finding significant "crowding out" of private funds, while other studies find evidence of either "crowding in" or ambiguous impact. Studies of symphony orchestras fall in the latter category (Brooks 2000; Smith 2007). Testing for the presence or absence of displacement effects requires a determination of whether larger government support is or is not associated with lower private contributions, after controlling for the effects of other influences on private contributions. Most displacement studies control for the effects of fundraising expenditures by arts organizations, ticket sales (which may influence private contributions), and variables capturing the economic capacity of communities to support the arts.

These studies also raise certain statistical issues that must be addressed before one can be sure of the direction of causality between private donations and government grants. A frustrating outcome of statistical diligence can be that a relationship that emerges with the use of one technique disappears when another technique is applied. Such is the case with the question of how government support of symphony orchestras influences private support. The strongest statement that can be made is that there is no evidence consistent with a displacement effect from government support for symphony orchestras (Smith 2007).

Alternative Forms of Government Support

Establishing a case for government financial support of orchestras does not establish a case for any particular method of support. Even the most respectable cases for public support of symphony orchestras remain mute on how that support should be delivered. Yet the method of government intervention determines how much money actually reaches artists and their endeavors, which members of the community determine the range of creative activities that will be defined as supportable art, and hence what artistic activities will receive public funding.

As mentioned in preceding sections, the method of direct public subsidies to arts organizations produces a significant arts bureaucracy devoted to channeling funds and lobbying for additional funds. This feature presumably reduces the fraction of public support actually spent on performances and other artistic activities. Moreover, direct subsidization inevitably requires relatively centralized approaches to determining which artistic activities will be supported. Whether that determination is made by government bureaucrats, designated peer review boards, or a legislative body, the process is likely to reflect the tastes and judgments of a relatively small number of people. In large measure, the potential audience for the arts has no say on which organizations get funded. Concerns over centralized spending decisions have surfaced frequently in U.S. legislative debates over public support of artistic enterprises. As we have observed, the ways in which legislative bodies have "resolved" these concerns have their own problems.

Direct subsidies are not the only way to deliver government support to symphony orchestras and other artistic endeavors, however. Considering alternative methods of support reveals how incompletely discussions of direct subsidies capture the overall effect of government on total nonperformance income. In particular, most discussions of public support overlook the impact of government policies on the amount of private giving.

Tax Expenditures

The most important government-related financial support received by U.S. symphony orchestras and other artistic organizations flows from tax policy. The Internal Revenue Code permits taxpayers to deduct contributions to most nonprofit organizations from their taxable income. Some 60 percent of U.S. taxpayers, who itemize their deductions rather than take a standard deduction, qualify for this tax break. Such "tax expenditures"—revenues that the government could collect and spend, but instead allows citizens to spend for specific purposes—constitute a major source of the funding for cultural organizations in the United States. As a result, the direct government subsidies for the arts discussed above constitute a decidedly incomplete measure of public support. The fact that government policies may influence the volume of private donations also greatly complicates the task of comparing government support by different countries (see chapter 10).

High-income U.S. taxpayers receive the strongest incentives to contribute to orchestras and other nonprofit organizations under this policy. Because high-income earners generally face the highest tax rates on their additional income, the government's effective share of their donations is largest. In the early 21st century, the highest marginal federal tax rate was 35 percent. When someone in this tax bracket contributed $1,000 to an orchestra, the federal government effectively "paid" $350 of the donation in the sense that, if the contribution had not been made, the taxpayer would have owed $350 more in federal taxes. The charitable deduction effectively reduces the "price" of contributions to orchestras. Changes in tax legislation can therefore alter the incentives for donations to symphony orchestras. In the mid-1980s, cuts in federal tax rates reduced incentives to contribute. In later years, the incentives gradually grew stronger as income tax rates slowly increased. In February 2009 President Obama released a national budget proposal that would have limited the extent to which taxpayers could deduct contributions to nonprofit organizations beginning in 2011. The proposed formula would have reduced the government's maximum share of a $1,000 donation from $350 to $280, irrespective of a taxpayer's income level.[4]

Supporting orchestras and other performing arts through tax expenditures does not require a government to establish an "arts bureaucracy" to designate supportable art. Instead, taxpayers decide which artistic activities merit support when they allocate their donations to different arts organizations. The tax expenditure approach decentralizes the determination of "supportable art" to taxpayers.

In decentralizing public support decisions, the tax expenditure approach brings a much broader range of tastes into the determination of artistic spending. This consideration is not unimportant in a society as heterogeneous as the United States, where ethnic and other diversity produces demands for a broader perspective on artistic activity than may be recognized by elites who may determine the distribution of public support in a regime of direct government subsidies. Not all tastes receive equal weight, however. The tastes of high-income people who gain the most from charitable deductions under the current tax code will receive disproportionately high representation.

When support flows directly from taxpayer decisions, taxpayers have a much stronger incentive to monitor the performance of the organizations they support and to ensure that their money is spent wisely. Organizations such as www.guidestar.org that evaluate the performance of various nonprofits and provide their ratings on the Internet greatly facilitate this task. Nonprofits seeking donations have an incentive to adopt policies that raise taxpayers' confidence in their performance. The tax expenditure approach is not without its costs, however. Orchestras and other arts organizations must invest in significant fundraising operations in order to attract contributions from individuals, businesses, and foundations.

There is also an important organizational consequence: indirect public support via tax expenditures is not a recipe for a quiet financial life for symphony orchestras and other arts organizations. The organizational implications were nicely captured by Dana Gioia, a former chair of the National Endowment for the Arts: "Similar [arts] institutions often have wildly differing results because of their locations, artistic talent, cultural philosophies, and management. Likewise, the dynamic nature of the system means that one decade's high-flying leader can suffer huge reversals in the next—just as in corporate America. While no one relishes the ups and downs of the cultural economy, it does have the healthy effect of keeping artists and institutions realistically focused on their goals and communities." (NEA 2007, p. vi)

Tax Expenditures for Symphony Orchestras

We have already observed that, by the measure of direct subsidies, there is considerably less public support in the United States than abroad—a discussion that will continue in chapter 10. To what extent does our view of public support change if we incorporate the value of government tax expenditures for orchestras?

It is much easier to pose this question than to answer it with official data on tax expenditures. The U.S. Office of Management and Budget (OMB) publishes information on the total value of annual tax expenditures in the nation, but it does not publish comparable information for symphony orchestras or even the performing arts collectively.[5] Lacking official data, one can estimate federal tax expenditures for orchestras using information on contributions received by orchestras from individuals and businesses. The schedules of federal income tax rates on individuals and businesses enable one to estimate how much money the federal government foregoes (that is, the tax expenditure) by permitting individuals and corporations to deduct contributions to symphony orchestras from their taxable income. Multiplying the applicable tax rate times the value of the individual or business contribution to orchestras provides an estimate of how much the government would have collected in taxes had it not permitted individuals and businesses to deduct their contributions.

Both individual and corporate income tax rates vary by income bracket. For married couples filing a joint tax return, tax rates ranged in 1987 from 11 percent (for taxable income under $3,000) to 38.5 percent (for income over $90,000). In 2005 the rates ranged from 10 percent (for income under $14,600) to 35 percent (for income over $326,450). For contributions to orchestras by individuals, table 7.3 provides estimates of tax expenditures for several tax rates. It seems likely that the 28 percent rate for incomes between $28 ($59.4) thousand and $45 ($119.9) thousand dollars in 1987

TABLE 7.3   DIRECT AND INDIRECT GOVERNMENT EXPENDITURES ON U.S.
SYMPHONY ORCHESTRAS

	1987		2005	
	Tax Rate (%)	Public Support	Tax Rate (%)	Public Support
Tax expenditures				
Individual donations	15	$9,493,462	25	$78,843,063
	28	17,721,129	28	88,304,230
	35	22,151,411	33	104,072,840
	38.5	24,366,552	35	110,380,290
Business donations	34	15,666,855	34	26,326,106
Government expenditures	—	11,007,964	—	4,457,365
Total government support at 28% individual rate		44,395,948		119,097,701
Percentage direct government expenditure		24.8%		3.7%

Source: League of American Orchestras; Tax Foundation; author's computations.

(2005) represents a suitable median income tax rate for the groups most likely to contribute to symphony orchestras, but the table offers estimates of individual tax expenditures at several tax rates. In both 1987 and 2005, corporations reached a 34 percent tax rate at $75,000 of income. Significant donations to orchestras are likely to come from corporations with income above this level, so 34 percent is used for the tax rate to estimate federal tax expenditures attributable to business contributions to orchestras, even though some corporations faced a higher income tax rate in each of these years.[6]

The table conveys two important facts about federal support for orchestras. First, federal tax expenditures for symphony orchestras dwarf direct government support. Second, tax expenditures have become the more important source of government support over time. When direct federal expenditures were near their peak in 1987, they constituted about one-quarter of total federal support to orchestras. Between 1987 and 2005, tax expenditures for orchestras grew rapidly in real terms. During this period, which included various congressional assaults on the NEA budget, *total* government support to orchestras *increased*. The growth of indirect support via tax expenditures more than offset the decline in direct federal subsidies. In the face of rising tax expenditures and falling NEA appropriations, direct subsidies to orchestras had became a trivial element (3–4 percent) of federal support for orchestras.

The paradox of declining direct subsidies and increasing tax expenditures is easily explained. The key point is the fact that the tax deduction is not targeted for the arts but for nonprofit organizations, of which orchestras and the arts compose a small fraction. Congress cannot easily challenge the tax expenditures that benefit orchestras and other performing arts without taking on the entire nonprofit community. Moreover, an effort to challenge tax expenditures would place a Congress that is generally suspicious of centralized arts support in the position of opposing an effective mechanism for decentralized arts support.

As impressive as they are, the estimates of federal tax expenditures in table 7.3 underestimate total U.S. tax expenditures for orchestras. State and local tax policies may encourage additional private contributions, but the extensive variation in those policies complicates efforts to estimate their value. It must suffice to note that incorporating state and local tax expenditures would further increase estimates of the role of indirect government support for orchestras.

One final point: the discussion of tax expenditures clarifies two sources of geographic variation in private support for orchestras and other performing arts. Federal tax incentives for private support are strongest in areas with a concentration of high-income individuals and businesses. Tax incentives vary further with differences in state and local tax policies and tax rates.

Government Support to Symphony Audiences

Under this approach, governments try to raise the performance income of performing arts organizations by subsidizing concert *attendance*. (In contrast, both direct government expenditures on the arts and tax expenditures subsidize concert *production*—determined in one case by designated arts elites and in the other by individual citizens and businesses when they choose the recipients of their philanthropic donations.) In subsidizing attendance, the government retains responsibility for providing financial support to the arts, but the support takes the form of vouchers that recipients can use to reduce the cost of admission to artistic events. The costs of distributing attendance vouchers are likely to be much lower than the costs of administering production subsidies.

An annual Museumkaart available in the Netherlands provides an example of how an orchestra or general arts performance voucher system might work. Individuals pay a fixed fee for the card, which enables them to visit a long list of public museums throughout the country at significant discounts. At the prices charged in the early 21st century, most Museumkaart holders are "in the money" after visiting four museums. By reducing the price per visit, the Museumkaart presumably increases the annual number of visits and visitors to a museum. If the exposure to a museum is pleasurable, the experience may change tastes in a way that builds future visits or even a demand for more museums. Since the voucher must be purchased, taxpayers fund only the administrative costs of the program. The Museumkaart scheme clarifies the issues that must be addressed with this approach to government support for orchestras.

A voucher scheme may raise attendance, but will it actually raise performance revenues? Revenues will increase if vouchers can be restricted to individuals who are least likely to attend a performance otherwise—an attendance voucher for young people, for example. In this instance, a voucher scheme becomes an example of the price discrimination approach to raising revenues first discussed in chapter 5. It may nonetheless be difficult to restrict public voucher schemes in this way. More likely, the vouchers would be available to anyone with sufficient interest to purchase one, but this would include many individuals who would have attended a symphony concert without the subsidy. From these attendees, the orchestra would receive less revenue than it would have before vouchers were available. If a voucher scheme is to raise performance revenues, it must stimulate a gain in revenues from new attendees that exceeds the loss of revenue on tickets that could have been sold without the discount. In economists' language, demand for attendance must be price elastic. The evidence presented in chapter 5, however, indicates that attendance at symphony concerts is price *in*elastic.

Of course, the government itself would gain revenues each year from the sale of vouchers—assuming they were sold to the public, like the Dutch Museumkaart. To some extent, the potential revenue losses of arts organizations might be offset by distributing these revenues to participating organizations. This would require a rule for distributing the revenues from voucher sales. Revenues might, for example, be distributed according to the volume of attendance in which a voucher was used.

A meaningful voucher system should provide consumers with choices as well as discounts. Indeed, subsidizing consumers further decentralizes artistic choices, a feature that provokes opposition from those members of the arts community who are heavily invested in lobbying for public production subsidies. Vouchers may raise the odds that individuals will attend a performance, but performing arts organizations that wish to attract more revenues must provide programs that attract audiences. In the United States, vouchers restricted to symphony orchestra concerts may provide insufficient choice, because except in the largest cities, consumers have practical access to only one orchestra. Culture vouchers that can be exercised at a variety of participating arts organizations therefore seem more attractive than symphony orchestra vouchers.

The words "participating arts organizations" remind us that voucher systems do not completely decentralize the demand for performances. Some entity—presumably a public agency—must announce the list of such organizations. In defining where vouchers may be used, that agency determines which artistic activities are likely to gain attendance and even which activities are likely to lose attendance, since the voucher effectively lowers the relative price of favored activities.

Carefully designed attendance vouchers offer governments a tool for building and broadening symphony audiences. But one should recall a key point from our broader look at concert attendance in chapter 5: the vast majority of orchestras in the United States cannot eliminate their performance deficits by filling their halls at each concert.

Concluding Comments

Direct public subsidies for symphony orchestras and other performing arts have always been a difficult political sell in the United States, and the past 45 years have witnessed a dramatic rise and fall of government subsidies. Since the late 1980s, support from federal and state governments has declined as the need for nonperformance income to cover growing performance deficits of orchestras has increased. Modest increases in local government support have provided only partial offsets to the federal and state declines. Orchestras and other arts organizations may continue to benefit from special short-term public expenditure programs to combat recessions, but in an era of large structural government budget deficits, a long-term growth of direct government support to orchestras seems unlikely in the United States.

Over the same period, the federal tax expenditures implied by private contributions to symphony orchestras grew rapidly. By 2005 over 95 percent of federal government support to U.S. orchestras came in the form of tax expenditures. Federal support of orchestras is now 20 times larger than one infers from looking at the value of direct government subsidies.

Both the importance of tax expenditures, which turn the distribution of support over to donors, and the methods for allocating the diminishing amount of direct U.S. government subsidies produce a highly decentralized system of government support for orchestras and other arts. The system resists capture by arts elites and facilitates the support of a more diverse range of artistic expression than might receive support in more centralized systems. Some of the themes that emerged in this chapter will be pursued further in the next chapter on private contributions and in the discussion of how foreign countries support orchestras (chapter 10).

Tax expenditures provide a more promising albeit still uncertain source of income to address the fundamental problem of ever-growing performance deficits. As incomes rise, more and more people move into the higher tax brackets that provide the strongest incentives to donate under current tax policy. There is no guarantee that such increases would be sufficient to cover the full growth of performance deficits, but unlike direct government subsidies, the trend is in the right direction. Future tax policy provides the main uncertainty. Faced with growing government budget deficits, tax revenues might be raised in two ways. If tax rates are increased, the incentives to contribute to nonprofit organizations will increase, and tax expenditures for orchestras are likely to grow more rapidly than under current tax policy. But tax revenues can also be increased by expanding the tax base (the range of income subject to taxation) while keeping tax rates unchanged. Reducing or eliminating charitable deductions—one approach to increasing the tax base—clearly would reduce the incentive to contribute to orchestras and other nonprofit organizations.

This chapter has demonstrated the importance of tax expenditures—a system in which private parties donate, but some of their donations are (foregone) government expenditures—for U.S. orchestras. We now turn to a full analysis of private support, recognizing that some "private" funds are truly public support distributed by private parties.

CHAPTER 8

Private Support of Orchestras

"The symphony orchestras were the first professional nonprofit arts groups in the United States to have patrons. . . . Long before the graduated income tax became a major incentive for private philanthropy, symphony orchestras were supported by the rich who wished to put their fortunes to good uses in public settings" (Ford Foundation 1974, p. 14). When a few committed patrons could cover deficits, professional fundraising operations were not necessary. As recently as the mid-1960s, many performing arts organizations had no systematic fundraising activities (Baumol and Bowen 1966, p. 324).

Over time, the relentless toll of increasing performance deficits required a broader base of support if orchestras were to survive. The previous chapter described how direct government subsidies have provided a transient and now diminishing source of nonperformance income. In this environment, private philanthropy—contributions from individuals, businesses, and foundations—plays the key role in offsetting performance deficits and in building endowments to address future variations in economic fortunes. To broaden the base of their financial support, orchestras must incur nonperformance expenses—notably for fundraising activities aimed at attracting private philanthropy. All orchestras now have significant fundraising operations, which constitute a steadily increasing if still modest share of their budgets.

This chapter describes the respective roles of contributions from these private sources and examines the determinants of contributions. Chapter 3 detailed how private contributions to orchestras vary with general economic conditions. We now go further and examine how private support varies with the economic characteristics of an orchestra's community, orchestra policies (particularly fundraising and audience development activities), and competition for philanthropy from other performing arts organizations.

Who Provides Private Support?

As direct government support for symphony orchestras declined between 1987 and 2005, private support increased and was mainly responsible for offsetting the growing performance deficits of orchestras. There is no guarantee, however, that private contributions will exactly offset those deficits in any given year or that they will grow sufficiently to completely offset growing performance deficits. After all, donations flow from the largely uncoordinated decisions of thousands of individuals, businesses, and foundations.

Public policies can influence the flow of private support in important ways. The previous chapter discussed the powerful effect of tax policies on philanthropic donations. The importance of tax expenditures effectively blurs the distinction between private and public support. But government policies do much more. Through their effects on general economic conditions and hence the well-being of potential donors, fiscal and monetary policies also influence the level of private contributions. Yet these policies cannot guarantee that private support will match symphony deficits.

Motivations beyond the reach of public policy also influence private support. Individuals are moved to donate by the quality of an orchestra's artistic expression and the belief that it raises the quality of life in a community. Some businesses focus their philanthropy on orchestras and other nonprofit organizations in their headquarters city, perhaps as a matter of civic pride or to raise their local profile. A business presence may also influence the level of individual contributions by signaling the value of the arts to their staff. Support from foundations is frequently tied to particular projects or foundation objectives.

While contributions to orchestras from all private sources have increased in both money and real terms since 1987, they have increased at different rates. The pie charts in figure 8.1 summarize how the structure of private support has changed since 1987 in the wake of those trends. The evolution of overall private support has been driven by the growth of individual giving, which now accounts for fully half of the private support

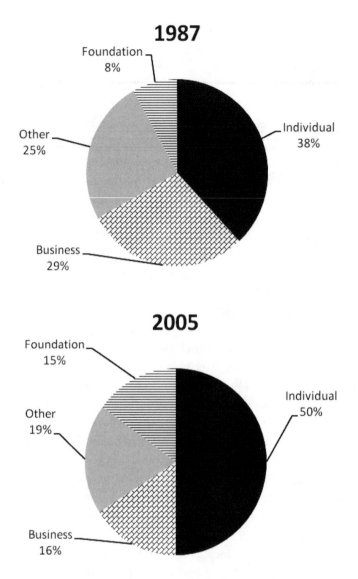

Figure 8.1. Distribution of Private Support for Orchestras, 1987 and 2005
Source: League of American Orchestras

received by the average orchestra. The share of private support provided by foundations has also increased, while the shares of businesses and "other" private support has declined. (Other private support includes in-kind or donated services, volunteer services, contributions from United Arts Funds, and the proceeds of special events.)

The pie charts describe the average pattern, but orchestras vary widely in the amount and composition of their external support. Philanthropic contributions from individuals ranged between 24 to 92 percent of the private support received by individual orchestras in 2005. Support from businesses ranged between 2 and 43 percent of private support; for independent foundations the range was from 0 to 43 percent. Shares also ranged widely over time for individual orchestras. The highly varied structure of non-performance income for these orchestras undermines any notion that they follow a common model of external financial support. Aside from a tendency for larger orchestras to have somewhat higher shares of foundation funding, the different patterns of private support cannot be explained by orchestra budget size. The varied patterns of private support occur within groups of large and small orchestras.

The previous chapter reviewed the requirements and restrictions that accompany government aid to U.S. symphony orchestras. Private philanthropy from individuals, businesses, and foundations also may arrive with strings attached. In 2005, for example, 19 percent of private contributions to the orchestras in our sample included temporary or permanent restrictions on how they could be used. Like the National Endowment for the Arts, some private foundations are more likely to provide project support than operating support. The former is easier to monitor, but may be directed at projects that reflect the enthusiasms of foundation staff or trustees more than the priorities of orchestras. Some orchestras have declined foundation support for projects that would divert them from the goals that they set for themselves. Less visible strings may also be attached to private support. Large donors—both businesses and individuals—may expect to acquire seats on an orchestra's board of trustees, for example, and in some instances may try to influence its artistic directions. Issues of orchestra governance raised by such efforts receive attention in the next chapter.

What Has Stimulated the Growth of Private Support?

The answer to this question most likely to occur to readers of the previous chapter is "tax incentives," because U.S. taxpayers are given significant incentives for charitable contributions. Moreover, the incentives make a difference. An econometric study of almost 30,000 corporations concluded that corporate charitable donations would decline by 30 percent if they could not be deducted from taxable income (Carroll and Joulfaian 2001).

This finding recalls a key point developed in the previous chapter—some "private" support is really indirect public support in the form of tax expenditures. But during the period covered by this study, the structure of tax incentives for philanthropy remained fairly stable. The challenge, then, is to explain why private support increased during a period of stable tax incentives. We must consider the role of three potential influences: the economic capacity of a community to support orchestras, symphony orchestra policies (such as fundraising and audience development policies), and competition with other performing arts.

Orchestra policies. Both fundraising and audience development policies may influence the level of private support enjoyed by a symphony. Audience development policies by orchestras have a double payoff to the extent that contributions are tied to concert attendance. Many individuals who attend symphony concerts—particularly subscribers—donate funds in addition to the amounts that they pay for their tickets. In fact, such "voluntary" contributions may be necessary to maintain the quality of one's seat assignments. The decline in the ratio of subscription to single-ticket sales has been a negative influence on individual contributions.

Economic capacity of community. Each orchestra has access to a distinctive set of private donors—local residents and businesses willing to support symphony activities—as well as national donors such as foundations that may fund many orchestras as part of a broad program of support to the industry. The distinctive local opportunities vary widely with the economic capacity of a community to provide financial support to its orchestra. The economic capacity may vary with the number of people in the community and its financial capacity, as indicated by its real per capita income and wealth. Per capita income, which influences the power of the tax incentive for charitable contributions, should be particularly important. Changes in stock market prices and housing prices may also influence private contributions through their effects on the value of assets.

Competition with other performing arts. Orchestras face competition for private philanthropic contributions from other arts organizations at both the local and national levels. Competition from other local performing arts organizations for philanthropic donations may not be as sharp as the competition for patronage discussed in chapter 5, because the time constraint that may influence current attendance choices is not relevant for philanthropic support. To the extent that the philanthropic budgets of individuals and organizations are limited, however, increased contributions to other performing arts organizations may come at the expense of lower contributions to orchestras, and conversely. Efforts by each arts organization to preserve or increase donations may produce escalating fundraising expenses. The contributions received by orchestras may be sensitive, for example, to the presence and fundraising activities of competing opera companies in the same community.

What Do Orchestras Get from Their Fundraising Activities?

Symphony orchestras and many other nonprofit organizations encourage private contributions through their fundraising or development activities. Few orchestras, however, appear to assess in any systematic way what they get for this growing source expenditure. Asked to justify a budget request, most fundraisers will divide the contributions received by an orchestra (or opera or university, etc.) by the fundraising budget and triumphantly reveal ratios in the range of 9 or 15 to 1—the annual averages in fact found in our orchestra data between 1998 and 2005. What organization would not expand the budget of a group that brought in over $9 for every dollar spent?

Unfortunately, this remarkable ratio invariably overstates the impact of fundraising activities on orchestra finances. In implying that larger fundraising expenses will replicate past fundraising achievements, the budget plea badly confuses average and incremental returns. Two difficulties underlie this confusion. First, fundraising operations cannot take full credit for all past returns. Symphony orchestras, like other performing arts organizations and universities, have loyal supporters who contribute year in and year out irrespective of the presence of a fundraising operation. As the opening paragraph of this chapter noted, orchestras survived on such support for decades before the advent of fundraising departments. All such contributions may be channeled through a fundraising department for "booking," but this mechanical procedure does not imply that the department attracted them. Orchestras that eliminated fundraising activities would no doubt receive less private support, but the amount would not be zero.

For assessing fundraising performance, the key questions are: What funds will an orchestra receive from additional fundraising expenditures? What return does the last fundraising dollar produce? Do *further* expenditures pay for themselves? This is where the second difficulty emerges: even if an orchestra's fundraising department could claim credit for all prior contributions, there is no guarantee that future expenditures will produce similar results. If fundraisers pursue the most generous donors first, for example, incremental expenditures will produce smaller returns than past expenditures. There may be alternative scenarios in which future expenditures produce larger returns than past expenditures. The main point is to be wary of predicting future outcomes from past experience. Fortunately, there are ways to assess the incremental productivity of fundraising resources.

General studies of the effects of fundraising on donations to nonprofit organizations often discover disquieting answers to these questions. One study reported that fundraising expenses rarely maximized the potential revenue available to a nonprofit (Okten and Weisbrod 2000). In some cases, organizations spent too little on fundraising in the sense that further expenditures would more than pay for themselves by attracting additional donations. In other cases, organizations spent too much, carrying fundraising to a point where each additional dollar spent attracted less than a dollar of new donations. In still other cases, there seemed to be no significant relationship between fundraising expenditures and donations to nonprofits. None of the nonprofit organizations studied were symphony orchestras, however.

Orchestra Fundraising Outcomes

Broadly speaking, orchestras receive three types of nonperformance income. Current operating funds, including unrestricted contributions and concert underwriting, come from current subscribers and local businesses. Many of these donations may be unsolicited, but they are stimulated by attendance at symphony concerts. Government support generally must be solicited from the relevant arts agencies or legislative bodies. Permanently restricted support, such as contributions to endowment, flows from individuals and in some cases foundations. As with current operating funds, some endowment support may be unsolicited and rest on the economic capacity of the community. Clearly, the influence of both fundraising and audience building policies on nonperformance income varies with the source and type of support.

The impact of these policies may be spread over time. Current fundraising expenses may lay the groundwork for significant contributions in future years. Expenses associated with the stewardship of past donors are intended in part to encourage additional giving in the future, for example. Planned giving commitments also require current costs to generate future income. These and other development strategies may produce a mismatch between current fundraising costs and returns. Efforts to evaluate the impact of fundraising and audience building activities should allow for lagged responses to expenditures.

Given these considerations, the statistical evaluation of orchestra policies discussed below includes three important features. First, it considers the impact of the policies on two measures of nonperformance income. One measure is current operating support from private donors—the measure of "private support" discussed earlier in this chapter. The annual orchestra reports to the League of American Orchestras label the second measure "fundraising income." This measure adds government support and permanently restricted funds to private operating support. Of course, the "fundraising income" label itself merits skepticism, since the question of how much of this measure is related to fundraising activities remains to be determined in the analysis. This measure is only available for years subsequent to 1998. Second, the analysis examines the role of both current and lagged fundraising and audience building activities on the two measures of nonperformance income. Third, the analysis also examines and controls for the influence of the community economic base and competition from other arts organizations for contributions. Once again a "fixed effects" statistical analysis examines how fundraising expenses and other factors are related to philanthropic contributions over time within symphony orchestras.[1]

The statistical analysis confirms the importance of a community's economic capacity for the level of private support received by an orchestra. Local real per capita income is significantly correlated with both "fundraising" income and private support for orchestras of all sizes. Donations are not significantly related to a community's population, however. As will become apparent below, simple ratios of total contributions to fundraising expense overstate the return on fundraising activities, in part because they credit fundraising with many contributions that result from an area's basic economic capacity. These results show once again how the financial security of orchestras depends in part on where they are located. They also signal on reasons why orchestras may face a certain financial inertia, since the factors that determine an area's economic capacity change slowly.

After controlling for the influence of a community's economic capacity, the payoff to fundraising is much lower than simple comparisons of

TABLE 8.1   PAYOFF PER DOLLAR OF FUNDRAISING EXPENDITURE
(YEAR 2000 DOLLARS)

	Private Support	"Fundraising" Income
1998–2005		
All orchestras	$1.20	$4.02
Large-budget orchestras	$1.29	$4.48
Small-budget orchestras	*	*
1987–2005		
All orchestras	$1.69	n.a.
Large-budget orchestras	$1.48	n.a.
Small-budget orchestras	$1.25	n.a.

Source: Appendix table A8.1.

"Fundraising" income = private operating support plus government support and permanently restricted support.

* No statistically significant effect.

n.a. = data not available.

fundraising expenses to contributed income imply. For the average orchestra, an additional dollar of fundraising expenditure yields slightly over $4 in "fundraising" income, but only $1.20 in private operating support, after controlling for the effects of the community economic base on donations (table 8.1). The difference between these estimates signals the importance of government and endowment support for much of the return to fundraising.

The analysis also reveals sharp differences in the payoff to fundraising activities in large-budget (total expenses over $9 million in 1999) and small-budget orchestras. (The $9 million cutoff divides the sample about in half.) Large-budget orchestras have significant positive returns per dollar of fundraising expense, but the relationship between fundraising expenditures and the measures of support is not statistically significant for the low-budget orchestras. Viewed over a longer period, however, the role of fundraising activities for small-budget (and other) orchestras seems more positive. A measure of private (operating) support to orchestras is available for the full 1987–2005 period; over that period, the average small- and large-budget orchestra respectively earned $1.25 and $1.48 per dollar spent on fundraising activities.

Efforts to identify a significant connection between past fundraising expenditures and current nonperformance income in the statistical analysis were not successful. Taken at face value, past fundraising expenditures either had either no reliable effect or implausible effects on private donations. (The implication in some analyses that increasing fundraising expenditures will *reduce* future "fundraising income" falls in the latter category.) While some fundraising approaches may drive donors away in the future, this seems to be an unlikely result for the industry as a whole. The more likely interpretation is that most fundraising activities in fact yield results within the year that they are incurred.

These findings emerge from statistical analyses that assume that the returns to fundraising do not vary with the level of fundraising expense. If fundraising departments pursue their best opportunities first, however, fundraising expenditures may eventually be subject to diminishing returns. Alternatively, where there are economies of scale in fundraising activities, contributions may increase disproportionately with expenditures. For the brief period covered by this analysis, there is no statistical evidence of either diminishing returns or increasing returns to overall fundraising activities.

Attendance-building activities have a modest but statistically significant payoff in raising current operating support for orchestras, but the attendance effect is not statistically significant for the broader measure of nonperformance income. Moreover, the effect on operating support is limited to small-budget orchestras. Community per capita income and fundraising remain the main influences on contributions to large-budget orchestras.

Competition between performing arts organizations for donations remains an understudied topic. An earlier study identified statistically significant evidence of modest competitive effects between orchestras and opera companies for nonperformance income (Flanagan 2008). Private contributions to symphony orchestras were lower in communities with at least one opera company. After holding the effects of an area's economic capacity and an orchestra's development/fundraising expenditures constant, there was evidence that higher development expenditures by an opera company raise support for the opera at the partial expense of the nearby symphony orchestra a year later. The effect is statistically significant but very small. Further work on the important topic of competitive interactions between performing arts organizations must await better data.

Past Growth and Future Prospects

This book has stressed that to achieve financial stability orchestras must discover ways to offset their ever-increasing structural operating deficits. Solving this year's budget emergency offers no respite from next year's larger deficit. Many of the approaches considered in earlier chapters may provide relief for temporary deficits, but they offer little hope for coping with growing imbalances.

Private philanthropy offers a promising exception, in principle. Private contributions to symphony orchestras could grow enough to offset increasing operating deficits and declining government support in the future, as they have in the past. But will they? Why have private contributions to orchestras continued to grow? Is the growth likely to continue? There is no guarantee that contributions will match needs in the future, but this chapter has provided a guide to the possibilities and risks that accompany a reliance on private support.

Chapter 3 of this book documented the trend of growth in real private donations to orchestras between 1987 and 2005 after controlling for cyclical influences. This chapter shows that this trend largely reflected the effects of growing real income and increasing fundraising efforts by orchestras, even though the effect of the latter activities on private support is much smaller than usually claimed. These results suggest that the future growth of private giving to orchestras rests on real income growth, increased concert subscriptions, and, with qualifications, increased fundraising expenses. Brief reflection, however, reveals that much private philanthropy rests on factors that are beyond the control of orchestras. The economic capacity of a community to support philanthropy changes slowly and is more likely to reflect government policies to promote economic growth than an orchestra's policies. The analyses discussed in this chapter confirm that orchestra policies to build audiences or increase outside contributions help defray operating deficits but also have significant limitations. The size of a concert venue ultimately limits the income growth possible from audience-building activities. Moreover, the analyses show how the returns to fundraising activities can be overstated. In fact, the relationship between private operating support and fundraising expenses indicates that, by this metric, fundraising activities barely pay for themselves.

Increasing competition for philanthropic donations raises further uncertainty regarding the future effectiveness of fundraising activities.

In a worst-case scenario, efforts to maintain shares of philanthropy could produce escalating fundraising expenditures among orchestras and other nonprofit organizations. The analyses reported in this chapter did not find evidence of the worst case between 1987 and 2005. Instead, they revealed statistically significant but quantitatively small indications of competition for donated funds between orchestras and operas in the same community. Viewed more broadly, the number of nonprofit organizations qualifying for tax-exempt contributions continues to increase rapidly, and the share of private philanthropy going to arts organizations has declined since the late 1990s (Kushner and Cohen 2010). In part this trend reflects growing philanthropic concerns with the problems of those at the bottom of national and international income distributions, while support for orchestras and other performing arts organizations targets the interests of people much higher in the income distribution (Strom 2007). Some observers suggest that doubts about orchestras themselves may account for these trends. The New England Conservatory of Music's president, a former orchestra manager, has commented that donors "are feeling fatigued by orchestras— the constant demands, the needs, the on-going and unresolved problems. They are questioning the role of 'orchestra monoliths' whose consumption of a community's philanthropic wealth is disproportionate to the value they produce. . . . these are the investors rethinking their priorities" (Woodcock 2011).

Orchestra endowments also provide support for current operations through the returns on endowment investments. Fundraising expenditures that increase endowment contributions therefore contribute indirectly to current needs, and when donations of restricted endowment funds are added to donations of operating funds, fundraising activities pay for themselves on average. Success in acquiring private support can be undermined by poor management of contributions. The management challenge is in part to control the growth of expenses and in part to manage endowment investments prudently. The scope of future activities that can be funded depends crucially on how these funds are invested and managed, the topic of the next chapter.

CHAPTER 9

Symphony Orchestra Endowments and Governance

When symphony orchestras encounter financial difficulties, attention focuses on building audiences, controlling expenses, raising contributions, concert programming, the quality of the music director, and so on—in short, virtually all aspects except the performance of the board of trustees, the group that ultimately has responsibility for oversight of the organization's economic health. One of a symphony board's most important tasks is to build and manage the orchestra's endowments to provide a reliable long-term source of annual support, and well-functioning symphony boards are successful in this endeavor. The following report summarizes what can happen when the board of an arts organization is inattentive to its responsibilities.

> The Museum of Contemporary Art has nearly killed itself. The museum has operated at a deficit in six of the last eight years, and its endowment has shrunk to about $6 million from nearly $50 million in 1999. . . . Now the California attorney general has begun an audit to determine if the museum broke laws governing the use of restricted money by nonprofit organizations. And local artists, curators and collectors, including current and former board members, are lobbying to remove the museum's director, . . . its board, or both. . . . [A] philanthropist . . . offered $30 million last month in support of the [museum], on the condition that half of it be matched by contributions from other donors. So far, no other donors have stepped forward. Part of the chal-

lenge may be that the very people who are considering the museum's options include those who oversaw its decline. . . . Some trustees have departed in recent years, frustrated with what they called the museum's financial recklessness and lack of leadership (Wyatt and Finkel 2008).

In describing the plight of a museum in Los Angeles, this report signals key issues encountered in the management of symphony orchestra endowments: What restrictions are placed on endowment support? How must an endowment be managed to avoid shrinkage? How do some boards of trustees manage to lose the participation of those with the most expertise to contribute? How does imprudent management of an endowment influence donor confidence in the stewardship of their contributions?

This chapter examines how endowments can be managed or mismanaged and discusses how orchestra boards organize themselves to manage endowments and provide oversight on a wide range of other issues. The chapter begins by discussing the opportunities and limitations associated with endowment support for symphony orchestras. It then reviews the current size of orchestra endowments and the support provided by the annual income flows from endowment investments. This discussion leads to a key issue raised by the report on the Museum of Contemporary Art—how investment strategies and endowment payout policies can sustain or undermine endowment support. The chapter concludes with discussions of the functioning of symphony boards and the prospects for using endowments to cover performance deficits.

Endowment Support

Most endowments are gifts of money or property donated to provide financial support in perpetuity. To reinforce the objective of long-term support, some endowments include a legal stipulation that only the returns from endowment investments may be used to support the organization's activities. The endowment principal must remain intact.[1] In the early days of endowments, only the annual flow of interest, dividends, and rent could be used to support current operations, but since the 1960s the capital appreciation of an endowment's assets has been recognized as an element of "investment returns." Endowments permit orchestras to provide activities beyond what current concertgoers and contributors are willing to support. In the words of an early study of symphony orchestra finances, "a substantial endowment is probably one of the most satisfactory assurances of financial stability. It permits long-range planning and the development of a varied program of community service, which make possible the building of an audience and hence of operating income" (Grant and Hettinger 1940, pp. 264–65).

Endowments take many forms. Some funds can be used to support virtually any activity of the organization. Such *unrestricted* endowments provide an orchestra with the most flexible assistance. Other endowments may only be used for purposes defined by their donors. Still, some *restricted* endowments may provide an orchestra with essentially the same flexibility as an unrestricted endowment. If a donor endows the concertmaster's position, for example, the operating funds that the orchestra would have spent on the concertmaster's salary become available for other purposes. Some donors may wish to create endowments that alter an orchestra's priorities, however. An endowment restricted to supporting the performance of an obscure composer's works might provide an example.

Endowments can provide for artistic independence that does not accompany other sources of funds. As mentioned in the previous two chapters, there is little pure philanthropy, even in the performing arts. Donations often arrive with strings attached. Orchestras that lack significant unrestricted endowment may have little choice but to elevate economic over artistic considerations and accept restrictions. Unrestricted endowment can reduce an orchestra's dependence on the artistic preferences of governments, foundations, and private donors.

These benefits do not arrive automatically, however. They depend on the ability of boards to raise and manage endowments to satisfy their long-term purposes. One of the greatest barriers to this task is the efforts of current claimants to obtain the benefits of endowment resources at the expense of future claimants.

How Large Are Symphony Orchestra Endowments?

For much of the history of symphony performance in the United States, only a few orchestras could rely on support from endowments. A study of orchestras in the late 1930s reported that endowments "are an important source of income for 6 of the major orchestras and a minor source for 4 more. The present value of the more important endowments ranges from approximately half a million to two or three million dollars [\$7–42 million

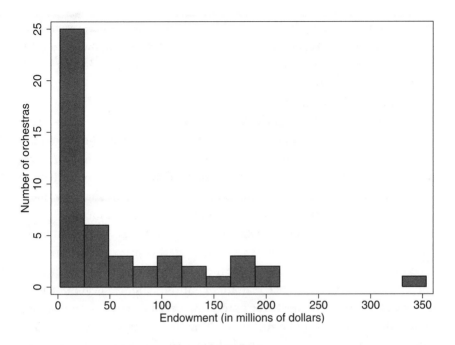

Figure 9.1. Symphony Orchestra Endowments, 2005
Source: League of American Orchestras

in 2005 dollars]. The yield on the endowments of major orchestras during the 1937–38 season was between 3.7 per cent and 4.7 per cent." (Grant and Hettinger 1940, pp. 261–62)

By the early 21st century, the endowment resources of major symphony orchestras were much larger, but widely dispersed. All but one of the 49 orchestras reporting data to the League of American Orchestras for the 2005 concert season had endowments, which ranged from $2.0 million to $ 353.5 million, a ratio of 1 to 177. Figure 9.1 provides a picture of the distribution of endowment values across orchestras. Clearly there are a few "outlying" orchestras with extremely large endowments, but the median endowment in the sample is $ 23.6 million. The majority of orchestras must confront their financial challenges and manage their artistic objectives with endowments under $25 million. Income from these endowments averaged 5 percent of orchestra income but ranged as high as 17 percent.

On average, orchestra endowments grew between the 1998 and 2000 concert seasons before declining during the subsequent recession. Beginning in 2003, the average orchestra endowment again grew rapidly until the recession beginning in early 2008. The pronounced cyclical variation in endowment size reflects the fact that endowment values follow the market value of their investments. Donations of new endowment also vary with cyclical changes in the value of contributors' financial assets. Historically, state laws prohibiting the use of endowment resources that fall below their initial value have further restricted access to endowment resources during the deepest recessions. Since 2006, however, a majority of the states have adopted the Uniform Prudent Management of Institutional Funds Act revisions, which permit some spending from endowment resources that are "underwater." In short, it becomes more difficult to maintain endowment resources just when an orchestra needs to rely on them the most.

Cyclical variations notwithstanding, most orchestra endowments increased significantly between the 1998 and 2005 concert seasons, the period for which data are available. The median orchestra's endowment value increased by 11.6 percent per year after controlling for cyclical influences. Endowment growth ranged from -10.2 to 101.4 percent per year among individual orchestras. (The real value of most orchestra endowments also advanced substantially over this period, since consumer prices increased by only 2.6 percent per year.) The remarkable variation in endowment growth reflects the variable success of orchestras in managing endowment funds.

How have the dramatic differences in endowment growth influenced the distribution of economic resources among symphony orchestras? Are the richer organizations getting richer while the poor get poorer? Has the inequality in endowment resources decreased over time? Broadly speaking, endowment growth was slower in orchestras that began the period with large endowments than in orchestras that began the period with small endowments. The inequality of endowment values declined slightly between 1998 and 2005.

Endowment Income

Income from endowment investments averaged about 7.5 percent of orchestra budgets between 1987 and 2005. This amounted to about 15.5 percent of the gap between performance revenues and performance expenses of the average orchestra, with considerable variation across individual orchestras. For reasons discussed above, the share of endowment income in total income or expenses is cyclically sensitive, declining in recessions and increasing when returns improve in economic expansions.

After taking account of the effect of business cycles, there was also a significant trend decline in endowment income as a share of total orchestra revenue. On average, the share declined by about 0.2 percentage points each year in the late 20th and early 21st centuries. If this trend continues, the share would drop by about two percentage points each decade. At first glance, it may seem counterintuitive that the trend in the *share* of endowment income has declined in a period in which endowments have generally increased. This finding does not mean that endowment income itself is decreasing. (In fact it has increased on average by about $29,000 per year for the average orchestra in the sample.) It simply means that other categories of orchestra income have been increasing more rapidly.

Managing Symphony Endowments

The long-term financial support that an orchestra derives from its endowment depends importantly on the returns on the endowment investments, whose management is a responsibility of the orchestra's board of trustees. All orchestras invest their endowments in the same national and international capital markets. The wide range of returns on endowment investments earned by individual orchestras may therefore come as a surprise (table 9.1).

While the impact of changing economic conditions on average returns is clearly visible in these figures, the overwhelming impression is one of highly dispersed annual returns. Year in and year out, there is considerable

TABLE 9.1   RETURNS ON SYMPHONY ORCHESTRA ENDOWMENT
INVESTMENTS (PERCENTAGES)

	24 Largest Orchestras		Next 24 Largest Orchestras	
Year	Median	Range	Median	Range
1998–1999	14.0%	4.9 to 27.9%	9.7%	4.4 to 23.2%
2000–2001	−9.7	−26.0 to 15.7	−5.4	−24.0 to 12.5
2001–2002	−7.4	−15.0 to 13.0	−5.9	−14.0 to 5.0
2003–2004	10.7	2.2 to 19.0	11.0	1.0 to 13.4
2005–2006	9.7	1.8 to 13.0	6.8	3.8 to 9.2

Source: League of American Orchestras, OSR.

variation in the investment returns experienced by individual orchestras. The dispersion of returns is largest in the larger orchestras. When the economy is strong, as in 1998, the endowment returns received by individual orchestras range from low single digits to almost 30 percent. When the economy is weak, as in 2001, returns range from negative double digits to a little above 20 percent. Neither group of orchestras consistently outperforms the other in endowment returns—the median return for the largest orchestras is higher in good times, while the median for the smaller orchestras is superior in a weak economy. With an improvement in economic conditions, as between 2002 and 2005, investment returns improved for most orchestras, but remained highly dispersed. Clearly, the investment of endowment resources ultimately yields substantially different opportunities for different orchestras.

Dispersed returns are not unique to symphony orchestras. Colleges and universities also rely heavily on endowment resources to achieve their objectives and earn different returns on their endowment investments. Of course, university endowments on average are much larger than orchestra endowments. In the 2004–5 academic year, the 20 largest university endowments ranged from $3.2 to $25.5 billion (Lerner et al 2008), several orders of magnitude larger than the $30 to $310 million range for the 20 largest orchestra endowments during that concert season. At 13 percent, the median return on investment for the top 20 university endowments was somewhat higher than the 11 percent return on the top 20 orchestra endowments. Both sectors experienced a wide range of returns on individual endowments. For universities, the returns ranged from 4.2 percent to 19.3 percent among the top 20 endowments; for orchestras, the top 20 range was from 5.7 to 18.8 percent. The overall impression is one of roughly similar dispersions of outcomes, notwithstanding the large differences in endowment size between universities and symphony orchestras.

Managing Endowment Returns

What accounts for the different returns on endowment investments experienced by different orchestras? Why do some orchestras experience low single-digit (or, worse yet, negative) returns on investments in years in which other orchestras earn significant double-digit returns on their investments? Why do symphonies differ so much in the resources that they generate per dollar of endowment? Answering these questions is the agenda for the rest of this chapter.

Those responsible for managing endowment investments must constantly balance considerations of investment returns and investment risk—the year-to-year variability in investment returns. Capital markets offer investors a tradeoff between risk and return. If investors consider two securities of equal risk, they will generally choose the investment offering the higher expected return, thereby bidding up the price (that is, reducing the expected return) on that investment and inducing a fall in the price (increase in the return) of the other investment. This market behavior soon equalizes the expected returns for the two equally risky investments. Sustained differences in return between investments reflect differences in their underlying risk. On average, investors require compensation in the form of higher expected return for assuming risk.

Investment portfolios, such as a bundle of securities purchased with endowment funds, offer opportunities to reduce the risk associated with endowment securities through careful diversification of the securities held. The risk of a portfolio need not be a weighted average of the risk of the portfolio's security holdings. When the returns to portfolio securities respond differently to underlying economic events, offsetting changes in the returns to individual portfolio securities reduce the variability of the portfolio's return. A key principle of diversification is therefore to select securities whose returns respond differently to underlying economic events—in more technical language, to select securities whose returns are not perfectly positively correlated. Diversification of an endowment portfolio then reduces the risk associated with a given expected return. Nobel laureate Harry Markowitz, who received the prize for his pathbreaking work in finance, reportedly remarked that by providing benefit (lower risk) without reduced expected return, portfolio diversification offered the only free lunch in economics.

The actual risk and return of the endowment portfolio of any particular orchestra depends significantly on the allocation of endowment resources across (1) stocks (equity investments), which over long periods offer higher returns and higher risk; (2) bonds (fixed-income investments), which offer less volatile but lower annual returns than equities; (3) cash, which provides liquidity, the least risk, and the lowest returns; and (4) high-risk investments, including real estate and venture capital. Risk and return will also depend on the choice of specific investments within each of these asset categories. On average, equities constituted 60–65 percent of endowment portfolios in our sample of symphony orchestras, but individual orchestras invested between 10 and 100 percent of their endowment investments in stocks. Fixed income securities averaged about one-third of endowment investments but ranged from 1 to 100 percent of the investments of individual symphonies. Extremely large shares of a particular asset category signal a lack of diversification that will threaten the returns that the endowment could yield and increase the risk to which the endowment portfolio is exposed. The share of cash and "other" investments was in the single digits for most orchestras in the sample. There was little change in the allocation of endowment resources across these investment classes during 1998–2005.

Investment managers may increase endowment portfolio returns by acquiring riskier securities, but the objective of diversification is to lower the risk (variability of annual returns) that must be incurred to achieve any particular expected return. In the words of a leading text on investments: "An efficient portfolio has less risk than any other with comparable expected return and more return than any other with comparable risk." (Sharpe 1985, p. 129)

By this standard, most endowment portfolios held by orchestras are not efficient. Figure 9.2 plots the average return on orchestra endowment investments between the 1998 and 2005 concert seasons (vertical axis) against a measure of risk (the standard deviation of annual returns on endowment investments over that period). Each dot in the figure shows the risk and return for a different orchestra's endowment portfolio. If all orchestras had efficient portfolios, differences in rates of return between orchestras would simply reflect different risk preferences. Visually, a distinct positive relation between risk and return would emerge, reflecting the fact that endowments with higher returns were invested in riskier (more volatile) portfolios. Instead, the figure shows no apparent relationship between the measures of endowment risk and return across orchestras—a conclusion confirmed by formal statistical analysis. Moreover, the same conclusion emerges from separate analyses of larger and smaller orchestras. Orchestras represented by dots across the top of the figure earned comparatively high returns given the risk of their endowment portfolios. In contrast, some orchestras earned returns on investment as much as 10 percentage points lower than the returns earned by other orchestras incurring the same level of risk. By replicating the portfolios of the first group of orchestras, these symphonies could get higher returns without incurring more risk.

Alternatively, the inefficiency of many symphony endowment portfolios can be seen by comparing orchestras on the left side of Figure 9.2 with

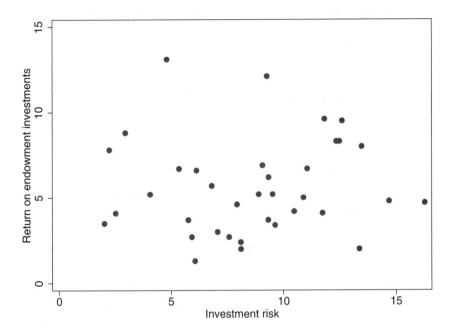

Figure 9.2. Investment Risk and Returns on Investment for Orchestras,
1998–2005
Source: League of American Orchestras

those on the right side. For any return on endowment (for example, 5 percent), the former orchestras have much less risky portfolios than the latter.
With superior endowment diversification, orchestras in the latter group
could maintain their current return with less volatility in annual returns.
Clearly many orchestras could increase the resources available for both
their current and future activities by improving the management of their
endowment portfolios.

Balancing the Interests of Current and Future Claimants

Orchestra trustees face an inherent conflict between supporting current
symphony activities and their legal obligation to preserve endowment assets to support artistic activities for future generations. Current claimants
have the edge over future claimants in presenting their interests. Orchestra musicians and staff, supported by their unions, may prefer higher current payouts from an endowment to maintain salaries and preserve current

employment security in the face of changes in general economic conditions. The orchestra's music director may want to perform more concerts or works requiring more musicians. In contrast, future beneficiaries—musicians and concertgoers alike—are an invisible constituency lacking the means to represent their interests. By default, the board of trustees is entrusted with representing these future interests in the face of the claims voiced by current beneficiaries.

How should trustees choose between these competing claims? What principles can guide them in deciding how much of an endowment's current return can safely be spent for an orchestra's current activities and how much should be preserved in order to maintain support for the orchestra's activities in perpetuity? Yale economist and Nobel laureate James Tobin crafted a classic statement of the endowment management principle that might guide boards of trustees: "The trustees of an endowed institution . . . want to know . . . the rate of consumption from endowment which can be sustained indefinitely. . . . [They want] the existing endowment . . . [to] continue to support the same set of activities that it is now supporting. This rule says that the current consumption should not benefit from the prospects of future gifts to endowment. Sustained consumption rises to encompass and enlarge the scope of activities when, but not before, capital gifts enlarge the endowment." (Tobin 1974)

This rule also implies that the endowment should be managed to preserve its purchasing power, but this objective raises difficult choices in a world of changing economic conditions. We have already noted how endowment returns are likely to decline just when orchestras need to draw on them the most to maintain financial stability. Drawing down endowment principal to provide financial stability violates the principle of preserving sufficient endowment purchasing power to provide equal support for an orchestra's activities for future generations. Drawing down orchestras' endowments to completely offset current performance income gaps endangers future orchestra activities. In the words of the manager of Yale University's endowment, "A clear, direct trade-off exists between preserving assets and supporting operations. To the extent that managers focus on maintaining purchasing power of endowment assets, great volatility affects the flow of resources delivered to the operating budget. To the extent that managers emphasize providing a sizable and stable flow of resources to the operating budget, substantial volatility influences the purchasing power of endowment assets" (Swensen 2000, p. 29).

Endowment Payout Policies

Preserving the purchasing power of an endowment so that it provides future generations with the same level of artistic experiences enjoyed by the current generation has considerable intuitive appeal. If an endowment supports a $300,000 salary for a concertmaster in 2005, the endowment should be managed so that it will support a much larger salary 10 years hence. If the salary of a concertmaster is expected to increase by 50 percent over the next decade, then the endowment principal must increase by 50 percent. Note that the criterion is how much the *costs* supported by the endowment are likely to increase. Maintaining purchasing power is often interpreted as increasing endowment value by the rate of inflation. But this broad principle will not serve symphony orchestras or other arts organizations well. Recall the basic point emerging from the discussion of the cost disease in chapter 2: in activities with low productivity trends, costs advance more rapidly than the rate of inflation. Therefore, endowments must be managed so that their value will increase as rapidly as orchestras' costs. Growing orchestra endowment value at the (lower) rate of inflation would favor current beneficiaries over future beneficiaries, since the endowment would be able to support fewer orchestra activities in the future.

Given these considerations, what rate of spending from an endowment keeps the growth of budget support from an endowment just equal to the growth of applicable expenses? Recognizing that inflation influences both nominal investment returns and orchestra costs, the endowment spending rate that preserves purchasing power and can be sustained indefinitely equals the long-run real total return on the endowment (earnings plus capital appreciation) minus the long-run real cost increase (Massy 1990, p. 28).

Orchestras that wish to spend 5 percent of their endowment each year and face, say, a 4 percent annual increase in costs must earn a 9 percent nominal return on the endowment portfolio to support a constant level of activities into the future. (Alternatively, with a 9 percent nominal return on the endowment and a 4 percent cost increase, an orchestra can sustain a payout rate of 5 percent of its endowment annually without changing its real value.) Spending at a higher rate will reduce future endowment values and ultimately prove to be unsustainable. Current beneficiaries—concert goers and musicians—will gain at the expense of future beneficiaries. Spending at a lower rate will increase endowment values and benefit future beneficiaries at the expense of current beneficiaries.

The fact that investment returns are volatile and sensitive to general business conditions presents a problem for the constant-spending-rate approach to endowment payout. Annual increases or decreases in endowment value produce large fluctuations in endowment support for current activities. The number and scale of concerts are not easily adjusted to such volatile swings in available resources. In short, providing stable current support while maintaining an endowment's long-run purchasing power requires a method of smoothing year-to-year fluctuations in the endowment's value. One popular approach is to apply the target endowment spending rate to a moving average of past market values of the endowment, but other approaches also have merit (Massy 1990, pp. 331–35; Swenson 2000, pp. 30–31). In the early 21st century, most symphony orchestras applied endowment spending rates to the endowment's average value over the past three years. A few orchestras used a five-year average, and a few others used only the prior year's value.

When endowment spending is based on past values of endowment, the effective spending rate will move counter cyclically. The spending rate rises in recessions, because the diminished current value of the endowment receives little or no weight in the moving average. Consider an orchestra that spends 4 percent of the average value of its investment over the past three years. If the endowment value was $ 1 million in each of the past three years, this year's draw from the endowment will be $40,000. But if the endowment loses 10 percent of its value this year, the effective spending rate will be 4.4 percent ($40,000/$900,000). Conversely, as economic conditions improve, the effective spending rate will decline because the appreciated current values receive little or no weight. Cyclical variations in the effective spending rate provide partial insurance against fluctuating endowment values.

As a matter of policy, most U.S. symphonies had established an annual payout rate by the early 21st century. Virtually all the rates fell in the range of 5 to 7 percent of an average of past endowment values. Payout rates above 4 to 5 percent tend to reduce the purchasing power of an endowment over time. Recall from the earlier discussion that the sustainable endowment spending rate equals the return on investment *minus* the inflation in an orchestra's costs. Most years, this rule implies that a sustainable spending rate would be three to five percentage points *less* than the return on endowment investment. Contrast this conclusion with the actual endowment spending of U.S. orchestras presented in table 9.2.

TABLE 9.2   SPENDING FROM ENDOWMENT

Year	Endowment Spending as Percentage of Market Value		Number of Orchestras Where Spending Exceeds Return on Endowment
	Median	Range	
	24 Largest Orchestras		
1998–1999	5.0%	3.13 to 8.0%	2
2000–2001	5.1%	0 to 10.5	17
2001–2002	6.2%	3.7 to 16	20
2002–2003	5.9%	1.7 to 12.2	8
2003–2004	5.3%	2.1 to 15.1	1
2005–2006	4.4%	3.2 to 7.1	2
	Next 24 Largest Orchestras		
1998–1999	5.0%	2.9 to 8.0%	2
2000–2001	3.8%	0 to 8.4	11
2001–2002	4.1%	2.6 to 8.1	13
2002–2003	4.7%	0.6 to 11.1	6
2003–2004	4.5%	0.1 to 7.4	2
2005–2006	4.3%	2.7 to 6.4	0

Source: League of American Orchestras, OSR.

Median endowment payout rates fall within the stated policy range, but each year payout rates vary substantially across individual orchestras. Those orchestras with annual payout rates at the lower end of the range should be able to sustain the real value of their endowment if the nominal return on their endowment portfolio is in the range of 6 to 8 percent. Higher rates of return will grow the real value of the endowment. But orchestras with payout rates at the upper end of the range would need returns on their endowment portfolio of 11 to 20 percent to maintain their real endowment value in the face of cost increases. Far from achieving sustainable payout rates that are less than the return on investment by the amount of cost inflation, many orchestras reported rates that *exceeded* the return on the endowment portfolio alone (right-hand column of table 9.2). This phenomenon is understandably at its worst during recessions. Even with more normal economic conditions, however, some orchestras spend from their endowments at rates that will diminish the range and scale of activities that can be supported from the endowments in the future. These observations raise the question of how an orchestra board might manage an endowment so that it can support desired spending.

Governance of Symphony Orchestras

The League has spent many years studying various aspects of orchestra operations in an attempt to isolate those factors which seem to predispose an orchestra toward failure or success. . . . Invariably, investigation of these factors leads back to the orchestra's governing board which holds the power to engage personnel, formulate and carry out basic policies of operation. The story of a successful orchestra is, in reality, the story of an effective orchestra board (Thompson 1958).

This quote from Helen M. Thompson, an early executive director of the League of American Orchestras and former manager of the New York Philharmonic, is as relevant today as it was in 1958. The board of trustees (or governors or directors) of a symphony orchestra is ultimately responsible for the conduct of its affairs and its economic fate. In addition to setting policies for the management of the orchestra's endowment, boards play a major role in determining a symphony's budget, raising nonperformance income, and selecting its music director, manager, and key administrative staff. The effectiveness of a board can have an immense impact on an orchestra's economic security and its ability to achieve its artistic goals.

In 2003 the average symphony orchestra board consisted of 32 members—large in comparison to the boards of profit-seeking organizations, but closer to the average board size of nonprofit organizations in general. Board size increased with the size of orchestra budgets, ranging from an average of 65 board members for the largest-budget orchestras to 13 members for the smallest-budget orchestras (Noonan 2006). The correlation between board and budget size signals one of the reasons why nonprofit boards are typically larger than corporate boards. Orchestras and other nonprofits require contributions to survive. The larger a nonprofit's budget, the more it needs to involve people who can donate and raise funds from others to support the organization. Board membership may require such involvement.

While all symphony board members are expected to generate funds for the orchestra, policies vary on whether trustees must commit to donating a specific amount or are left to choose "an amount that seems reasonable."

Not all board members keep their promises. In Columbus, Ohio, whose orchestra's financial crisis in 2008 is described in the opening pages of this book, each trustee was "expected to raise at least $25,000 for the symphony, from themselves or from others," while actual individual pledges ranged from $2,500 to $1.75 million (Grossberg 2008). Some trustees regularly attend symphony performances and work diligently and selflessly to improve the orchestra's economic security and organizational effectiveness. Others rarely attend orchestra concerts and have limited engagement with the board's financing and governance endeavors. This kind of situation can occur when businesses receive seats on the board in exchange for contributions but then fill those seats with employees with little interest in orchestral music.

Well-functioning boards develop methods for limiting the impact of nonperforming trustees. The key is to avoid indefinite periods of service. Term limits, which provide for severance after a standard period of board service, meet that test but limit the service of performing and nonperforming board members alike. Term limits with a requirement that a board member may not stand for reelection for a certain period provide more flexibility (Bowen 2008).

Board members who fully meet their financial commitments, but expect to acquire influence over the artistic direction of an orchestra in return, present a different kind of concern. The best way to limit the leverage of any particular donor is to develop a large and diverse number of funding sources. Although there appears to be no formal study of this issue, donor artistic leverage seems most likely to arise in the small boards of low-budget orchestras, if it arises at all.

Potential Conflicts of Interest

Why do boards that can invest endowment resources in the same national and international capital markets achieve such different outcomes? Any answer to this question must recognize that the management of endowment resources may present some board members with potentially significant conflicts of interest, and boards that successfully counter these conflicts are likely to generate superior returns on endowment resources.

While there have been no systematic studies of conflicts of interest on symphony orchestra boards, experienced board members and endowment managers are quite forthright about the dangers. An authoritative board member for both profit-seeking and nonprofit organizations remarked that

"nonprofits are subject to the same risks as for-profits that personal friend-
ships, and social or political relationships, will influence judgments. Moreover, it can be very awkward to terminate a business relationship—with, for
example, a money management firm—when the organization providing a
service is led by a board member" (Bowen 2008, p. 148). Major university
endowment managers are even more specific. William F. Massy, a former
vice president for business affairs at Stanford University, observed that
some trustees may "see the situation with eyes conditioned by values other
than those of the endowed institution. Trustees can be subjected to considerable pressure to entice the institution to 'take advantage' of investment
opportunities being offered by their friends or business associates" (Massy
1990, p. 128). Similarly, the manager of the Yale University endowment has
stated that "nearly every aspect of funds management suffers from decisions
made in the self-interest of the decision-makers, not in the best interest of
the fund. Culprits range from trustees seeking to make an impact during
their term on the investment committee, to portfolio managers pursuing
steady fee income at the expense of investment excellence, to corporate
mangers diverting assets for personal gain" (Swensen 2000, p. 4).

The interests and investment enthusiasms of board members and donors can interfere with a diversification strategy. Encouraging or retaining
investments favored by current or former trustees, former donors, or prospective donors all alter the optimal diversification. By lowering the return
on endowment or raising the riskiness of endowment investments, departures from an optimal diversification strategy will reduce the capacity of an
orchestra to achieve its artistic goals.

A 2005 survey of U.S. nonprofit organizations indicated that the potential for such conflicts of interest is great. Forty-one percent of the nonprofits surveyed with budgets over $10 million reported that they had pur-
chased or rented goods from board members or associated companies over
the prior two years. (About two-thirds of the orchestras in our sample fell
in this budget category in 2005.) Of these organizations, 60 percent reported having a written conflict of interest policy. A bare majority of nonprofits reported that these transactions involved goods or services provided
at below-market cost—a fact that explains the resistance among nonprofit
firms to an absolute ban on such transactions (Ostrower 2007).

There are defenses against such conflicts of interest and the damage
that they might do to orchestras or other nonprofit organizations. In the

2005 survey, 60 percent of the nonprofits reporting financial transactions with board members had a conflict-of-interest policy, 42 percent required board members to disclose any financial interests in companies doing business with the nonprofit, and 82 percent required other board members to review and approve such transactions beforehand. Only two-thirds of the largest nonprofit organizations required the latter approval, however (Ostrower 2007). The Internal Revenue Service now requires orchestras and other nonprofits to include a self-dealing statement in their annual tax return. Boards themselves may require their members to recuse themselves from voting on decisions in which they have a personal interest and publicly disclose the affiliations of trustees, the portfolio of endowment investments, and the identity of investment managers.

Can Current Endowments Achieve Financial Balance?

How large would endowments have to be for prudent annual endowment spending to offset the performance income gaps of symphony orchestras? Table 9.3 provides the estimates of the required endowment for the median orchestra and for orchestras at the 25th and 75th percentile of performance income gaps.[2] Estimates of required endowment are provided for three endowment spending rates (4, 5, and 6 percent) along with the actual endowment of orchestras at each position in the distribution. The table shows that actual endowments are not sufficiently large to cover performance deficits at these endowment draw rates. To make the same point a different way: with endowment levels that existed at the beginning of the 21st century, it would take an unsustainable endowment payout rate of over 30 percent to fully offset the performance income gap for the median orchestra. This point applies more broadly. *None* of the orchestras in the sample have endowments large enough to completely offset performance deficits at prudent 4 to 5 percent endowment payout rates. Payout rates that would offset performance deficits in the short run are so high that they would cannibalize endowment and exceed the investment policy statements governing most endowments.

The future incapacity of current symphony orchestra endowments to offset performance deficits is in fact larger than the presentation in table 9.3 suggests. Recall that the performance income gap tends to get worse over time, even after controlling for cyclical fluctuations. Estimates

TABLE 9.3   ENDOWMENT REQUIRED TO OFFSET PERFORMANCE INCOME
GAP, 2005 (MILLIONS OF DOLLARS)

Orchestra at	Endowment Spending Rate			Actual Endowment
	4%	5%	6%	
25th percentile	$98.4	$78.7	$65.6	$8.7
Median	$188.0	$150.0	$125.0	$22.3
75th percentile	$349.0	$279.0	$233.0	$92.7

Source: League of American Orchestras, OSR; author's computations.

of the required endowment at any particular time—such as the year 2005
in table 9.3—ignore the endowment growth that would be needed to offset
future increases in performance deficits.

To summarize, symphony orchestras that pursue financial stability
solely through endowment policies face three challenges. First, they require
extremely large increases in current endowments to offset current performance deficits using prudent endowment payout rates. Second, endowments must continue to grow at rates sufficient to offset the trend increase
in performance deficits assuming prudent payout rates. Third, the highly
dispersed endowment returns indicate that many orchestras could increase
the resources available for artistic activities by improving the management
of endowment portfolios.

Potential and Practice

Symphony orchestras in the United States vary greatly in their access to
endowment resources. That said, the inequality in orchestra endowments
diminished somewhat as their value advanced substantially in the late 20th
and early 21st century—the period in which there is sufficient data to track
their progress.

Endowment growth itself reflects the interplay of three factors: contributions of new endowment funds, the rate of return on endowment investments, and the rate of payout from endowment funds. The choices made
by an orchestra's board of trustees determine both endowment growth and
the extent to which current and future claimants on the endowment are
treated equably.

The evidence reviewed in this chapter indicates that orchestra boards vary remarkably in their ability to augment endowment resources through successful investment strategies. By developing different endowment portfolios, a number of orchestras could earn higher returns with no increase in risk (annual volatility). There also is evidence that some orchestras have paid out endowment funds at a rate that is not sustainable, given the rate of return on endowment investments and the general advance of orchestra costs. Without an adjustment in these payout policies, those orchestras will subordinate the interests of future employees and patrons to the interests of current claimants. Ultimately, boards of trustees have the responsibility to resist the conflicts of interest and the superior bargaining power of current claimants that may produce inferior long-term outcomes.

Even with better-managed endowments, however, the scale of endowment would have to be an order of magnitude larger to cover performance deficits. Moreover, because structural deficits grow over time, endowments also must grow continually to achieve their goal. As with many other topics addressed in this book, larger endowments will help, but by themselves are unlikely to solve, the problem of growing performance deficits.

The foregoing discussion of board behavior is necessarily incomplete because some important board activities fall outside the scope of this book's focus on orchestra economics. In particular, the emphasis on board stewardship of endowments falls well short of a full discussion of orchestra governance. This crucially important topic concerns the division of responsibilities and authority among orchestra boards, managers, and musicians. Resolving the ongoing tensions between these three groups remains one of the crucial, but not primarily economic, issues facing orchestras (Wichterman 1998).

If none of the three grand strategies outlined early in the book—raising performance revenues, growing expenses more slowly, and raising non-performance income—are likely by themselves to achieve financial balance for U.S. orchestras, why do we not observe more bankruptcies of orchestras in other countries? How do orchestras in the rest of the world solve the problem of balancing revenues and expenses? We address these provocative questions in the next chapter.

CHAPTER 10

How Do Other Countries Support Their Orchestras?

Symphonic music and symphony orchestras emerged in Europe during the 17th century. Courts and churches financed the earliest orchestras, which accompanied operas and sacred texts composed for performance in those venues. There was a dark side to supporting this musical establishment: "Hand in hand with the brilliant development of court and church music went the inquisition and the ruthless exploitation of the lower classes by means of oppressive taxes" (Bukofzer 1947, pp. 394–95).

By the early 18th century, the original sponsors of orchestras became less able to cover the ever-increasing costs of a stable of musicians and composers. Musical activity shifted from the courts and churches to cities and towns, where the tastes of the public at large became more important (Weber 2008). Symphonies had to be composed "not for aristocratic salons where the audience might number perhaps a hundred, but for big public halls where the audience might number a thousand" (Taruskin 2005, vol. 2, p. 556). The financial burden of presenting symphony concerts shifted to the organizers of public subscription concerts, whose emerging middle-class patrons supplanted royalty and the clergy as the main source of financial support. Insecure about their knowledge of music, the middle class associated quality with music that had stood the test of time. Between 1800 and 1870, the dominant orchestra repertoire shifted from the music of contemporary composers, which had dominated performances in the courts and churches, to the music of earlier composers (Weber 2008). In the view of one informed writer, "the concert hall had effectively become a museum." (Taruskin 2005, vol. 3, p. 680)

The richness of the European orchestral tradition offers little protection from the same economic forces that buffet U.S. orchestras. No symphony orchestra in any part of the world earns enough from ticket sales, broadcasts, and recordings to cover its expenses. Instead, the methods by which performance deficits are financed distinguish U.S. from European orchestras. While U.S. orchestras mainly rely on private contributions to offset deficits, direct government subsidies have come to dominate the nonperformance income received by most foreign orchestras since the end of World War II. This chapter documents the wide differences in the sources of nonperformance income in the United States and abroad and explores the ramifications of these differences for orchestras. Drawing on foreign experience, this chapter also shows how the design and administration of government support influences the financial balance of orchestras. More than the risk of bankruptcy is at stake when governments decide to subsidize orchestras, however, and this chapter considers how national policies may influence the nature of artistic endeavor.

Government Support of Foreign Orchestras

Symphony orchestra bankruptcies, an unwelcome feature of the U.S. classical music scene, are essentially unheard of abroad, although foreign orchestras are no more likely to cover their expenses with earned income than U.S. orchestras. In fact, most foreign orchestras report *larger* performance deficits. The dearth of foreign orchestra bankruptcies instead reflects their different sources of nonperformance income.

Previous chapters have explained that private donations dominate nonperformance income in the United States and have stressed that there is no guarantee that donations will continue to cover the ever-growing gap between performance revenues and expenses. When donations persistently fail to cover performance deficits, bankruptcies can and do occur, as the musicians and classical music patrons in several U.S. cities are only too aware.

The private donations that are so important to U.S. orchestras play a minor role abroad. Instead foreign governments seem united by their willingness to provide significant subsidies to their cultural institutions. In effect, foreign governments have not let their orchestras and other cultural institutions die, even though the specific content of national cultural policies varies widely. The National Endowment for the Arts estimated that, in the mid-1990s, direct expenditures on the arts by the governments of 10 industrialized nations ranged from 0.02 percent (USA) to 0.47 percent (Finland) of GDP (NEA 2000). (The median percentage for this group of countries was about 0.23 percent of GDP.) More recent data show that public funding of culture ranged between 0.2 percent and 1 percent of GDP in the vast majority of European countries between 2000 and 2005 (European Parliament 2006a, p. 28). By late 2010, however, there were indications of a weakening in the historical government support of orchestras and other cultural institutions in some European countries—a development we shall return to later in this chapter.

Of course, European countries define "culture" much more broadly than "symphony orchestras" or even "performing arts," but in the wake of these policies, the structure of nonperformance revenues in foreign orchestras differs substantially from that in the United States. Private support for foreign cultural activities and institutions is many times smaller. Between 2000 and 2005, for example, private support to the arts and culture in Europe ranged from 0.13 percent (Bulgaria) to 6.5 percent (UK) of public support (European Parliament 2006a, p. 99).

The comparison of revenues for U.S. and Australian orchestras in chapter 4 provided a preliminary sense of how revenue sources might differ around the world. The private contributions from individuals, businesses, and foundations that compose most nonperformance income for U.S. orchestras barely exist in Australia, where government subsidies cover most operating deficits. But which pattern of support is typical? A broader international comparison of orchestra revenues shows that the Australian revenue structure is closer to the international norm (table 10.1). U.S. orchestras are an anomaly in their lack of access to direct government subsidies, which constitute a majority of orchestra income in most foreign countries. Continental European and Scandinavian countries mimic Australia in providing subsidies from national, regional, and local government agencies that make up about 60 to 90 percent of the revenues of most orchestras. With about 30 to 40 percent of their revenues from government sources, orchestras in Canada and the United Kingdom present an intermediate case.

In turn, the private philanthropy and investment income so essential for U.S. orchestras barely exists in countries with such large and reliable

TABLE 10.1   SOURCES OF ORCHESTRA INCOME (PERCENTAGES)

Country (concert season)	Earned Income	Public Subsidies	Private Donations	Other*
Australia (2003)	28	61	9	2
Range for 8 orchestras	14–83	46–81	2–16	1–4
Canada (2005–6)	32	41	26	1
Range for 3 orchestras	19–42	20–61	1–9	0–7
Finland (2006)	12	87	0	1
Range for 14 orchestras	5–24	75–95	0	0–7
France (1986–87)				
Orchestre de Paris	28	72	0	0
Orchestre de Toulouse	10	90	0	0
Netherlands (2006–7)	21	75	4	0
Big 3	31	64	5	0
5 regional	14	80	6	0
United Kingdom (1998–99)	58	33	9	0
4 London orchestras	63	23	10	4
7 regional	46	36	9	9
5 BBC	46	52	1	1
United States (2005–6)	37	5	45	13

Sources: Australia (2005, chap. 2); Association of British Orchestras (2000, p. 69); Association of Finnish Symphony Orchestras; *Cultural Trends* (1990: 5, p. 29); League of American Orchestras; Netherlands Ministry of Education, Culture and Science; Statistics Canada 2000.
* Includes investment income.

government subsidies. Private support to orchestras can be so insignificant abroad that it is not even recorded in tabulations of orchestra revenues. Taxes in most foreign countries transfer a much larger share of GDP to the public sector than in the United States, and even people who value the arts may feel that they have already provided significant support through their comparatively high tax payments.

Within each country, the importance of public subsidies for the survival of individual orchestras varies substantially. The Australian government supports a symphony orchestra, as well as a ballet and opera orchestra, in each Australian state. Public support ranges from a low of 48 percent of revenues (for the Sydney Orchestra) to a high of 81 percent of revenues (for the Tasmanian Orchestra). The orchestras in the large urban centers of Sydney and Melbourne, where concert attendance is high, rely least on government subsidies. Private donations average 9 percent of the income of Australian orchestras (Australia DEWHA 2005).

In European countries, regional orchestras also receive proportionately higher public support. The public share of orchestra revenues is highest in Finland (at 95 percent) for the Pori Symphony. The limited data for France indicate a similar pattern, with government support ranging from 72 percent of the revenues of the Orchestre de Paris to 90 percent of the revenues of the Orchestre de Toulouse. In the Netherlands, the share of public support is smallest for the three most prominent orchestras—the Concertgebouw, the Rotterdam Philharmonic, and the Residentie Orkest in The Hague—and much higher for regional orchestras.

A clear picture of public support in the United Kingdom emerges by comparing three distinctive groups of orchestras: the four principal London orchestras, a sample of contract (regional) orchestras, and the five British Broadcasting Corporation (BBC) orchestras (located in Cardiff, Glasgow, Manchester, and London). The four London orchestras (the London Symphony Orchestra, the Philharmonia Orchestra, the London Philharmonic Orchestra, and the Royal Philharmonic Orchestra) are self-governing—managed by the orchestra musicians. Contract orchestras provide their members with full-time contracts and salaries, as in most U.S. orchestras. The BBC orchestras broadcast many concerts and have received a significant corporate subsidy over the years. We again see a familiar pattern: the share of government support in revenues is lowest for the London orchestras, about twice as high on average for regional orchestras, and almost twice as high again for the BBC orchestras. In short, governments that support the arts tend to provide disproportionate subsidies to orchestras with weaker earning capacity—a policy that increases access to live classical music outside of the largest cities.

Design and Implementation of Subsidies

Classical music lovers in countries that lack significant subsidies to the arts often see direct government support as a solution to the economic challenges faced by their orchestras. Subsidies might enable orchestras to increase audience size by charging lower concert ticket prices, to raise the pay of symphony musicians, and to lengthen concert seasons. They also might permit presentation of more works requiring a large orchestra and chorus.

But public subsidies to orchestras also may produce unintended negative consequences. By reducing the risk of financial failure, subsidies may induce moral hazard, encouraging inefficiencies in the management of orchestras that exacerbate cost pressures. Orchestras that can count on public support to fill their performance deficits have less incentive to develop ticket-pricing strategies or marketing activities to raise performance revenues and attendance. They also have less incentive to pursue fundraising activities that they might consider in countries in which bankruptcy was a real possibility. In fact, the fundraising skills and activities that are so important for the survival of U.S. orchestras barely exist in countries with significant government support. Concert production and administrative costs may be higher in well-subsidized orchestras.

Government support may also alter labor relations in symphony orchestras. Strikes by musicians, a signal of management resistance to some collective bargaining demands, are rare in countries with substantial public subsidies. (Union–management collaboration to raise subsidies is a more likely collective action.) Artistic costs may also be larger to the extent that the assurance of subsidies reduces management resistance to the wage bargaining demands of musicians and other employees. More generally, under a regime of public subsidies, managers may find it easier to avoid the inevitable conflicts that arise from efforts to control costs.

How Governments Subsidize Their Orchestras

The arresting figures in table 10.1 obscure the variety of ways in which public subsidies may be designed and delivered. But these are exactly the details that determine the impact of subsidies on the financial balance and artistic achievements of orchestras. A few examples illustrate how details of subsidy design and implementation effectively govern the extent to which moral hazard may undermine the objectives of a subsidy program.

Australia. The Australian Broadcasting Corporation (ABC) originally assumed responsibility for the support and centralized management of broadcast orchestras established in the capital city of each Australian state. During the 1990s, these orchestras became subsidiary companies of the ABC in an effort "to move towards making each orchestra accountable for its own performance both financially and artistically" and to enable the orchestras "to respond more flexibly and effectively to issues and opportunities in local environments" (Australia DEWHA 2005).

In the guarded language of official reports, a study of the Australia's symphony management arrangements remarked that subsidy policies "may have had the effect of insulating some orchestras to varying degrees from the pressures and changes in their marketplaces. In addition, it appears there may have not been sufficient realism about the financial performance of orchestras, or the size of orchestra ensemble in relation to audience, or different levels of salaries able to be supported in different locations. In the context of today's marketplace and governance arrangements, the conditions and standards associated with that structure are not sustainable going forward."

In the early 21st century, the Australian government tried to combat these concerns by setting a base grant for each of the six state orchestras and raising the base grant annually at a rate that allowed for some cost inflation. The inflation rate (initially 2.27 percent—the rate applied to other government agencies) was reduced by an "efficiency dividend," initially one percentage point, "as a means of ensuring that bodies drawing public funding can demonstrate ongoing efficiencies in their operations" (Australia DEWHA 2005). Australian orchestras could no longer count on blank checks from their government: not only did gaps between an orchestra's costs and government support have to be covered by raising performance revenues and private contributions, but the presence of the efficiency dividend also implied that the real value of government funding would decline over time. The government report noted that "if government funding accounts for 60 per cent of an orchestra's total revenues and its costs increase by an average of 4 per cent per annum (broadly the average cost movement of recent years), it will need to increase its income from non-government sources by as much as 8 per cent per annum in order to maintain even a neutral financial position. For orchestras with higher levels of dependence on government funding the size of the challenge is even greater." (Australia DEWHA 2005)

The Australian approach provides incentives for orchestras to minimize costs, maximize performance revenues, and cultivate nonperformance income from private sources, but it may underappreciate a basic message of the cost disease: the gap between performance revenues and expenses tends to grow over time. Even when orchestras maintain efficient operations, their costs inherently rise faster than in the rest of the economy, producing a need for ever-increasing amounts of nonperformance income. Declining real support from government sources produces extraordinary pressure for raising funds from a society accustomed to government support of the arts.

The Netherlands. The Dutch experience also illustrates how the design of a subsidy system can have a crucial impact on economic outcomes. Consider the following description of two approaches to delivering arts subsidies in the Netherlands:

> Up to the mid eighties subsidies were based on the projected annual deficit of performing arts organizations and were given in advance. . . . A higher deficit than the one projected involved an additional amount of subsidy. On the other hand, if the deficit was lower than the one projected, the difference had to be refunded.
>
> The system did not provide incentives to performing arts organizations to operate efficiently and to generate income from other sources. . . . Since 1985 . . . symphony orchestras receive a fixed budget rather than a compensation based on their annual deficit. Budgets are allocated as a lump sum to performing arts organizations, leaving the positive and negative risks of the activities and the spending decisions to the organizations. From 1988 performing arts organizations receive a fixed budget for four years. (Goudriaan, de Haart, and Weide 1996, p. 1)

Following the policy change, Dutch orchestras faced much stronger incentives to increase revenues from ticket sales and to seek other sources of nonperformance income. The orchestras responded by increasing ticket prices and raising the share of performance income in total revenue. Between 1985 and 1995, orchestra ticket prices increased by 11.3 percent per year, while consumer prices increased by only 1.7 percent per year (Goudriaan, de Haart, and Weide 1996). In the Netherlands, as in other countries, demand for concert tickets is inelastic, so that ticket price increases raise the total revenue from concerts. Moreover, without the tradition of private giving that is so important in the United States, there is little risk of significant losses of contributions from individuals who decide not to attend in the response to higher ticket prices. In fact, attendance at Dutch orchestra concerts rose during this period, possibly reflecting intensified marketing activities, increasing incomes, and changes in programming. (The share of nonartistic costs, which include marketing and fundraising, increased following the policy change.)

The four-year Dutch subsidy cycle now begins when the government publishes a "cultural policy document" setting out cultural policy principles for each period. A council of professional experts then appraises the applications for support submitted by Dutch cultural institutions. "Quality is the main criterion . . . it is inconceivable under the Dutch system that a politician and his or her civil servants should judge the content and quality of art or culture. The Council's opinion is the decisive factor" (Bina 2002).

Following the assessment of the applications for support, the Ministry of Education, Culture, and Science allocates subsidies for the next four years. Debate and passage by the Dutch parliament completes the process. The key objectives of cultural policy are "to enhance the quality and variety of culture available and to encourage cultural participation by the Dutch population. The first two goals are much easier to achieve than the third one. . . . Subsidies, however, have only an indirect effect on cultural participation by making admission tickets cheaper" (Bina 2002).

Germany. In contrast with the prior examples, local governments are the principal source of public support in Germany, where subsidies average over 80 percent of orchestra budgets. Remittances by theaters and operas constitute about 15 percent of the subsidies for orchestras, but direct expenditures from local government budgets dominate the support received by orchestras and other performing arts. Consequently, local circumstances and politicians influence the amount of public funding.

One study found that German orchestra subsidies varied with population size and the fiscal strength of localities. This same study did not find significant correlations between the size of orchestra subsidies and local differences in income and education, even though one would expect areas with relatively affluent and well-educated populations to prefer more public support of performing arts (Schulze and Rose 1998).

France. Experience in France shows that large public subsidies may have the perverse effect of worsening orchestra deficits. During the 1970s and 1980s, the state controlled the administrative and financial operations of orchestras. Large orchestra concerts were viewed as a public service that enhanced the reputation of French music. Orchestra musicians received job security and salaries indexed to civil service salaries. Like the earliest of the Dutch systems, the size of public subsidies to orchestras was based on their prior deficits, along with the economic balance of similar orchestras and the artistic priority of one orchestra over another. A former manager of the Orchestre de Paris argued that this system led orchestra managers to disregard costs, hoping that they would be saved by subsidies. Given the role of subjective artistic priorities in establishing subsidies, orchestras could also favor comparatively expensive performances that might enhance the orchestra's image for its subsidizers (Guillard 1985).

In short, foreign experience shows that subsidies are not necessarily an instant cure for financial strain. A subsidy policy may even induce further need for subsidies, raising the question of how far a government is willing to support orchestras. The Australian report noted that, even with a government subsidy, only half of the eight major Australian orchestras avoided an overall deficit, and the orchestra sector as a whole experienced an overall deficit (Australia DEWHA 2005). Faced with these facts, governments are increasingly reexamining their orchestra subsidy policies and looking for alternative financing models. In June 2010, for example, the new British government announced emergency budget cuts that included a reduction of 25 percent for the budget for the department in charge of arts over four years. Later in the year, a new Dutch government proposed cutting funding to the arts by $274 million over five years. As part of this initiative, the government would close the Netherlands Broadcasting Music Center and four musical organizations associated with it—a radio symphony orchestra, a radio chamber ensemble, a radio choir, and a pop and jazz orchestra (Service 2010).

The search for alternatives includes greater financial participation by private parties—an approach that resembles the U.S. model described in earlier chapters. While many in the United States see greater government support as a solution to orchestras' financial challenges, classical music lovers in foreign countries envy the private support that keeps many orchestras performing in the United States.

The remainder of this chapter compares the experience of orchestras in countries offering significant subsidies to symphonies with the experience in the United States. We begin by showing that, despite the stark difference in sources of nonperformance income, U.S. and foreign orchestras share many economic circumstances.

Shared Circumstances

The different methods that many foreign governments adopt to support symphony orchestras may divert attention from a wide range of economic circumstances shared by orchestras around the world. In the words of an Australian report, "Over the past decade or more, many orchestras in Australia and around the world have had to confront a number of harsh realities, including flat or declining attendances, an ageing audience profile, shifting audience expectations, a declining base of subscriptions, increases in guest artist fees, reductions in corporate sponsorship and private philanthropy, dwindling cash reserves, and increased demands for accountability from governments" (Australia DEWHA 2005).

A cautionary note: Accessible information on the finances and operations of foreign orchestras is sparse outside of the United States. While a few countries offer detailed data for several years, others at most have special one-time or occasional analyses of the financial health of orchestras. Nonetheless, available data support several conclusions.

Performance Deficits

To what extent do foreign orchestras cover their expenses with the revenues they earn from concerts, broadcasts, and recordings? The available data suggest that these revenues lag well behind expenses. No foreign orchestra comes close to covering its expenses with its earned income (table 10.2).

TABLE 10.2   PERFORMANCE INCOME RATIOS[a] AROUND THE WORLD (PERCENTAGES)

	1998	2000	2004
Australia	n.a.	n.a	28[b]
Sydney symphony	n.a.	n.a.	44[b]
Melbourne symphony	n.a.	n.a.	30[b]
6 regional orchestras	n.a.	n.a.	20[b]
Canada	41	35	36[b]
Finland	11	11	11
	(5–22)	(5–28)	(5–25)
Netherlands	40[c]	42	50
Big 3	75[c]	77	93
5 regional	18[c]	21	24
United Kingdom	58	n.a.	n.a.
4 London orchestras	67	n.a.	n.a.
7 independent contract	54	n.a.	n.a.
5 BBC orchestras	48	n.a.	n.a.
14 chamber/freelance	62	n.a.	n.a.
United States	48	44	41

Sources: See table 10.1.

Figures in parentheses show range of outcomes for individual orchestras.

n.a. = not available.

[a] Ratio of performance revenues to performance expenses × 100.

[b] 2003.

[c] 1997.

TABLE 10.3   PER-CONCERT AUDIENCE, PERFORMANCE REVENUE,
AND EXPENSES

	Years	Audience	Revenue	Expenses
Australia	(2001–3)	505	$8,917	$41,207
Canada	(2001–3)	1399	$45,213	$116,624
Finland	(2001–3)	576	$3,047	$53,213
Netherlands	(2001–3)	990	$20,408	$141,700
United Kingdom	(1995–99)	943	$17,735	n.a.
United States	(2001–3)	1470	$31,036	$86,153

Sources: See table 10.1.
n.a. = not available.

The fraction of performance expenses covered by the revenues of U.S. orchestras declined from 46 to 41 percent between the early 1990s and the 2005–6 concert season. With the exception of the United Kingdom, performance income covers an even smaller share of expenses in foreign countries. Some of the differences are quite dramatic: At 11 percent of expenses, the average performance income ratio for Finnish orchestras is well below the lowest ratios experienced by any orchestra in the other countries in the table. There is considerable variation in the performance income ratios of individual orchestras. Orchestras with access to large, urban populations cover the highest proportion of their expenses with performance income.[1]

The evidence that U.S. orchestras generally report smaller performance deficits than orchestras in most foreign countries may surprise some readers. At the least, it signals possible moral hazard in countries that subsidize the arts substantially. A closer look at the performance revenues and costs of foreign orchestras can help us understand some of the sources of their eye-catching deficits.

On the revenue side, foreign orchestras generally play to smaller audiences. Attendance per concert ranges from one-third to two-thirds of the U.S. average (table 10.3). Performance revenues per concert can be even lower, ranging from 1 percent (Finland) to 65 percent (the Netherlands) of the average per-concert receipts in the United States. Variations in revenue that cannot be explained by differences in attendance signal the importance of ticket pricing policies, but we lack sufficient data on the levels and structures of foreign concert ticket prices. With the exception of the

Netherlands, foreign countries have lower per-concert expenses than the United States. Canada provides a contrast with overseas experience.

Stagnating Concert Attendance

At a time when they would benefit from higher concert revenues, foreign orchestras have encountered another parallel with the U.S. experience—stagnating attendance. Surveys indicate that the fraction of the adult (15 years and older) population attending at least one classical music concert in a year was remarkably similar among countries in the early 21st century (table 10.4). (In these surveys, "classical music" includes orchestra, chamber, and choral concerts.) The reduced inclination to attend live classical concerts in the United States is hardly unusual, given this international perspective. (The Netherlands presents the exceptional case, with a noticeably higher attendance rate.)

In country after country, larger proportions of the population attended classical music concerts in the 1980s and 1990s than in the early years of the 21st century. For the 1990s, Bina (2002) cites attendance rates of 31 percent in Belgium, 16 percent in Denmark and the Netherlands, and 10 percent in Finland. Not all countries survey cultural participation regularly, but where comparisons over time are possible, attendance rates declined.

Foreign countries also have similar demographic patterns of concert attendance. Attendance rates everywhere tend increase with age. Rumors of growing audiences of younger listeners in some countries remain unconfirmed by national surveys. Occasionally, as in Australia and the Netherlands, there is concrete evidence of growing proportions of older listeners, but there are too few surveys in most countries to determine definitively whether the aging of symphony audiences continues generally.

National surveys do confirm that more educated and affluent people are more likely to attend classical concerts in all countries. Yet declining attendance rates are observed for all education levels and virtually all ages. As in the United States, successive cohorts of foreign populations are increasingly less likely to attend a classical music concert irrespective of education, income, or age. The surveys also confirm that women are.more likely to attend classical music concerts than men, but ethnic minorities are less likely to attend than whites—a finding that bodes poorly for audience growth in countries with substantial immigration.

TABLE 10.4   FRACTION OF POPULATION ATTENDING CLASSICAL CONCERTS (PERCENTAGES)

Age Range	Australia	Canada		Ireland		Netherlands[d]			UK	United States		
	(2005–6)	1992	1998	1994	2006	1983	1995	2007	2007	1982	2002	2008
All Ages	9	12	8	9	7	13	17	14	8	13	12	9
15–19	6[a]	—	6	—	4	—	10	7	3	11	8	7
20–24	—	—	6	—	—	⎱	—	10 ⎰	—	—	—	—
25–34	7	—	6	—	7	⎰	14	⎱	4	13	9	7
35–44	8	—	7	—	5	—	21	10	6	16	11	9
45–54	12	—	11[b]	—	8	—	—	—	10	15	15	10
55–64	13	—		—	13	—	27	22	14	13	16	12
65+	11	—	10[c]	—	13	—	18	23	12	10	11	11

Sources: Australian Bureau of Statistics (2009); Statistics Canada Culture Research Program (2000); Ireland Arts Council (2006); Arts Council of England (2007); NEA (2009).

[a] Ages 18–24.

[b] Ages 45–59.

[c] Ages 60+.

[d] Age breaks for the Netherlands are 12–19, 20–34, 35–49, 50–64 and 65+.

But in the face of growing national populations, do declining attendance *rates* imply declining attendance? In most countries, they do—population growth is not sufficient to offset declining attendance rates. In Canada adult attendance declined from 2.6 million to 2 million between 1992 and 1998, a drop of 23 percent. Over the same period, business conditions improved and the unemployment rate fell from 10.6 to 7.7 percent, a cyclical improvement that should have raised attendance. Detailed data for orchestras in Finland and the Netherlands also show decreasing total attendance at symphony concerts during the late 20th and early 21st century. In Finland the total number of concerts performed by the top 14 symphony orchestras declined by 36 percent, from 1,760 in 1994 to 1,121 in 2008. Despite declining unemployment rates, total attendance at Finnish symphony concerts also declined, although at a slower rate than the number of concerts. In short, as total attendance declined, Finnish orchestras were presenting fewer concerts to somewhat larger audiences.

The overall number of concert performances offered by the eight largest orchestras in the Netherlands declined by 22 percent between 1997 and 2007, while annual concert attendance fell by 24 percent. As a result, there was no significant trend in audience per concert. In large measure, Dutch orchestras compensated for the decline in concert audiences by increasing educational programs and other musical activities. Audiences for these alternative activities grew throughout the period and offset the decline in concert audiences.

The three years of data available for Australia show fluctuating attendance with no clear trend. As in the United States, there has been a decline in the proportion of subscribers and an increase in the share of single-ticket sales.

From an international perspective, therefore, the U.S. concert attendance experience seems unexceptional. The changing levels and patterns of classical attendance appear to be a global phenomenon that limits the concert revenues available to orchestras. The evidence of worldwide declines in attendance suggests that influences identified in one country may also apply elsewhere. In examining the U.S. experience, we stressed that concert attendance involves *both* time and money costs (chapter 5). The importance of time costs appears in Europe as well. When a survey of European cultural participation inquired about barriers to attending concerts, the most frequent response (cited by 42 percent of the respondents) was a lack of time. Time constraints were particularly important for more educated people, whose opportunity cost of time was relatively high. In contrast, only 29 percent claimed that concerts were too expensive. Increasingly lower percentages of respondents cited lack of interest (27 percent), lack of information (17 percent), or insufficient background (13 percent) as reasons for not attending (European Commission 2007, p. 31).

Rising Expenses

Chapter 2 detailed how orchestra expenses in the United States have risen more rapidly than costs in other economic sectors, consistent with the predictions of the cost disease argument. If orchestra productivity grows more rapidly elsewhere in the world than in the United States, or orchestra pay rises less rapidly, foreign symphonies could escape the cost disease and its consequences.

Information on foreign orchestra expenses is scarce, but for Australia, Finland, the Netherlands, and the United Kingdom we may compare increases in cost per symphony concert with increases in the Producer Price Index (PPI), a measure of the costs per unit of manufactured products computed and published by many governments (table 10.5). Chapter 2 (see fig. 2.1) presented parallel information for the United States. The orchestra expense data include both artistic and nonartistic costs.

One key point emerges from table 10.5: around the world, orchestra expenses increase much more rapidly than costs in the manufacturing sector. With concert costs increasing more rapidly than the cost of many consumer goods, either the relative price of concert tickets must increase over time in these countries or the flows of nonperformance income must continually increase if the orchestras are to maintain financial balance.

Artists and Artistic Costs

What is the economic position of orchestra musicians in societies with substantial public support of the arts? How do the salaries of foreign and U.S. orchestra musicians compare? Where do orchestra musicians stand in their national income distributions? The answers to these questions speak to both the welfare of symphony musicians and the artistic costs incurred by orchestras.

TABLE 10.5   COMPARISON OF ORCHESTRA AND MANUFACTURING
             COST INCREASES (PERCENTAGE INCREASE)

Australia (2001–3)	
Expense per concert	10.5
Producer Price Index	0.7
Finland (1994–2007)	
Expense per concert	114.0
Producer Price Index	14.1
Netherlands (1997–2004)	
Expense per concert	56.8
Producer Price Index	13.7
United Kingdom* (1995–98)	
Expense per concert	7.0
Producer Price Index	2.4
United States (1994–2005)	
Expense per concert	67.3
Producer Price Index	24.1

Sources: ABO 2000, p. 79; Association of Finnish Symphony Orchestras; Australia 2005; League of
American Orchestras; OECD 2009b.
*Three independent contract orchestras.

Discussions of musicians' incomes begin with the basic fact that the
number of well-trained musicians seeking positions in symphony orchestras worldwide exceeds the number of positions available. As in the United
States, collective bargaining arrangements between musicians' unions and
symphony management or employer associations generally counter the
downward pressure on pay and working conditions produced by the large
supply of qualified classical musicians. Nevertheless, bargaining arrangements vary widely. Some countries follow the U.S. practice of conducting
separate negotiations with each orchestra. In principle, this decentralized
arrangement offers the greatest opportunity for weighing special local circumstances in negotiations. In other countries, industry-wide negotiations
between a musicians' union and an orchestra employers' association determine pay and working conditions of musicians at all orchestras. Industry-
wide negotiations typically provide for some pay differentiation within and
between orchestras. Seniority and the special responsibilities of leading an
instrumental section also drive pay differences between musicians in foreign orchestras.

Industry-wide bargaining does not rule out some market influence on musicians' pay. Pay differences between Dutch orchestras increasingly reflect differences in labor market pressures. In the 2006–7 collective bargaining agreement, musicians in four Dutch orchestras received the base rate, while musicians in three other orchestras received 110 percent of that rate. Musicians in the Rotterdam Philharmonic Orchestra, commonly viewed as the second best in the Netherlands, received 115 percent of the base rate. Musicians in the Concertgebouw Orchestra, rated in some polls as the best symphony orchestra in the world, received still higher pay, driven by the fact that in the open labor market of the European Union, the Netherlands was in danger of losing some of its finest musicians to German orchestras paying higher salaries. In the face of continuing market competition, the Concertgebouw eventually agreed to pay 150 percent of the base rate.

Local bargaining in the United Kingdom has produced considerable variation in orchestra musicians' salaries. Some salary differences between orchestras reflect the greater diversity of organizational forms in the United Kingdom. As noted earlier, the four major London orchestras are self-governing, a form of organization adopted only by a very few U.S. orchestras emerging from bankruptcy. The player boards of the four London orchestras have direct control of the strategy and operations of the entire organization, including the selection and retention of each orchestra's musical director and managing director. With that power, the musicians bear responsibility for the economic consequences of their decisions.

The self-governing London orchestras also have established greater internal pay equality than other orchestras. The following description of musician pay differentials at the London Symphony Orchestra contrasts sharply with pay practices in the United States and other countries: "The importance of equality as a core LSO value was underscored by the orchestra's compensation system. All players in a given category were paid the same. There were no exceptions to standard rates, regardless of a player's seniority or musical prowess—although compensation was higher for principal players and for some others who had special responsibilities. Moreover, pay levels were public—known to all members, and accepted by most" (Lehman and Galinsky 1994, p. 8).

During the 1998–99 concert season, musicians in the BBC orchestras received the highest average salaries (£2,105, or $3,445, per month), followed by musicians in the opera and ballet orchestras (£2,046 or $3,350) and independent contract orchestras (£1,978 or $3,235). Each of these

TABLE 10.6   ANNUAL PAY OF SYMPHONY MUSICIANS AND
              ORCHESTRA MANAGERS

Country	Average[a]	Range[b]	Percentage of Mean Income[c]
Australia (2003)			
Minimum	$28,990	$24,325–$41,728	65–111%
10 years experience	$36,390	$30,475–$50,075	81–134%
Finland (2005)			
Section principal	n.a.	$30,840–$52,440	105–178%
Deputy principal	n.a.	$27,180–$48,960	92–166%
Musician	n.a.	$25,500–$42,660	87–145%
Netherlands (2007)			
Minimum	n.a.	$35,820–$41,196	84–97%
10 years experience	n.a.	$46,140–$53,040	109–125%
United Kingdom (1998–99)			
Independent contract	$38,930	$36,005–$41,845	137–160%
BBC	$41,426	$37,195–$49,200	142–188%
United States (2003)			
52-week schedules			
Minimum	$86,315	$57,720–$104,520	137–248%
Average	$100,480	$63,700–$127,556	151–303%
30 largest orchestras			
Minimum	$71,497	$28,000–$106,000	67–252%
Average	$84,168	$33,280–$134,514	79–319%

Sources: See table 10.1 and OECD 2009a table I.

[a] All salaries have been converted into U.S. dollars using the average interbank foreign exchange rate for each period. Data at Oanda.com.

[b] Data are for the six state orchestras in Australia, fifteen orchestras reporting to the Association of Finnish Symphony Orchestras, eight orchestras in the Netherlands, and six orchestras in the UK.

[c] Adjusted for differences in purchasing power.

n.a. = not available.

amounts was below the minimum salaries of musicians at the top U.S. orchestras during the 1998 concert season.

In short, the salaries of orchestra musicians reflect the interplay of market forces and a variety of institutional influences. Table 10.6 presents information on musician salaries from five different countries between

1998 and 2007. For each country, the annual salaries of symphony musicians have been adjusted to U.S. dollars, using currency exchange rates for the relevant period. The table includes average salaries (when an average is available) and the salary range among major orchestras. The exact years represented and other details vary from country to country with the availability of data. For Australia and the Netherlands, one can compare the minimum salary with the salary of musicians with 10 years of experience with an orchestra. For Finland, a basic musician's salary can be compared with the salaries for section leaders and their deputies. For the United States, one can compare the minimum salary with the average musician's salary, which includes the effects of seniority and section leadership responsibilities. Separate information is provided for the 13 U.S. orchestras with 52-week schedules and for the largest 30 orchestras. Since most foreign orchestras offer annual contracts, the former information is most appropriate for international comparisons.

In dollar terms, it is clear that orchestra musicians in other countries earn considerably less than U.S. symphony musicians (columns 1 and 2). Musicians' salaries at the top U.S. orchestras are at least twice as high as salaries at top orchestras abroad, some of which are rated as the best orchestras in the world. Clearly, government subsidies for orchestras abroad have not produced distinctively higher relative salaries for foreign musicians. Indeed, lower artistic salaries may account in part for the lower expense per concert reported by foreign orchestras.[2]

Two additional perspectives on salaries may help assess the economic position of orchestra musicians in different countries. Individuals in all professions sometimes express more concern with *relative* than *absolute* salaries. Where do the salaries reported in table 10.6 place musicians in their national distribution of income? Secondly, the level and structure of prices facing consumers varies between countries, influencing the purchasing power of a given salary. How do the salaries of orchestra musicians in different countries compare in terms of purchasing power? These two additional perspectives are combined in column 3, which shows how the lowest and highest salaries of symphony musicians compare to average wages in each country, adjusted to U.S. purchasing power parity.[3] For example, when adjusted to U.S. purchasing power equivalents, the 2003 data for Australia in column 3 show that the minimum salary of Australian symphonic musicians (recorded in column 2) ranged from 65 percent to 111 percent of average national wages. In contrast, the minimum salary for U.S. orchestra musicians on 52-week schedules ranged from 137 percent to 248 percent of U.S. average income. Other data in the table may be interpreted accordingly. The United States again stands out, not only for the salary level but also for the comparatively high position of symphony musicians in the national income distribution.

The data in table 10.6 also permit some limited international perspective on the pay structure within symphony orchestras. Seniority premia seem comparatively high in some foreign countries. Ten years of service yields pay premia of 25 to 28 percent in Australia and the Netherlands, whereas 10 years of service with a top 52-week orchestra in the United States will yield a premium equal to 1 to 5 percent of annual salary. As the earlier discussion of the London Symphony Orchestra indicates, however, some foreign orchestras also establish quite moderate seniority premia.

The same may be said of pay premia for section leaders. Concertmasters at top U.S. orchestras received from 2 to 3.5 times the minimum salary for orchestra musicians (see chapter 6). The differential is much lower—about a 40 percent premium—in Finland, the only foreign country providing salary information by orchestra position.

The limited information available for foreign orchestras suggests that management pay is also lower than in the United States. During the 1998–99 concert season, the pay of the chief executive officers of four independent contract orchestras in the United Kingdom averaged just under £60,000 ($98,160). This salary was about 2.5 times the average pay for an orchestra musician—a much smaller differential than is found in most U.S. orchestras (see chapter 6). Heads of finance averaged about £32,000 ($52,350), while heads of marketing and of development (fundraising) received about £28–29,000 ($46–47,000) annually—respectively, 1.3 and 1.2 times average musician's pay. The salaries of management personnel in British chamber orchestras were considerably lower (ABO 2000). The British orchestra data indicate increasing relative salaries for development directors (reflecting increased emphasis on fundraising) and decreasing relative salaries for directors of education and community work (ABO 2000). In Finland the average pay range for orchestra managers was roughly 1.5 times the average musicians' salary. These pay structures reveal less differentiation than is typical in the United States. In fact, pay distributions are generally less dispersed in these countries, and the lower relative pay of managers may reflect less remunerative outside market opportunities.

Subsidies and Tax Expenditures

There is a danger that this chapter's focus on direct government subsidies to orchestras may encourage the view that foreign governments support their orchestras, while the U.S. federal government does not. As chapter 7 showed, adherents to this view badly caricature the relation between government and the performing arts in the United States by ignoring the impact of tax expenditures. Some of the "private" orchestra support recorded in table 10.1 and elsewhere in this book should instead be thought of as "public" support—money that otherwise would have been paid to the government. Emphasizing direct support through subsidies to the exclusion of indirect support from tax expenditures understates public support and overstates private support for orchestras.

While emphasizing the role of direct subsidies overstates international differences in government support for orchestras, most foreign governments do not appear to offer tax benefits comparable to those in the United States for donations to the arts. An early study of tax expenditures abroad concluded that "tax expenditures are of only marginal financial importance in . . . other countries," and "in the United States tax expenditures are a significant source of indirect aid to the arts, whereas in the other countries their impact is minimal" (Schuster 1985, pp. 44, 54).

Where tax benefits for donating to the arts exist, they appear to be limited by regulations that have no parallel in the United States. Tax expenditures may become more important as foreign countries seek to maintain some public commitment to arts without funding increasing deficits, but the data remain too elusive to track trends in the early 21st century. Official documents provide some guidance on the scope and limitations of European tax expenditure policies, but no estimate of how they compare in importance to direct government subsidies (European Parliament 2006a, p. 84).

Subsidies, Art, and Innovation

Some of the international preference for government subsidies over private support of orchestras and other performing arts stems from suspicion of the quality of artistic tastes that might be expressed through market dynamics. Fear that private choices would lead to low-brow, unsophisticated programming and stifle innovation in classical music often underlies preferences for direct government funding. Two considerations, however, challenge the influential view that government support produces superior artistic outcomes.

There is, first, the experience of countries that provide little direct public support for the performing arts. The United States, with its decentralized approach to funding the arts, is the leading example. Has the quality of American orchestras suffered under the regime of largely private financing? The testimony of an international group of classical music critics who regularly evaluate the live and recorded performances of orchestras around the world suggests that such is not the case. Asked by *Gramophone* magazine to name the world's top 20 orchestras, the critics included seven U.S. orchestras. In the ranking developed from these evaluations, U.S. orchestras placed 5th (Chicago), 7th (Cleveland), 8th (Los Angeles), 11th (Boston), 12th (New York Philharmonic), 13th (San Francisco), and 18th (Metropolitan Opera Orchestra) (*Gramophone* 2008).

Even well-informed rankings are subject to debate, and the *Gramophone*'s orchestra rankings were no exception. But the critiques invariably voiced disagreements about *which* U.S. orchestras belonged on the list, not about *whether* U.S. orchestras belonged on the list. Frequent invitations for international touring and foreign performances further signal the quality of musicianship and performance that can emerge from a decentralized system of support. Admittedly, a convincing test of the hypothesis that private support will degrade symphony orchestra programming choices (or direct government support will improve programming) remains elusive. What one can say is that when experienced critics look around the world, they find superior orchestras surviving in both regimes of direct and indirect public support, despite the different parties who make decisions on financial support.

The assumption that a regime of direct government subsidies enhances artistic quality and innovation is in fact subject to challenge. Self-interested individuals administer public subsidies, and their interests may not reliably advance artistic innovation and quality. How government support for orchestras is organized and administered influences what is considered to be art and who is considered to be an artist.

In practice, three broad approaches to distributing subsidies to orchestras and other arts organizations have emerged in European countries. In the most centralized support systems, bureaucrats and politicians determine both the budget for the arts and how that budget will be distributed among orchestras and other arts organizations. The choices of politicians and bureaucrats effectively define supportable art. The decision-making process usually lacks transparency and may favor large showpiece or "prestige" projects (Van der Ploeg 2006, p. 1208). In discussing centralized government subsidy policies, Dana Gioia, former chair of the U.S. National Endowment for the Arts, commented: "In countries like France, Germany, Mexico, or China, most arts funding comes from the government—either at a federal or local level. For the most part, these systems tend to be centralized, often located in a large ministry of culture. These organizations are also typically political, as arts personnel are usually either members of civil service or political appointees from the ruling party. These systems provide smooth and stable planning for arts organizations, but they run the risk of dividing the cultural world into insiders and outsiders. The insider institutions tend to be well subsidized with large annual grants while the outsiders survive on the margins of the culture, if they survive at all" (NEA 2007, p. v).

At the other extreme, bureaucrats and politicians determine the size of the arts budget but leave the responsibility for allocating the budget to a semiautonomous arts council. This system, which prevails in the United Kingdom, shifts allocation decisions from politicians and bureaucrats to an arts elite from which arts councils seek advice on the artistic merits of alternative proposals for support. The policy increases transparency, but in removing opportunities for politicians and bureaucrats to determine the funding of specific organizations and projects it also limits the opportunity for government to influence the general direction of cultural policy or broad selection criteria.

An intermediate approach used in the Netherlands seeks a middle ground that permits the government to determine general directions in government policy but uses an independent arts council to determine the artistic merit of proposals for support. Well in advance of proposal evaluation, the government publishes a policy document setting out the priorities, criteria, and budgets that should inform the arts council's decisions. Later the council submits its funding recommendations based on evaluations of artistic merit to a government minister, who makes the final allocation decisions. The minister may depart from the recommendations if the arts council has not followed the general goals stated in the policy document. But the system also permits ministers to depart from the recommendations in response to various forms of special pleading.

Each of these approaches has its strengths and weaknesses, but none leaves artistic choices to groups that can claim reliably superior tastes to the public at large. *Elected politicians* in principle respond to the electorate, but in practice they are subject to the influence of well-financed interest groups. "Established and, therefore, essentially culturally conservative group interests have a larger say than those promoting innovative forms of culture. The latter are, almost by definition, unorganized and therefore politically weak, as they represent future, still unknown forms and types of art" (Frey 2000, p. 14).

Government arts administrators may protect their reputations by endorsing and defending past choices for support. Changing direction to support new art forms casts doubt on the wisdom of past decisions. "Arts administrators therefore have an interest in defending established art. Most importantly, they have an incentive to fight off outsiders—but this is exactly where creative and innovative art comes from. Leaving cultural decisions to art administrators introduces a marked conservative bias" (Frey 2000, p. 15).

Members of the *arts establishment* (for example, music critics, music historians, major philanthropists) may have conservative tastes because established art is their field of competence through education and practice. A report on European cultural policy recently observed that the experts who judge art are often part of the art world themselves, and their personal survival may be linked to the survival of the art with which they are familiar (European Parliament 2006b).

Musicians and other artists themselves may be too centered on their own style and training to be unbiased judges of the work of others in their field. Furthermore, who *are* the artists? Those who graduate from certain schools? (Which schools?) Those who belong to certain associations? (Which associations?) Those who make a living from art? Those who believe that they are artists? Each definition of an artist will produce a different slant to decisions on supporting the arts.

In short, critics of decentralized support for orchestras and other arts have not advanced a convincing case for the inferiority of choices by the public at large. From a different perspective, a former director of the Netherlands Ministry of Education, Culture, and Science noted that "one should not forget that supply subsidies allocated by committees of experts might lead to high culture for a small elite" (Van der Ploeg 2006, p. 349).

Symphony Economics at Home and Abroad

There have been few dramatic examples of symphony orchestra failures outside of the United States. Yet foreign orchestras face the same economic challenges encountered by U.S. symphonies. This chapter has documented a worldwide erosion of concert audiences and increase in cost pressures. In fact, the study of foreign orchestras reveals a seeming paradox: comparatively large performance deficits accompany their comparatively stable finances. Foreign orchestras have not discovered the secret of earning enough income from concerts, broadcasts, and recordings to cover their expenses. In this respect, their economic performance is worse than the record of U.S. symphonies.

Instead, different sources of nonperformance income largely account for the differences in financial stability in the face of common economic challenges. Most foreign orchestras can count on significant subsidies from local, state, or national governments, while most U.S. orchestras cannot. The subsidies provide a more consistently reliable method of filling gaps between performance income and expenses than the private support on which U.S. orchestras mainly rely. This important difference is often telescoped into the following statement: foreign orchestras benefit from government support, while U.S. orchestras do not. This chapter and chapter 7 have tried to clarify that this statement is a caricature, because U.S. symphonies receive significant government assistance that takes a different form—tax expenditures.

These different approaches to providing government support have far-reaching consequences. Direct subsidies can reliably cover performance deficits, but if subsidies remove all financial risks, performance deficits may grow larger. A kind of moral hazard may emerge in which orchestras may devote less effort to raising performance revenues and reducing performance expenses. Countries that directly subsidize orchestras may avoid overt failures (bankruptcies) but may be subject to a slow erosion of economic balance from the forces of moral hazard—an outcome requiring ever-increasing subsidies. Much depends on how the subsidy system is designed, and many governments that offer direct subsidies to the arts are insisting on greater accountability by arts organizations and searching for models that counter moral hazard. The difficulty of finding such models is signaled by the envy that arts officials in other countries increasingly express for the system of "private" support that they believe prevails in the United States.

Both systems of government support to orchestras and other performing arts remain vulnerable to efforts to reduce government deficits. By 2011, it was becoming all too apparent that nations confronting large budget deficits are finding it easier to impose larger cuts on the arts than national security and entitlement programs.

CHAPTER 11

The Economic Future of Symphony Orchestras

The "perilous life" of orchestras noted in this book's title signals the tension between significant artistic achievements and the challenging economic circumstances that most orchestras live with. Symphonic music probably never has been performed better than today, yet orchestras at all levels of achievement confront ongoing economic distress. This book has tried to provide an up-to-date diagnosis of the economic challenges and an appraisal of the main strategies for addressing them.

Diagnosing Financial Distress

The diagnosis of a symphony's perilous economic life begins with the limited opportunities for ongoing productivity growth. With the labor required for performances more or less frozen for all time by the composers of the symphonic repertoire, there are few opportunities for orchestras to take advantage of the technical changes that have raised productivity in many other sectors of the economy. Yet the pay of orchestra employees must increase at roughly the same rate as pay in high-productivity-growth industries, or orchestras will find it increasingly difficult to retain artistic and nonartistic personnel. When pay rises more rapidly than productivity, the costs of presenting symphony performances grow relative to the costs of producing products in high-productivity industries—a fact documented in chapters 2 and 3 for the United States and in chapter 10 for other countries. Performance (operating) deficits will not just persist in these sectors—they will *grow over time*. Without a cure or offset for this phenomenon, growing operating deficits threaten the sustainability of orchestras.

Forty-five years after the publication and analysis of this cost disease scenario, discomfort with its unwelcome implications still leads many people in the arts community to deny its validity or argue that it may be offset. Yet none of the common objections are supported by the facts of orchestra economics in the late 20th and early 21rst century. On the contrary, chapter 3 documented the relentless decline in the fraction of expenses covered by performance revenues, even after controlling for the notable influence of business cycles on orchestra finances. Moreover, no orchestra in the world has succeeded in growing performance revenues rapidly enough to offset its ongoing cost increases. Increasing structural deficits thus remain a fact of life for symphony orchestras around the world. All organizations with limited productivity growth—including other performing arts, universities, and some government agencies—must find methods to offset their growing gaps between operating income and expenses.

The diagnosis continues by noting developments in concert attendance and orchestra costs that in principle are reversible (unlike the productivity problem). Attendance per concert has fallen for virtually all types of concerts offered by orchestras, despite steady increases in the proportion of the population with a college education (the demographic most likely to attend symphony concerts). Groups that provided the most support in the past now attend less frequently. Efforts to raise attendance by offering more concerts encounter sharply diminishing returns. Indeed, total concert attendance has declined, even after adjusting for cyclical influences on patronage. Worse yet, declining attendance has been accompanied by the sale of fewer subscription tickets and more single tickets—a development that raises an orchestra's marketing costs per concert. A distinct minority of orchestras receive opportunities to supplement home concert revenues with concert tours and recordings. Many orchestras have tried to counter these trends with innovative experiments in marketing and in the timing and content of orchestra concerts. The data analyzed for this study incorporate whatever impacts these experiments have had on concert attendance. Without them, attendance presumably would have been even lower.

The pay of musicians has not just matched pay growth elsewhere in the economy, as assumed in some versions of the cost disease argument; it has increased faster. Since 1987 the pay of symphony musicians has grown more rapidly than the pay of most other labor market groups, and collective agreements have changed the artistic expenses of symphony orchestras from variable costs into fixed costs. Most alarming for the size of an orchestra's structural deficit, pay changes show little sensitivity on average to the financial balance of orchestras.

Increasing concert attendance and slowing the growth of orchestra costs would limit the future growth of symphony deficits, but it would not eliminate them, given the underlying productivity problem. Hence, symphony orchestras cannot survive as private profit-seeking business organizations. Self-supporting status is an elusive goal. Instead they generally organize as nonprofit entities and try to cover the growing gap between performance revenues and expenses with some combination of contributed support, direct government subsidies, and investment income from endowments.

The final step in the diagnosis considers the prospects for whether these sources of nonperformance income will in fact cover the structural deficits of orchestras. The key point is that, in large measure, U.S. symphony orchestras do not control the main factors influencing their nonperformance income. The flow of nonperformance income to an orchestra reflects the largely uncoordinated decisions of individual contributors, businesses, foundation personnel, politicians, arts council employees, and symphony boards of trustees. The prospect that the diverse interests motivating these sources of nonperformance income would produce an annual flow of income just equal to performance deficits is staggeringly small—a fact confirmed by the observation that no U.S. symphony orchestra, however prominent, has been able to maintain a consistent record of financial balance.

Consider first the significant but underappreciated role of government in supporting orchestras. Most discussions of the topic consider only the flow of direct government subsidies, which in the United States have declined dramatically since the late 1980s and which are small in comparison with the subsidies that many foreign governments provide to their orchestras. But this focus overlooks the fact that tax expenditures for symphony orchestras dwarf direct government support in the United States; federal tax expenditures alone increased from 75 to 96 percent of the public support for orchestras between 1987 and 2005 (chapter 7). In foreign countries, such indirect government support appears to be quite small in comparison to direct subsidies. Viewed in international perspective, *combined* direct and indirect government support for orchestras may not be unusually low in the United States. At the same time, the fact that tax expenditures dominate government support adds to the financial uncertainty facing U.S. orchestras, given that the amount of indirect support depends on the decisions of thousands of individuals, businesses, and foundations rather than the centralized decisions of a government arts agency.

If tax expenditures alter our perception of government support for orchestras, they must also alter our perception of the scope of private support, for some fraction of what orchestras report as private support is in fact tax expenditure—money that the government could have collected and spent but instead allowed taxpayers to contribute to orchestras. Orchestras categorize donations by their immediate source, so all sums received from individuals, businesses, and foundations are considered as "private" contributions, even though a significant fraction has effectively been donated by the government.

The growth of such "private" donations has been crucial for whatever financial balance U.S. orchestras have been able to achieve. The surge of private donations in the late 1990s, for example, offset both declining government subsidies and the rising performance deficits of orchestras. But the late 1990s were years of stable tax rates and growing real incomes. As income growth moved increasing numbers of people into higher tax brackets, contributions to orchestras and other nonprofits became more attractive. Periods with slower income growth or different tax rates could produce quite different flows of "private" donations. Once again, no mechanism guarantees that donations will match deficits.

Investment income, largely the earnings from endowment investments, constitutes the final source of nonperformance income. This can be an important resource for symphonies, but building an endowment requires private contributions that are subject to the incentives and uncertainties mentioned in the previous paragraph. Once endowment funds are acquired, the opportunities that they create for an orchestra depend on the skill with which its board of trustees manages the endowment. Evidence presented in chapter 9 shows that orchestra boards vary widely in their stewardship skills. Some orchestras earn much lower returns on their endowment investments than others with similarly risky portfolios. Moreover, some orchestra boards have approved imprudent endowment payout rates, effectively diverting endowment resources from future to present generations of orchestra personnel and patrons.

The orchestra reports analyzed for this book document an impressive variety of economic structures. Revenue and expense structures, patterns of contributed support, returns on investments, and endowment payout practices all vary widely. While this is not an industry in which competitive forces may provoke an aggressive search by individual orchestras for better practices, the variance in actual practice at least raises the question of how much symphony orchestras learn from each other's policies and experience. It also has provided the opportunity to study how such variation is related to the size of structural deficits and the ability of orchestras to offset them with nonperformance income.

Performance deficits are not new to orchestras anywhere in the world, and most orchestras have managed to survive despite periodic budget crises. Nonetheless, recent experience shows that orchestras cannot count on an extrapolation of the past any more than private organizations can. The issue is not whether symphony orchestras will survive, but whether they will survive at the same level as in the past. The facts support the view that access to live symphonic performances could gradually become more concentrated.

Analyses reported in this book confirm that a community's economic capacity influences both the size of operating deficits and the nonperformance income needed to offset these deficits. Less populous, lower-income communities support lower attendance and lower ticket prices, reducing performance revenues and limiting the nonperformance income that an orchestra can expect. With lower performance revenues and lower contributions, orchestras in communities with limited economic capacity can only survive if their costs are also comparatively low.

In this setting, efforts to equalize pay between orchestras can jeopardize the survival of orchestras in communities with weaker economic capacity. Pay equalization efforts invariably try to raise the lowest pay. To the extent that such efforts are successful, pay will not be reliably sensitive to the financial balance of orchestras, as discussed in chapter 6.

In the United States the pattern of symphony orchestra bankruptcies also signals the importance of a community's economic base. While top orchestras in major cities are not immune from significant financial pressures—particularly in the depths of a serious recession—most bankruptcies have occurred in smaller communities. The fact that orchestras eventually re-formed in many of these communities hardly restored the status quo for musicians and concert patrons. The new organizations typically played shorter concert seasons, paid lower wages, and used fewer full-time musicians. In most foreign countries, subsidy policies do not permit bankruptcies, but regional orchestras invariably require proportionately larger subsidies to counter their weaker economic capacity (chapter 10). In some instances, governments attempt to reduce subsidies by encouraging the merger of deficit-ridden regional orchestras.

What can poorer communities do to counter the risks that they face? The economic base limits individual and business contributions for operating support or for building endowments. The strongest tax incentives for private contributions occur in high-income (high–tax rate) areas. Direct government support is more likely to decline than to grow. This leaves foundations, whose support is usually project-driven. Would foundations consider offsetting location disadvantages by indexing their support to community economic conditions? How does one structure a grant program so that it supports long-term orchestra goals rather than short-term pay increases? A natural response is to increase fundraising activities, but since 1998 the level of fundraising expense incurred by low-budget orchestras has not been significantly related to private contributions.

Addressing Financial Distress

The research reported in this book clarifies how orchestras may address the economic challenges reviewed in the prior section. Orchestras first should recognize the difference between the temporary, reversible challenges flowing from weak business conditions and structural performance deficits. Practices addressing cyclical deficits are discussed at the end of chapter 3. As that chapter demonstrates, however, structural performance deficits grow over time and remain with an orchestra even after the return of normal economic conditions. Curing structural deficits requires changing some aspects of an orchestra's business model, as discussed below.

Orchestras next should recognize that many proposed cures for structural deficits fail to address the key characteristic of such deficits—their growth over time. Consider several common proposals for addressing orchestra budget crises: fill every seat in the existing concert hall; build (and fill) a larger hall; freeze the pay of orchestra personnel; cut the pay of orchestra personnel; get a gift from a new donor or a larger gift from a prior donor. Each of these proposals may help solve this year's budget crisis, but each provides *only one-time relief.* If an orchestra's structural budget deficit were constant from year to year, these proposals, alone or in combination, would contribute to a permanent solution. Unfortunately, orchestras face a far more serious challenge.

As explained in chapter 2 and documented in chapter 3, the cost disease has a continual, cumulative effect on an orchestra's financial balance. Since performance revenues cover a decreasing fraction of an orchestra's performance expenses over time after holding cyclical influence constant, orchestras face growing structural performance deficits. Economic security requires solutions that *grow with the deficits*: ever-growing audiences (or ever-growing ticket prices that they are willing to pay); a permanent slowdown in the rate of growth of orchestra costs, ever-increasing gifts, and ever-growing endowments.

Finally, orchestras should recognize that none of the three broad strategies available to orchestras—raising performance revenues, slowing the growth of expenses, and increasing nonperformance income—*by itself* is likely to cure structural budget deficits. Most orchestras prefer policies that fall under the first and third strategies in order to avoid the inevitable conflicts with employees and some patrons that accompany efforts to mitigate the growth of costs. But taking any strategy off the table raises the economic peril to which an orchestra is exposed. The contributions and limitations of each strategy are reviewed below.

Enhancing Performance Revenues

Orchestras have adopted many experiments intended to enhance performance revenues by attracting new generations of concertgoers. Conductors may speak directly to an audience to provide some background on a concert program. Orchestras may offer abbreviated concerts in late afternoons or early evenings to attract commuting professionals or educational concerts to interest youth in classical music and its performance. Occasionally, a major television project, such as the *Keeping Score* series mounted by Michael Tilson Thomas and the San Francisco Symphony Orchestra for PBS, will seek to illuminate key works from the orchestral literature in a way that attracts the general population to live performances. Some of these approaches seek to increase interest in symphonic music, while others seek to reduce the time costs of attending symphony performances.

We have seen in chapter 5, however, that these inventive approaches to audience development encounter a key fact: even if the experiments succeed in filling all the seats at concerts, they will not balance most orchestras' books at current ticket prices. For the vast majority of U.S. orchestras, filling the halls must be accompanied by *increasingly higher* ticket prices if performance revenues are to offset rising performance expenses. To balance an orchestra's books, audience-building policies must create preferences for symphonic music that are relatively insensitive to the price of attendance.

Performance revenues could be raised further at some orchestras by combining audience-building activities with greater ticket-price differentiation. While orchestras may be reluctant to maximize ticket revenues by auctioning off individual seats, as the Boston Symphony Orchestra did early in the 20th century, many could increase revenues by matching ticket prices more closely to the amount that concert patrons are willing to pay for different seats—charging higher prices for the most preferred seats and lower prices for the least preferred seats. Chapter 5 indicates some ways to achieve such strategic ticket-price differentiation. Implementation of this intuitive principle normally results in increased ticket-price differentiation to match the pricing to the preferences. Orchestras that currently offer little ticket-price differentiation are likely to gain the most from this approach.

In the past many orchestras sought improved performance revenues by offering more concerts. Two facts undermine this seemingly straightforward approach. First, additional concerts incur additional costs—performance expenses rise. Second, additional concerts produce diminishing financial returns. When orchestras increase the number and variety of concerts that they provide, attendance per concert declines sharply. Moreover, those who attend concerts are increasingly likely to purchase single tickets rather than season subscriptions. With attendance and hence revenues diminishing as the number of concerts increases, each additional concert offers a smaller contribution toward balancing the books.

To summarize, raising performance revenues can reduce structural performance deficits, but most revenue-raising proposals narrow the current deficit without slowing the growth of future deficits. Filling a concert hall may narrow this year's performance deficit, but by itself will not further narrow the larger structural deficits that will arrive in subsequent years. The same may be said of changes in the structure of ticket prices. Once the hall is filled and a new ticket price structure is in place, performance revenues can only grow if ticket prices increase annually. Since most orchestras would not eliminate their current deficits even if they could fill their halls at current ticket prices, it is unlikely that future price increases would eliminate growing deficits. In short, efforts to raise attendance and change ticket pricing structures reduce, but cannot by themselves eliminate, structural deficits. Securing that objective requires supplementary strategies.

Reducing the Growth of Expenses

Policies to slow the growth of expenses can productively supplement efforts to raise performance revenues. At several points, this book has stressed that orchestras can increase efficiency by assessing the *incremental* benefits and cost of their activities. The evidence in chapter 5 that incremental marketing expenditures provide diminishing attendance gains signals a risk that marketing activities can be conducted to a point where they do not pay for themselves, for example. The incremental approach also reveals that a substantial volume of donations to orchestras reflects the economic capacity and dedication to the arts of a community rather than fundraising activities per se. Moreover, the amount spent on fundraising is not reliably related to subsidies received from any level of government. Although the overall return on fundraising activities is positive for most orchestras, it is much smaller than is frequently claimed.

The pay of artistic personnel constitutes the largest element of an orchestra's costs. Discussions of pay levels and growth are inherently conflictual, because artistic pay is both a cost to the organization and the income of skilled professionals. This book has established some facts relevant to discussions about the evolution of pay in U.S. orchestras. In recent decades, the pay of U.S. orchestra musicians rose more rapidly than the pay of most other groups in society, despite the fact that the supply of well-trained classical musicians continues to exceed the demand for their services (chapter 6). Current pay levels exceed the pay of orchestra musicians in other high-income countries, including the musicians at what music critics consider some of the top orchestras in the world, and place U.S. musicians at a comparatively high position in their national income distribution. In most years, the pay of orchestra musicians is not responsive to changes in the financial balance of orchestras—a fact that contributes to the distinct worsening of the performance income ratio in recessions. Instead, musicians' pay responds to private donations to an orchestra, making it difficult for orchestras to improve their financial balance through such donations.

Collective bargaining strategies that gave more weight to the financial condition of orchestras would reduce the odds of bankruptcies and the hardships endured by the musicians and concert patrons who are the victims of those bankruptcies.

Negotiating practices and techniques may have an important impact on collective bargaining outcomes. When conflicts between musicians and orchestra management are poorly managed by negotiators, the result may be a strike that imposes costs on patrons (lost concerts), musicians (lost pay), and the orchestra itself (lost donor support). Seemingly small details can be important. The degree of conflict and ultimate outcome of negotiations can rest on factors such as the methods by which each side establishes its goals and ranks priorities, the ability of each side to elevate the pursuit of contract priorities over the expression of accumulated anger, the use of evidence rather than assertions in motivating proposals, and the procedures used by each side for contract approval.[1]

Most concerts include guest soloists, whose fees can be quite high. Does the presence of soloists attract a sufficiently larger audience (or higher ticket prices) to justify the expense? Do orchestras know? Do they even raise the question? As with the other strategies discussed in this chapter, reducing the number of soloists will not balance an orchestra's books by itself—soloists comprise too small a proportion of an orchestra's costs. But when soloists do not pay for themselves, a reduction will narrow an orchestra's performance deficit.

To a degree, orchestras and the other performing arts compete with each other for the support of time-constrained patrons. Such competition can raise costs in each arts organization. The extent and consequences of such competition has been all but ignored in past studies. This study explored competitive interactions between symphony orchestras and opera companies—two performing arts that share rich musical traditions—and identified statistically significant but quantitatively small tendencies for some gains in attendance and contributions by one art form to occur at the expense of the other. At the moment, only a small amount of the returns on marketing and fundraising activities by an orchestra result in losses of opera attendance or donations (chapters 5 and 8).

But the performing arts as a whole compete with other uses of leisure time for patronage and contributions. If the trends emerging from the NEA surveys of arts attendance in the United States and similar surveys elsewhere in the world continue (chapters 5 and 10), the more important element of competition will be with uses of leisure time outside the performing arts, an issue that merits much more investigation. Forming coalitions of performing arts groups may be a productive and cost-reducing approach to competing for the attention of those whose leisure activities and philanthropy do not presently include the performing arts. There are certainly opportunities for economies of scale. Each arts organization in turn can reduce marketing and fundraising costs, since at least some of the costs currently incurred may be directed at enticing patrons or contributions from other arts or defending against such predation. There are also opportunities to expand the demand for the individual arts participating in the coalition as patrons initially attracted to one art form find other forms enjoyable. The main resistance to such efforts will come from those who are currently employed performing those tasks for specific arts organizations. Economies of scale imply fewer personnel in those functions, and personal concerns may receive more weight than the overall effort to raise support for the arts.

Reducing the growth of expenses also will slow the growth of structural deficits, but some proposals mainly narrow the current deficit without slowing the growth of future deficits. Others, such as reducing the growth rate of salaries, mainly reduce future deficit growth. Clearly, these policies can increase the economic security of orchestras, but by themselves are unlikely to eliminate structural deficits, since there are limits to how much salary growth can be reduced without threatening the loss of valuable personnel.

Raising Nonperformance Income

Even when an orchestra has done all that is possible to grow performance revenues and to slow the growth of expenses, the remaining gap between performance revenues and expenses may continue to grow and must be covered by nonperformance income. Every U.S. orchestra has years in which the gap is covered and years in which it is not. But can orchestras avoid the conflicts and costs associated with the first two strategies by simply relying on the growth of nonperformance income?

Consider first the prospects for government support. Political support for the arts has always been controversial in the United States, and the trend in direct government subsidies has been negative since at least 1987. Declining government spending on orchestras effectively raises the importance of policies to grow performance revenues, slow the growth of performance expenses, and increase investment income and private donations. By the end of the first decade of the 21st century, the prospects for increasing public subsidies to orchestras and other performing arts seem dimmer than ever in the face of increasingly large budget deficits at all levels of government. Faced with such deficits, governments are more likely to reduce than expand direct financial commitments to the arts and other activities enjoyed by a relatively small number of people in the upper reaches of the national income distribution.

Most foreign governments offer far more generous direct subsidies to orchestras, but many of these same governments are increasingly troubled by their subsidy policies. Few governments seem to have anticipated that, even under the best of circumstances, a policy of support implies ever-increasing payments to meet the industry's ever-increasing structural performance deficits. Even fewer may have understood the challenges of designing subsidy policies that provide economic security to orchestras but remain free of moral hazard. Orchestras in countries with reliable government subsidies face negligible bankruptcy risk, but they also face few incentives to take action to achieve genuine financial balance. Chapter 10 documented the comparatively large structural deficits of foreign orchestras. The resulting budgetary commitments will become increasingly troubling as governments must address large general budget deficits. In 2010, for example, a new Dutch government proposed terminating three state-supported orchestras, while in 2011 major British orchestras faced an 11 percent funding reduction from the Arts Council of England through the 2014–15 concert season.

More difficult to evaluate is the future of the tax incentives in the United States for private contributions to orchestras. The same government deficits that diminish the prospects for increased direct public subsidies for orchestras are creating pressure for increasing tax revenues at all levels of government. To an extent, the future growth of private contributions rests on how the public sector decides to raise tax revenues. General tax-rate increases raise the incentive to donate, because the government effectively "pays" for a larger fraction of each contribution for orchestra supporters who itemize their deductions. But if governments choose to maintain current rates and expand the tax base by reducing or eliminating the deduction for charitable contributions, the incentive to donate will fall. As this book is published, the future need for private giving is much clearer than the future of the tax incentives that stimulate such giving.

Ultimately, a society pays for performance deficits, whether by taxes paid directly to the government (in societies with direct government support of the arts) or by taxes diverted from the government because they are spent on orchestras (as in the United States). Symphony orchestras may incur less immediate pressure in the former societies, because changing tastes will register more slowly than in countries where the arts must rely on private donations.

More broadly, most private giving to orchestras by individuals, businesses, and foundations rests on influences beyond the reach of orchestra policies. Once the underlying tax policies are set, contributions depend on the growth of personal incomes, which in turn reflect general economic conditions and a community's economic capacity. Federal government monetary and fiscal policies influence the former, while the population size and industrial mix of a community influence the latter. Fundraising activities, the only orchestra-controlled influence on donations, exert a secondary influence whose effectiveness may be limited to larger orchestras (chapter 8).

Earnings on endowment investments constitute an important source of nonperformance income for U.S. orchestras (but not for symphonies in countries with significant government support of the performing arts). No U.S. symphony orchestra currently has sufficient endowment earnings to offset its structural deficits. More important, no orchestra has anywhere near the endowment required to finance growing deficits in the future at prudent rates of endowment draw (chapter 9). Symphony orchestras that pursue financial stability *solely* through endowment policies face three challenges. First, they require extremely large increases in current endowments to offset current performance deficits using prudent endowment payout rates. Second, endowments must continue to grow at rates sufficient to offset the trend increase in performance deficits assuming prudent payout rates. Third, the highly dispersed endowment returns indicate that many orchestra boards could increase the resources available for artistic activities by improving the management of endowment portfolios.

The reluctant conclusion of this discussion is that nonperformance income growth alone is unlikely to cover future structural budget deficits, unless supplemented with actions to narrow the deficit itself by both raising the growth of performance revenues and slowing the growth of expenses.

Symphony Orchestras and Universities

The economic challenges and choices facing U.S. symphony orchestras may be clarified by examining why universities do not lead similarly perilous economic lives. After all, universities also face increasing relative costs and growing structural deficits as a result of the same slim productivity gains that characterize orchestras and other cultural institutions. How do universities avoid living closer to the edge, threatened by deficits and bankruptcy?

Differences in demand for services are an important part of the answer. While attendance at symphony orchestra concerts averages 70 percent of capacity and even the most renowned orchestras do not completely fill their concert halls for most concerts, most universities continue to experience excess demand. Qualified applications for admission regularly exceed the number of slots, with as few as 10 percent of the applicants offered admission at top universities. Facing excess demand, most universities are able to raise tuition significantly (although few charge anywhere near an amount that would clear the market). As incomes have advanced, society has been more willing to pay for higher education than for live classical music.

Nevertheless, the comparatively robust demand for higher education does not permit universities to cover operating costs with operating revenues from tuition, research funds, licenses, and so on. Universities, too, must rely on government support, private contributions, and investment income to balance their books. Like orchestras, they benefit from the generosity of donors who wish to support their basic mission, and they seek to augment the normal flow of donations through development and fundraising activities.

Universities also have advantages over orchestras in the quest for "nonperformance" income to offset operating deficits. With less political controversy over public support for education and research than for culture, the flow of government funds to universities has remained larger and more assured than to orchestras and other cultural institutions. (The existence of public universities provides merely one indication of the different political attitudes historically.) Moreover, universities are able to draw on a much broader pool of private support than orchestras. Each year a new cohort of alumni graduates from their universities with the knowledge that they have paid a modest fraction of the costs of their university education. As their careers develop around the globe, many of these alumni will contribute regularly, motivated by loyalty and reciprocity. Each year the alumni base is renewed and, with declining mortality, expanded.

In contrast, symphony orchestras have much more limited access to nonperformance income. Chapter 7 detailed how government support has declined. Private support is largely restricted to the local communities, with occasional outside support for special projects such as a foreign concert tour or television program. The impact of community characteristics is often significant, but they are the factors that are least likely to change rapidly and they are unlikely to be changed by the policies of symphony organizations. To some degree, symphonies must live with the luck of where they are located.

These comments also pertain to investment income, which largely flows from endowment investments. Private donations establish endowments, so the scale of an orchestra's endowment will largely reflect its local base for support. Not surprisingly, university endowments exceed orchestra endowments (and their budgets dwarf orchestra budgets). For better and for worse, both institutions have a checkered history of endowment management. The inefficiencies in some orchestra endowments received attention in chapter 9. While some of the most astute writing on endowment management has emerged from universities, that sector has also provided examples of dramatic mismanagement.

Concluding Observations

The economic challenges faced by U.S. orchestras are not uniquely American. Orchestras in most countries face large structural deficits and weakening attendance. Governments in all countries assist orchestras in meeting their economic challenges, although the form that assistance takes varies widely, and significant uncertainties surround the scale of future government assistance.

No undiscovered "silver bullet"—a single solution that eliminates these challenges—emerges from the analyses of the financial and operating data of U.S. symphony orchestras in earlier chapters. Indeed, taken as a whole, this book documents the futility of single solutions. Most orchestras cannot achieve economic stability solely by selling out their concert halls, or by ever-increasing marketing expenditures, or by drawing prudent amounts from their endowments, or by relying on direct government support. Some readers may consider this implication obvious, but then why do many orchestras address their deficits with a single-minded focus on building audiences or finding a new major donor?

In the conflict-ridden world of U.S. symphony orchestras, it is pertinent to note that the futility of single solutions usually signals the absence of a single "devil" that is responsible for an orchestra's plight. At the same time, the analyses reported in this book do not provide managers, musicians, or trustees with a "free pass." Instead the analyses point to actions by each group that can increase the economic security of orchestras, while showing that no single group can solve the problem by itself.

Symphony Orchestras Included in the Analysis

Alabama	Hartford	Omaha
Atlanta	Honolulu	Oregon
Baltimore	Houston	Pacific
Boston	Indianapolis	Philadelphia
Buffalo	Jacksonville	Phoenix
Charlotte	Kansas City	Pittsburgh
Chicago	Knoxville	Richmond
Cincinnati	Los Angeles	Rochester
Cleveland	Los Angeles Chamber	Sacramento
Columbus	Louisville	Saint Louis
Dallas	Memphis	Saint Paul
Dayton	Milwaukee	San Antonio
Denver	Minnesota	San Diego
Detroit	Naples	San Francisco
Florida Orchestra	Nashville	San Jose
Florida Philharmonic	National	Seattle
Florida Symphony	New Jersey	Syracuse
Fort Wayne	New Mexico	Toledo
Fort Worth	New World	Tulsa
Grand Rapids	New York	Utah
Grant Park	North Carolina	Virginia

Each orchestra was in the top 50 symphony orchestras by budget size for at least two years between the 1987–88 and 2005–6 concert seasons.

Cycle and Trend Analyses of Symphony Finances

This appendix describes the statistical analysis underlying the discussion of the cycle and trend behavior of orchestra revenues and expenses in chapter 3. The analysis first explores the extent to which the ratio of performance revenue to performance expenses (the performance income ratio) varies with cyclical and trend influences. Cyclical influences stem from changes in overall economic conditions, while trend influences reflect the operation of structural influences that are not correlated with the general state of the economy. The primary structural influence is the markedly limited productivity growth in symphony orchestras (discussed in chapter 2).

The statistical analysis was conducted on the annual panel data for 63 orchestras over 19 concert seasons (1987–2005) used throughout this book. The statistical evidence in this and most other chapters emerged from *fixed-effects analyses* of the panel data. Fixed-effects estimates depend on how variables change over time for each orchestra. They ignore variations in the level of variables between orchestras. This approach avoids biases that might arise, for example, from inter-orchestra differences in measurement and reporting practices. By focusing on the effects of changes over time *within* orchestras, fixed-effects analysis also adopts the perspective that is most relevant for assessing the effects of policy changes by individual orchestras.

The first line of table A3.1 reports the results of fixed-effects regression of the performance income ratio (the fraction of performance expenses covered by performance revenues) on the unemployment rate in the area where each orchestra is located (capturing the general state of economic conditions), a linear time trend that tested for the ongoing budgetary impact of Baumol and Bowen's cost disease and other structural influences on the balance between performance revenues and costs. It includes a post-2000 comparison (to evaluate claims of extraordinary change in symphony finances following the 9/11 tragedy). If the cost disease scenario were not relevant for symphony orchestras, the time trend would lack significance. In fact, the analysis reveals both pro-

TABLE A3.1   CYCLE AND TREND ANALYSIS OF ORCHESTRA REVENUE,
            1987–2005

Dependent Variable	Unemployment Rate	Time Trend	Post-2000 Trend	R^2
Performance income ratio	−0.695	−.223	−.030	.12
	(.209)*	(.067)*	(.008)*	
Natural logarithm of:				
Total income	−.014	.029	.001	.40
	(.007)***	(.002)*	(.0002)*	
Performance revenue	−.038	.019	−.0001	.19
	(.008)*	(.002)*	(.0002)	
Nonperformance income	−.015	.035	.002	.50
	(.008)***	(.003)*	(.0003)*	
Government subsidies	−.042	−.044	.001	.14
	(.015)*	(.005)*	(.006)**	
Private support	−.011	.044	.0001	.54
	(.007)***	(.002)*	(.0002)	
Individual	−.006	.048	.001	.48
	(.010)	(.003)*	(.0003)**	
Business	−.017	.017	−.0007	.05
	(.011)	(.004)*	(.0004)***	
Foundation	−.015	.087	−.002	.25
	(.023)	(.008)*	(.001)**	
Investment Income	−.086	.055	.005	.17
	(.034)**	(.011)*	(.001)*	

Fixed-effects estimates.
All revenues in year 2000 dollars.
The performance income ratio = (100) (performance revenues)/performance expenses.
*p < .01, **p < .05, *** p < .10

nounced cyclical and trend influences on the performance ratio. (The numbers in parentheses are robust standard errors, asterisks denote the level of statistical significance, and results with no asterisk do not reach conventional levels of statistical significance.) Chapter 3 addresses the implications of these findings.

The remaining regressions in table A3.1 examine the cycle and trend behavior of the major categories of real income received by orchestras. (Revenues and expenditures are expressed in constant year 2000 dollars by deflating the nominal figures by the GDP deflator.) In these regressions, the natural logarithm of each type of revenue is regressed on the local unemployment rate, a linear time trend, and the variable testing for a post-2000 change in the trend.

TABLE A3.2   CYCLE AND TREND ANALYSIS OF ORCHESTRA EXPENSES,
                1987-2005

Dependent Variable	Unemployment Rate	Time Trend	R^2
Total expenses	−.011	.027	.49
	(.004)*	(.001)*	
Performance expenses	−.012	.027	.49
	(.004)*	(.001)*	
Artistic	−.004	.021	.37
	(.004)	(.001)*	
Concert production	−.013	.055	.64
	(.007)***	(.001)*	
General administration	−.018	.024	.24
	(.007)*	(.001)*	
Marketing	−.028	.042	.48
	(.007)*	(.001)*	
Fundraising expenses	.002	.041	.22
	(.012)	(.003)*	

Fixed-effects estimates.

All expenses in year 2000 dollars.

All dependent variables in natural logarithms.

*$p < .01$, *** $p < .10$

Each regression coefficient in the Unemployment Rate column indicates the proportionate response of the associated dependent variable to a one percentage point change in the unemployment rate in each symphony's local area, holding the effect of the time trend constant. Each coefficient in the Time Trend column indicates the response of the dependent variable to a one-year change, holding the effect of the local unemployment rate constant. The statistical results show that each percentage point increase in the local unemployment rate significantly reduces the performance income ratio of the average orchestra in the sample by about seven-tenths of a percentage point (regression 1). This result signals an important difference in the responsiveness of performance revenues and performance expenses to changes in business conditions. Each one percentage point increase in the unemployment rate reduces real performance revenues by 3.8 percent (regression 3), while real performance expenditures fall by only 1.2 percent (regression 2 in table A3.2). With performance revenues more responsive to general economic conditions than performance expenses, the performance deficit gets worse in recessions and improves when unemployment declines during economic expansions. The trend increase in real performance expenses is about one and one-half times as large as the trend in real performance income, so over this period the perfor-

mance deficit grew. For the average symphony, the performance income ratio fell by
0.2 percentage points per year after controlling for cyclical influences.

The remaining findings reported in table A3.1 clarify the cycle and trend movements in the sources of nonperformance income—private philanthropic contributions,
government subsidies, and investment income—that may be used to address the growing deficits. Like performance income, all three sources of nonperformance income
decline in recessions and grow in economic expansions. Nonperformance income declines when orchestras need it most. The trend growth in total nonperformance income
obscures very different trends for government and private support. Real government
support declined by 4.4 percent per year for the average symphony in the sample (regression 5 in table A3.1). Increases in the much larger volume of private support from
individuals, foundations, and businesses more than countered the declining government support. An upward trend in real investment income of 5.5 percent per year also
helped to offset the trend deterioration in performance deficits.

The remaining findings reported in table A3.2 clarify the sources of the comparative cyclical insensitivity of performance expenses, which produces larger deficits
during recessions. All categories of performance expenses except the largest—artistic
expenses—are cyclically sensitive. This is the major source of cyclical inertia in orchestra expenses. Fundraising expenses, which constitute a much smaller fraction of
orchestra budgets, also are not significantly related to general economic conditions.

Total orchestra income (performance and nonperformance income combined)
and total expenses vary with overall economic conditions, but total income is more
cyclically sensitive than total expenses. As a result, the overall financial balance of symphony orchestras is cyclically sensitive—moving further into deficit when unemployment rises and toward surpluses when unemployment declines. The trend in total income is slightly higher than the trend in total expenses, so the overall financial balance
improved slightly between 1987 and 2005, after controlling for the effects of general
economic conditions.

APPENDIX TO CHAPTER 5

Chapter 5 addresses issues encountered by symphony orchestras trying to raise their performance revenues. This appendix reports the statistical analyses underlying the discussions of cyclical and trend movements in concert attendance, the effect of the number of concerts performed on concert attendance, and influences on attendance per concert.

Concerts and Attendance

Debates about trends in concert attendance frequently confuse short-term cyclical impacts on concert attendance with long-term trends. Attendance unquestionably falls as economic conditions deteriorate and rises as conditions improve, producing fluctuations around the attendance trend. Since observed attendance in any year includes both cycle and trend influences, changes in economic conditions tend to obscure actual attendance trends. Identifying the concert attendance trend requires statistical techniques that will hold the cyclical influences on attendance constant, a task that is well-suited for multiple regression analysis.

The trends in concert attendance discussed in chapter 5 are estimated in a fixed-effects regression analysis of the annual panel data on 63 U.S. symphony orchestras for 1987–2005. The reported results therefore reflect the annual variation *within* individual orchestras and ignore differences between orchestras. The dependent variable is the natural logarithm of total attendance for the concert season. The first regression in table A5.1 isolates both a statistically significant cyclical influence (reflected in the coefficient on the local area unemployment rate) and a significant negative trend in total attendance (the coefficient on the trend variable) that remains after controlling for the cyclical influence. The regression indicates that, on average, attendance falls by 3.8 percent when the local unemployment rate rises by one percentage point and in addition

TABLE A5.1   CYCLE AND TREND ANALYSIS OF TOTAL ATTENDANCE, 1987–2005
(COEFFICIENTS AND STANDARD ERRORS)

	I	2	3	4
Unemployment rate	−0.038	−0.041	−0.044	−0.038
	(.009)*	(.008)*	(.009)*	(.009)*
Time trend	−0.011	−0.019	−0.016	−0.018
	(.002)*	(.002)*	(.002)*	(.002)*
Natural log of concerts		0.466		
		(.025)*		
Number of concerts			0.001	0.003
			(.0001)*	(.0002)*
Concerts squared				−0.000019
				(0.0000018)*
R^2	0.039	0.288	0.126	0.214
Number of concert years	1,041	1,041	1,041	1,041

Dependent variable: natural logarithm of total attendance.

Fixed-effects estimates.

* $p < .01$, ** $p < .05$, *** $p < .10$

declines by about 1 percent per year (the trend), all other things being equal. Much of the variation in total attendance remains unexplained, however, indicating a potentially important role for other explanatory variables.

During the 1987–2005 concert seasons, most symphony orchestras increased the number of concerts performed in an effort to increase concert attendance and performance revenues. Some of the trend estimated in regression 1 may simply reflect increases in the number of concerts performed rather than increasing attendance per concert. To check this, the second regression in table A5.1 adds a new variable: the natural logarithm of total concerts performed. The statistically significant results indicate that a 1 percent increase in the number of concerts performed is associated with a 0.5 percent gain in attendance, after controlling for the effects of cycle and trend. Notice that after controlling for the number of concerts, the negative trend in attendance remains, but the regression model now explains much more of the variation in total concert attendance. Attendance per concert clearly declined throughout the period.

Two additional regression specifications were compared to check the possibility that additional concerts achieve diminishing returns in audience gains. In regression 3, the actual number of concerts enters linearly; in regression 4 it enters as a quadratic, a nonlinear specification that tests for the presence of increasing or diminishing returns. The latter specification provides a better fit of the data. Moreover, the pattern of signs in regression 4 confirms the importance of diminishing attendance gains from additional concerts.

Influences on Attendance

Chapter 5 also examines how symphony orchestra policies, economic character-istics of the community in which an orchestra performs, and competition from local opera companies influence concert attendance at regular season and pops concerts. The dependent variable in the underlying regression analyses is attendance per con-cert. Orchestra policy variables include average ticket prices for the respective concerts and marketing expenditures reported by each orchestra. The average price data were constructed by dividing ticket revenue by the number of tickets sold (separately for regular and pops concerts). Measures of community economic characteristics include population, per capita income (U.S. Bureau of Economic Analysis 2006), and the lo-cal unemployment rate (U.S. Bureau of Labor Statistics 2006a). The ticket price and marketing expenditures of opera companies in the same market area were used to test for possible competitive interactions between orchestras and operas (Opera America). Annual data on all variables were available for 1987–2003.

Random-effects and fixed-effects models of attendance per concert were estimated for both regular season and pops concerts. A log-linear model provided a superior fit of the data. The results confirm the statistical and economic significance of both pric-ing policies and marketing expenditures for attendance at regular season (table A5.2) and pops (table A5.3) concerts. The price elasticity of demand for seats is about -0.5 for regular season concerts and -0.3 for pops concerts. Both media advertising and telephone/mail campaigns are associated with higher attendance per regular season concert, but each activity is subject to diminishing returns. The quadratic specifica-tion of marketing expenditures (regressions 3 and 4 in table A5.2) that support this conclusion fit the data better than the linear specification (regressions 1 and 2). Only expenditures on telephone and mail campaigns were significantly correlated with at-tendance per pops concert, and they too yielded diminishing returns. Of the commu-nity economic characteristics, only the area population was usually significantly corre-lated with attendance. Always insignificant in trial regressions, the area unemployment rate was dropped from the reported regressions. (A variable for the proportion of the population with at least a college degree, potentially an important indicator of tastes for symphony music, was available for too few years to be used.)

Turning to competition from other performing arts, neither the presence of an opera company nor attendance at local opera performances are significantly correlated with regular season concert attendance. Marketing expenditures by a local opera have a small, marginally significant, but positive correlation with symphony attendance at regular season concerts (table A5.2, regression 5). The effects of ticket pricing by lo-cal opera companies on attendance at regular season symphony concerts is sensitive to how an orchestra's marketing expenditures enter the analysis, however. When the regression analysis controls for *total* marketing expenditures (regression 6), an increase in the relative price of opera season tickets (effectively, a decrease in the relative price of symphony tickets) is associated with higher symphony attendance—presumably because some arts patrons who would have attended the opera go instead to a sym-

TABLE A5.2 ANALYSIS OF ATTENDANCE PER REGULAR SEASON CONCERT, 1987-2003 (REGRESSION COEFFICIENTS AND STANDARD ERRORS)

	1	2	3	4	5	6	7
Ticket price	-.525 (.039)*	-.549 (.042)*	-.554 (.038)*	-.571 (.042)*	-.632 (.045)*	-.516 (.039)*	-.633 (0.047)**
Media ads	.00013 (.00004)*	.00012 (.00004)*	.00034 (.00008)*	.00033 (.00008)*	.00019 (.00008)*		.00020 (0.00009)*
(Media ads)^2			-1.37E-07 (4.39E-08)*	-1.33E-07 (4.42E-08)*	-7.22E-08 (4.20E-08)***		-7.28E-08 (4.35E-08)***
Phone/mail	.00016 (0.00003)*	.0014 (.00003)*	.00040 (0.00006)*	.00035 (0.00006)*	.00034 (0.00006)*		.00035 (0.00007)*
(phone/mail)^2			-7.09E-08 (1.71E-08)*	-6.13E-08 (1.77E-08)*	-6.02E-08 (1.66E-08)*		-6.20E-08 (1.71E-08)*
Marketing expense						0.143 (0.025)*	
Population	.105 (.036)*	.280 (.176)	.068 (.037)***	.205 (.175)	.315*** (.193)	.221 (.150)	.390 (.206)***
Real income	.277 (.132)**	.192 (.170)	.128 (.133)	.037 (.171)	.109 (.182)	.019 (.125)	.137 (.198)
Opera ticket price						0.029 (.015)***	0.018 (.016)
Opera marketing expense					.028 (.017)***		
(Marketing expense)^2					-3.90E-08 (6.67E-09)*		
R^2	.194	.295	.253	.322	.402	.353	.404
Number of concert years	591	591	591	591	421	511	379
Estimation method	RE	FE	RE	FE	FE	FE	FE

Dependent variable: logarithm of attendance per regular season concert.

$* \; p < .01$, $** \; p < .05$, $*** \; p < .10$

TABLE A5.3. ANALYSIS OF ATTENDANCE PER POPS CONCERT, 1987–2003 (REGRESSION COEFFICIENTS AND STANDARD ERRORS)

	1	2	3	4	5	6
Ticket price	−.263	−.330	−.278	−.344	−.286	−.340
	(.046)*	(.053)*	(.047)*	(.052)*	(.050)*	(.055)
Media ads	−6.99E-06	−.00004	.00022	.00020	−.00020	−.00029
	(.00007)	(.00007)	(.00015)	(.00016)	(.00018)	(.00018)
(Media ads)^2			−2.07E-07	−2.16E-07	7.27E-08	1.10E-07
			(1.31E-07)	(1.33E-07)	(1.34E-07)	(1.37E-07)
Phone/mail	.00013	.00011	.00035	.00035	.00048	.00051
	(.00005)*	(.00006)**	(.00013)*	(.00014)*	(.00013)*	(.00014)*
(Phone/mail)^2			−9.49E-08	−9.76E-08	−1.45E-07	−1.59E-07
			(5.20E-08)***	(5.40E-08)***	(5.20E-08)*	(5.48E-08)
Population	.019	.756	−.025	.715	−.101	.338
	(.058)	(.268)*	(.061)	(.267)*	(.085)	(.303)
Real income	−.063	−.268	−.123	−.366	−.085	−.046
	(.193)	(.276)	(.196)	(.278)	(.231)	(.309)
Opera marketing expense					.053	.040
					(.024)**	(.027)
R^2	.067	.124	.075	.136	.094	.211
Number of concert years	487	487	487	487	326	326
Estimation method	RE	FE	RE	FE	RE	FE

Dependent variable: logarithm of attendance per regular season concert.

* $p < .01$, ** $p < .05$, *** $p < .10$

phony concert. While statistically significant, this effect is quantitatively small. When the analysis controls for the effects of media and phone/mail expenditures separately, however, the price of opera tickets is not a statistically significant determinant of attendance at symphony concerts (regression 7). Opera ticket prices are not significantly correlated with attendance at pops concerts.

APPENDIX TO CHAPTER 6

This chapter discusses the salaries and working conditions of musicians, conductors, and orchestra senior staff. Information on salaries and some working conditions for orchestra musicians affiliated with the International Conference of Symphony and Opera Musicians (ICSOM) are available from the archive of *Senza Sordino* (the official ICSOM newspaper), available at http://www.icsom.org/senzarchive.html. The League of American Orchestras also collects data on musician salaries and other provisions of collective bargaining agreements from their member orchestras. (The two sources agree closely. The interorchestra correlation for minimum weekly salary data from the two sources exceeds 0.99 for each year, providing confidence that the more comprehensive League data may be used for the salaries of workers in non-ICSOM orchestras.)

Chapter 6 includes a discussion of annual salary structures within large-budget and small-budget orchestras in 2005, based on data reported in table 6.1. To estimate annual minimum and average salaries for orchestra musicians, their reported weekly salaries were multiplied by the number of guaranteed weeks of work at each orchestra. All the large-budget orchestras guaranteed 52 weeks per year, but the smaller-budget orchestras guaranteed fewer weeks.

The fourth section of the chapter examines the relationship between musicians' salaries and the financial condition of their orchestra. It reports the results of a regression analysis of an unbalanced panel of 63 orchestras from the 1987–88 through the 2003–4 concert seasons (Flanagan 2010). The dependent variable in the analysis is the natural logarithm of the negotiated minimum weekly salary of musicians in symphony i during year t. The analysis tests the responsiveness of musicians' wages to measures of the financial strength of symphony organizations, both across orchestras and within orchestras over time. The broadest measure of economic strength is overall financial balance (total revenues minus total expenses), which captures the extent to which nonperformance income offsets operating deficits. Disaggregating the overall balance permits examination of the respective roles of performance and nonperformance financial balances in union wage determination. This approach separates financial strength into the gap between performance-related revenues and expenses, and the contributed support from private and government sources, in both cases as a percentage of performance expenses. The analysis also examines whether general economic conditions, represented by the local area rate of unemployment, influence the salaries of symphony musicians independently of their effect on an orchestra's economic balance.

Differences in musicians' salaries *between* orchestras are *not* significantly correlated with current and lagged measures of the financial balance of orchestras. Neither variation in the overall financial balance nor the performance deficit (the gap between performance revenues and expenses) are significantly correlated with wage differences between orchestras. Instead, inter-orchestra salary differences are tightly correlated with differences in the size of the nonartistic budgets (total expenses) of orchestras. (The artistic budget was removed to avoid regressing wages on wages.) Variations in total expenditures accounted for 63 to 86 percent of the wage differences between orchestras in the years between 1987 and 2003, with an elasticity of weekly salaries with respect to nonartistic budgets of about 0.45. Scale of operations appears to be a more important determinant of wage differences between orchestras than current or past financial strength.

Cross-orchestra correlations may provide a poor guide to how wage levels may change in response to the changing financial circumstances of individual orchestras, however. Fixed-effects analysis of a panel of orchestras provided a stronger test of the sensitivity of union wage policy to changes in the financial circumstances of individual orchestras. The statistical model is:

$$W_{it} = a_0 + a_1 \, BALANCE_{it} + a_2 \, SUPPORT_{it} + a_3 \, RUN_{it} + \varepsilon_{it}$$

in which RUN_{it} is the local area unemployment rate for an orchestra i in the year t, an orchestra's overall financial balance and performance deficit provide alternative measures of $BALANCE_{it}$, and private and government support provide alternative measures of $SUPPORT_{it}$. Although the dependent variable is (the logarithm of) a wage *rate* rather than a measure of total wage payments to musicians, payments for musicians' services influence measures of financial balance and create ambiguity about the direction of causation between the wages and the balance measures. In an effort to address this concern, current and lagged measures of financial balance were tested in alternative regressions (Flanagan 2010). Chapter 6 describes the results of the analysis.

In contrast, private support from individuals, businesses, and foundations (as a percentage of total and performance expenditures, respectively) is significantly positively correlated with the contractual minimum salary, whether or not it is lagged. The results support an interpretation of a bargaining process in which an orchestra's level of private support, rather than measures of financial balance, influences wages. There is a clear causality question here: does contributed support determine union demands, or do collective bargaining agreements determine fundraising goals (and hence contributed support)?

Finally, regression analyses of pay supplements (the ratio of average weekly salary to minimum weekly salary) found no significant correlations with the independent variables. As developed in chapter 6, these supplements (mainly seniority and over-scale payments) depend on characteristics of an orchestra's musicians (for example, seniority and the number of section leaders) and hence should not be sensitive to the financial conditions of orchestras.

Chapter 7 examines how government support received by U.S. symphony orchestras evolved in the late 20th and early 21st centuries. The definition of government support used in the analysis differs from legislative appropriations, the concept used in most discussions of the role of government in the arts. For reasons noted in the chapter, appropriations provide an unreliable guide to the government support actually received by orchestras and other arts organizations.

The chapter analyzes and contrasts the support received from three levels of government. Orchestras receive local grants and in-kind support from cities, counties, or boards of education. State support includes grants from state arts councils or state legislatures as well as in-kind support. Grants from the National Endowment for the Arts and other federal agencies constitute most federal support. In-kind support consists of donated services, including office space in government-owned buildings.

The second section of the chapter discusses cycle and trend variations in nominal and real (nominal values deflated by the GDP deflator) support to orchestras from the three levels of government. Changes in general economic conditions influence government revenues in ways that could produce cyclical fluctuations in public support. In the statistical analysis, the local unemployment rate for each orchestra provides an indicator of general economic conditions. Public support also reflects long-term, noncyclical changes in the willingness of governments to provide funds for the arts. A time trend tests for such trends—positive or negative—in public support.

The following fixed-effects statistical model estimates the cycle and trend variations in government support:

$$\ln (\text{GOVERNMENT SUPPORT})_{it} = a_0 + a_1 \text{ UNEMPLOYMENT RATE}_{it} + a_2 \text{ TREND}_{it} + u_i + e_{it}$$

The dependent variable is the natural logarithm of government support for orchestra i at time t. The independent variables are the local unemployment rate and a

TABLE A7.1 CYCLE AND TREND ANALYSIS OF GOVERNMENT SUPPORT, 1987–2005 (COEFFICENTS AND STANDARD ERRORS)

	Real Government Support				Nominal Government Support			
	Total	Federal	State	Local	Total	Federal	State	Local
Unemployment rate	-.029	0.05	-.066	-0.047	-.026	0.053	-0.064	-0.045
	(.014)**	(.017)*	(.017)*	(.021)**	(.014)***	(.017)*	(.017)*	(.021)**
Time trend	-.036	-.093	-.036	.007	0.014	-0.071	-0.014	0.029
	(.003)*	(.004)*	(.004)*	(.004)***	(.003)*	(.004)*	(.004)*	(.004)*
R²	.14	.48	.10	.01	0.02	0.36	0.03	0.07
Number of orchestra years	1,042	859	980	844	1,042	859	980	844

Dependent variable: natural logarithm of real or nominal government support.

Fixed-effects estimates.

*p < .01, **p < .05, ***p < .10

time trend. The variable, u_i, is an orchestra fixed effect, which captures ongoing measurement errors or ongoing differences in government support between orchestras. The error term is e_{it}. The coefficients, a_i, are estimated from fixed-effects regression analyses of the panel of 63 orchestras between 1987 and 2005. Table A7.1 reports the results of separate analyses of support received by orchestras from each level of government. The regression results for real total government support indicate that a one percentage point increase in the local unemployment rate reduces the total amount of public support received by a symphony orchestra by about 2.9 percent on average. After holding the effect of general economic conditions constant, total government support fell by about 3.6 percent per year. Both results meet normal standards for statistical significance.

Other regressions show that changes in state and local support to orchestras account for most of the cyclical variation in public support; federal support moved countercyclically. Nonetheless, a long-term decline in real federal support (over 9 percent per year) is the dominant factor behind the trend decline in government support. State support has also declined over time (at 3.6 percent per year). A weak trend increase in real local government support provides only a partial offset. The regression results for nominal support show that more than inflation was at work. Changes in nominal appropriations contribute to the trend developments at all levels of government.

The third section of chapter 7 discusses the criteria that may guide the distribution of public funds to orchestras by different levels of government. The cycle-trend analysis was expanded to include possible distributional criteria. The results of the following random-effects regression model are discussed in the chapter:

$$\text{GOVERNMENT SUPPORT}_{it} = a_0 + a_1 \text{ REAL INCOME}_{it} + a_2 \text{ POPULATION}_{it} + a_3 \text{ PERFORMANCE INCOME RATIO}_{it} + a_4 \text{ BUDGET}_{it} + a_5 \text{ DEVELOPMENT EXPENSE}_{it} + a_6 \text{ UNEMPLOYMENT RATE}_{it} + a_7 \text{ TREND}_{it} + e_{it}$$

The real per capita income of an orchestra's market area captures the economic capacity of an area to support orchestras. The variable was included to determine whether government support equalizes ($a_1 < 0$) or exacerbates ($a_1 > 0$) the inequality of private resources likely to be available to orchestras. If political processes favor the equalization of per capita payments, government support will be positively related to the population of an orchestra's community ($a_2 > 0$). If support is instead distributed to equalize the total nonperformance income of orchestras, $a_2 < 0$, since communities with a larger population normally have higher levels of private donations.

The performance income ratio (the ratio of performance revenues to performance expenses) measures orchestra i's performance deficit in year t and captures the extent to which orchestra need governs the distribution of public support. Orchestra budget size tests the extent to which public support favors large organizations. ("Budget" is defined as total expenses minus fundraising expenses, in order to separate a size effect from differences in the fundraising capacity.) A separate variable for development expense tests the effectiveness of orchestras' fundraising operations in attracting government subsidies. All variables except the performance income ratio, unemployment rate,

TABLE A7.2 DETERMINANTS OF FEDERAL, STATE, AND LOCAL GOVERNMENT
SUPPORT, 1987-2005

Independent Variables	Federal	State	Local	All Levels
Per capita income[a]	−1.160	−.188	1.504	−.074
	(.335)*	(.546)	(.623)**	(.394)
Population	.159	.054	.272	.143
	(.060)*	(.103)	(1.22)**	(.076)***
Performance income ratio[b]	−.002	−.010	−.004	−.006
	(.002)	(.003)*	(.003)	(.002)*
Budget[a,c]	.806	.575	.267	.382
	(.082)*	(.135)*	(.161)***	(.099)*
Development expense[a]	.021	.001	−.022	.170
	(.054)	(.061)	(.078)	(.046)*
Unemployment rate	.011	−.062	−.009	−.036
	(.016)	(.019)*	(.022)	(.014)**
Time trend	−.101	−.051	−.032	−.055
	(.007)*	(.011)*	(.012)*	(.008)*

Dependent variables: natural logarithm of real government support.
Random-effects regressions. All variables except performance income ratio,
unemployment rate, and time trend are natural logarithms.
[a] Adjusted for inflation.
[b] Ratio of performance revenues to performance expenses.
[c] Total expenses minus development expense.
* $p. < 01$; ** $p. < 05$; *** $p < .10$

and time trend are expressed as natural logarithms. Table A7.2A reports the results of
the analyses, which are discussed in the chapter text.

Chapter 7 also discusses how U.S. orchestras benefit from indirect government
support when taxpayers deduct donations to orchestras from their taxable income.
Table 7.3 provides estimates of federal government tax expenditures for symphony
orchestras. Estimated tax expenditures (tax revenues that the federal government did
not collect because contributors have lower taxable income) equal the value of donations, as reported by the orchestras themselves to the League of American Orchestras,
multiplied by the appropriate marginal federal tax rate. The table reports separate estimates for individual and corporate tax expenditures based on their respective levels of
contributed support and the marginal tax rates that they face.

Which marginal tax rates should be used? Both the individual and corporate tax
codes include a schedule of tax rates that rise with income levels. The data on contributions to orchestras provide no information on the income levels of contributors,

however. The chapter suggests that 28 percent and 34 percent constitute reasonable estimates of the average marginal tax rate faced by individual and corporate contributors respectively. At those tax rates, table 7.3 shows that individual contributions to orchestras produced federal tax expenditures of $17.7 and $88.3 million in 1987 and 2005, respectively. Adding these amounts to the tax expenditures associated with business contributions (assuming a 34 percent marginal tax rate) and direct government expenditures produces estimates of total government support ($44.4 million in 1987 and $119.1 million in 2005).

Table 7.3 also provides estimates of individual tax expenditures if individual contributors are assumed to face alternative marginal tax rates. Reestimating the table with alternative tax rates does not change the basic message: tax expenditures provide the dominant federal government support to symphony orchestras. At the 15 percent marginal tax rate, the share of direct government expenditure in total federal support rises from 24.8 percent to 30.4 percent in 1987 and from 3.7 percent to 4.1 percent in 2005. At marginal rates above 28 percent, the share of direct expenditures is even smaller.

Chapter 8 discusses the composition and determinants of private philanthropic contributions to symphony orchestras in the United States. The annual Orchestra Statistical Reports submitted to the League of American Orchestras provide considerable information on support received from individuals, businesses, foundations, and other sources. Prior to 1998, "private support" from each source consisted of the sum of general (unrestricted annual) support, project (restricted operating) support, and concert underwriting. Beginning in 1998, the reports added a new concept, fundraising income, while maintaining the previous definition of private support. Fundraising income equaled private support (as defined above) plus government support plus "other" support (volunteers, in-kind, etc.). Beginning in 2002, the concept of private support was expanded to include unrestricted operating contributions, other unrestricted donations designated by the orchestra's board of trustees for other purposes, contributions with temporary donor restrictions on when or how the funds may be used, and permanently restricted contributions, which include contributions to endowment. To maintain a consistent definition of private support for 1987–2005, the concept was restricted in this analysis to operating funds through 2005. Fundraising income includes permanently restricted funds.

The third section of chapter 8 discusses the outcome of a fixed-effects regression analysis of how these two concepts of private donations (expressed in year 2000 dollars) respond to orchestra policies, a community's economic capacity, and competition from other performing arts. Fundraising expenditures and annual concert attendance constitute the key orchestra policy variables. Exploratory analyses tested for both linear and nonlinear relationships between fundraising expenditures and both fundraising income and private support. (The nonlinear specifications tested for the possibility that the influence of incremental fundraising expenditures on contributions depends on the overall level of fundraising expenditures.) The linear specification provided superior

TABLE A8.1   ANALYSIS OF EXTERNAL SUPPORT FOR U.S. ORCHESTRAS (REGRESSION COEFFICIENTS AND STANDARD ERRORS)

Orchestras	Dependent Variable	Real Per Capita Income	Area Population	Concert Attendance	Fundraising Expense	Orchestra Years	R^2
All (1998–2005)	Fundraising income	693.98 (240.52)*	0.64 (.263)**	-5.99 (4.64)	4.02 (1.00)*	422	.10
All (1998–2005)	Private support	136.11 (49.97)*	-.025 (.055)	2.14 (.96)**	1.20 (.21)*	422	.12
Large (1998–2005)	Fundraising income	1,006.92 (462.77)**	.086 (.356)	-4.74 (6.88)	4.48 (1.42)*	206	.13
Large (1998–2005)	Private support	160.73 (97.15)***	-.030 (.075)	2.34 (1.44)	1.29 (.30)*	206	.14
Small (1998–2005)	Fundraising income	568.73 (193.16)*	-.166 (.630)	-5.00 (5.73)	-2.28 (1.68)	207	.06
Small (1998–2005)	Private support	129.44 (37.28)*	0.05 (.12)	2.23 (1.11)**	.23 (.32)	207	.10
All (1987–2005)	Private support	273.69 (12.66)*	.04 (.05)	.58 (.47)	1.69 (.13)*	1,021	.54
Large (1987–2005)	Private support	370.49 (20.70)*	.02 (.07)	.42 (.68)	1.48 (.17)*	499	.60
Small (1987–2005)	Private support	155.58 (11.02)*	.02 (.10)	1.78 (.53)*	1.25 (.22)*	478	0.49

Fixed-effects estimates. All monetary variables are in year 2000 dollars.

*$p < .01$, **$p < .05$, ***$p < .10$

statistical results. The concert attendance variable tested the view that concert patrons also provide a significant flow of donations to orchestras. If that view is correct, audience development policies are doubly beneficial: they expand both ticket sales and philanthropic contributions. Local real per capita income and population measure an area's economic capacity for philanthropy. The text discussion relies on the estimates in table A8.1, which presents separate results for all orchestras in the sample, large orchestras (total expenses above $9 million in 1999), and small orchestras.

The analyses confirm the importance of an area's real per capita income for private donations to both large and small orchestras. Orchestras benefit from the long-term growth of per capita income but also encounter variations in support as real per capita income fluctuates during recessions and expansions. There is no significant relationship between the private support received by an orchestra and the population size of its market area, however.

Turning to orchestra policies, private support and concert attendance are significantly positively correlated, although the experience of smaller orchestras accounts for most of the statistical action. Yet fundraising income, which adds government support and restricted contributions to endowment to private operating support, is not significantly correlated with attendance. Attendance-building policies are most likely to have their impact in private operating support.

Table A8.1 also reports estimates of the relationship between fundraising expenditures and the private support and fundraising income received by orchestras. Underlying this analysis is the question of whether fundraising expenditures pay for themselves. The answer to this question varies with the size of orchestras and, to an extent, with the definition of private nonperformance income. Additional fundraising expenditures by large orchestras pay for themselves, although the gains in private donations associated with such expenditures are much lower than simple comparisons of contributions and expenses suggest. Between 1998 and 2005, the average large orchestra received about $4.74 in fundraising income ($2.34 in private support) for each dollar spent on fundraising. During the same period, there was no statistically significant relationship between fundraising expenditures and returns for smaller orchestras, however.

For the much longer period (1987 through 2005) for which only private support data are available, both larger and smaller orchestras registered positive to returns on fundraising expenses ($1.48 and $1.25 per dollar spent, respectively), although the returns were lower for smaller orchestras.

NOTES

Chapter 2. Why Are Surpluses So Difficult to Maintain?

1. There have been three comparatively recent reversions to musician ownership of an orchestra. The Denver Symphony Orchestra failed in 1989 and re-formed the following year as the Colorado Symphony; the New Orleans Symphony ceased operations in 1990 and re-formed for the 1991–92 season as the Louisiana Symphony; and musicians from the Tulsa Philharmonic, which failed in 2002, established the Tulsa Symphony Orchestra in 2005. The symphony musicians own each orchestra. At least three prominent European symphony orchestras are organized as self-governing musicians' cooperatives: the London Symphony Orchestra, the Vienna Philharmonic, and the Berlin Philharmonic.

Chapter 3. Cost Disease or Business Cycles?

1. To minimize the impact of distortions that might be introduced into the data by possible variations in reporting practices by different orchestras, this study adopts a statistical technique known as *fixed-effects analysis*. Fixed-effects analysis considers only how variables change over time for each orchestra and ignores differences in the level of variables in different orchestras. Therefore, interorchestra differences in financial or operating variables that might be biased by different reporting practices play no role in the analysis. By focusing on the effects of changes over time *within* orchestras, fixed-effects analysis adopts the perspective that is most relevant for assessing the effects of policy changes by individual orchestras.

Chapter 5. The Search for Symphony Audiences

1. The average experience should not obscure the varied experience of individual orchestras. Of the orchestras reporting sufficient data for analysis, 14 experienced a

general increase in attendance over the period, while 31 experienced declining attendance, as did the six orchestras that went bankrupt.

2. Details about regression analyses of attendance appear in the appendix for this chapter.

3. Ticket price data were not available for later years. See the chapter appendix for technical details.

4. The appendix for this chapter includes the technical details of the statistical analysis underlying this discussion.

5. Not everyone pursues revenue maximization in pricing musical events. At major rock concerts, for example, a single price often applies to all seats (Connolly and Krueger 2006).

6. Regression analyses also turned up evidence that actual seating capacity declined during this period for the average orchestra in this sample. Seating capacity, which is linked to the size of concert venues and the number of regular season concerts performed during a year, exhibits no cyclical sensitivity (in contrast to the percentage of seats sold). The sources of this trend could not be determined with the data available for this study.

Chapter 6. Artistic and Nonartistic Costs

1. See http://www.icsom.org/pdf/orchestrasalaryfacts.pdf, accessed June 16, 2007.

2. According to the AFM website, the national union "recognized the International Conference of Symphony and Opera Musicians (ICSOM) as an organization representing orchestral musicians within the union." See http://www.afm.org/about/our-history/1960–1969, accessed January 30, 2008.

3. Most collective bargaining agreements also provide for musicians' health care and pensions. There are a variety of health-care arrangements, with 100 percent of the contributions usually paid by the symphony employer. Orchestras used to have a variety of private defined benefit plans, but most orchestras now use a plan administered by the American Federation of Musicians.

4. See http://www.icsom.org/pdf/orchestrasalaryfacts.pdf, accessed June 16, 2007.

5. A remarkable example of these protocols occurred at Tanglewood in July 1986, when Midori, who was then a 14-year-old Juilliard School student, broke a string on her violin while performing the final movement of Leonard Bernstein's *Serenade* with the Boston Symphony Orchestra, conducted by Bernstein himself. According to the *New York Times*, "She quickly turned to Malcolm Lowe, the concertmaster, who looked nonplussed but finally handed over his Stradivarius. There was a moment's pause while Miss Dori [*sic*] fitted her chin rest onto the new violin. But then she proceeded absolutely unfazed. Then it happened again—another snapped E string. By this time Mr. Lowe was playing the Guadagnini of the acting associate concertmaster, Max Hobart, and Mr. Hobart had retuned Miss Dori's and was playing it, 'faking' his way around the missing E string. Miss Dori took Mr. Hobart's Guadagnini from Mr. Lowe, thinking at first it was her own violin, restrung. Realizing that it wasn't, and unwilling

once again to interrupt the music, she played on, perfectly . . . and finished the piece on Mr. Hobart's violin" (Rockwell 1986). The incident may be viewed at http://www.youtube.com/watch?v=Rkp8YSuePPM.

6. From www.guidestar.org, accessed May 2009.

7. Contrary evidence occasionally surfaces. In March 2008, a time of deteriorating economic conditions, the La Crosse, Wisconsin, *Tribune* reported that "The La Crosse Symphony Orchestra has received 226 applicants from all over the world for the position of music director and conductor"—a part-time position paying in the range of $45,000 to $55,000 (Rindfleisch 2008).

8. The appendix for this chapter contains technical details of the analysis.

9. For an informed discussion of the myriad of factors that may be involved in the bankruptcy of a symphony orchestra, see Wolf and Glaze 2005.

10. The Birmingham Symphony Orchestra declared bankruptcy in 1993 and reformed as the Alabama Symphony Orchestra by 1996. The Denver Symphony Orchestra went bankrupt in 1989 and later re-formed as the Colorado Symphony Orchestra, and the New Orleans Symphony Orchestra went through a similar process, emerging as the Louisiana Philharmonic Orchestra. (The last two successor orchestras now operate as labor cooperatives.) Hawaii's orchestra closed for several seasons in the mid-1990s before renewing operations as the Honolulu Symphony Orchestra, which itself declared bankruptcy in 2009. Orchestras in Louisville and San Diego have also filed for bankruptcy but eventually reorganized and reopened. Orchestras in Oakland, Sacramento, and San Jose never reopened.

Chapter 7. Government Support of Orchestras

1. For reviews of the troubled political history of the NEA, see Frohnmayer 1993, Alexander 2000, and Heilbrun and Gray 2001.

2. Faced with additional budget reductions, the NEA proposed to end its Jazz Masters program in the 2012 budget proposal submitted to Congress in February 2011.

3. See the appendix for this chapter for technical details of the analysis supporting this discussion.

4. Specifically, the budget document proposed to limit the tax rate at which high-income taxpayers could take itemized deductions to 28 percent. The administration's expectation that the provision would raise $318 billion over 10 years provides a rough idea of the scale of total tax expenditures in the United States (U.S. Office of Management and Budget 2009).

5. Instead, OMB reports annual estimates of tax expenditures for three categories of charitable contributions: education, health, and "other than education and health." Donations to symphony orchestras and many other nonprofit organizations are buried in the last category. In 2007, tax expenditures in the "other" category amounted to $36.8 billion for individuals and $1.4 billion for corporations (U.S. Office of Management and Budget 2008, pp. 287–331), but donations to symphony orchestras would be a very small proportion of this total.

6. Businesses with income between $100,000 and $335,000 in 1987 faced a 39 percent income tax rate. By 2005, rates exceeding 34 percent applied to corporations with income over $10 million.

Chapter 8. Private Support of Orchestras

1. The appendix for this chapter reports technical details of the statistical analyses.

Chapter 9. Symphony Orchestra Endowments and Governance

1. As always, there are exceptions: "term" endowments permit spending of original principal at a prespecified rate, but these funds constitute a distinct minority of endowments.

2. The estimates in table 9.3 use the average of the performance income gaps for 2004 and 2005. The average performance income gaps are divided by the alternative endowment draw rates to obtain the estimates of the required endowments. The actual endowment figures are also averages of 2004 and 2005.

Chapter 10. How Do Other Countries Support Their Orchestras?

1. Whether the performance revenues of foreign orchestras fall short of their performance expenses by ever-increasing amounts, as in the United States, remains an open question. It is difficult to discern long-term trends without first holding cyclical influences on orchestra revenues and expenses constant (chapter 3), and foreign orchestras generally report insufficient data to permit separation of trend and cycle influences.

2. By ensuring the survival of orchestras, subsidies remove some of the risks associated with becoming a symphony musician and thus attract more people to the profession. By raising the supply of musicians, subsidies may even reduce musicians' incomes. This provocative hypothesis is difficult to test for orchestra musicians, but Abbing (2004, chap. 6) reports that enrollments in fine arts programs leveled off and dropped with discontinuation of Dutch artist subsidy program.

3. For each country, the wages of orchestra musicians (converted to U.S. dollars using official currency exchange rates) are compared to the country's average wage in U.S. dollar purchasing power equivalents, as published by the Organization for Economic Cooperation and Development (OECD 2009a).

Chapter 11. The Economic Future of Symphony Orchestras

1. For a fascinating case study of how the San Francisco Symphony used training in negotiating techniques to move from the aftermath of a disastrous strike to a more productive negotiating relationship, see Mnookin 2010, chap. 8.

REFERENCES

Abbing, Hans. 2004. *Why Are Artists Poor? The Exceptional Economy of the Arts*. Amsterdam: Amsterdam University Press.

Aguiar, Mark, and Erik Hurst. 2006. "Measuring Trends in Leisure: The Allocation of Time over Five Decades." NBER Working Paper no. 12082. Cambridge, MA: National Bureau of Economic Research.

Aldrich, Richard. 1903. "'Permanent Orchestra' Season a Bad One." *New York Times*, May 3.

Alexander, Jane. 2000. *Command Performance: An Actress in the Theater of Politics*. New York: Public Affairs Press.

Arts Council England. 2007. *Informing Change: Taking Part in the Arts, Survey Findings from the First 12 Months*. London: Arts Council England.

Association of British Orchestras (ABO). 2000. *Knowing the Score*. London: ABO.

Association of Finnish Symphony Orchestras. Various years. *Member Orchestras: Facts and Figures*. Helsinki: Suomen Sinfoniaorkesterit.

Atlanta Symphony Orchestra. 2009. "Atlanta Symphony Orchestra Musicians Join ASO Executive and Artistic Leadership and Administration in Compensation Reductions." http://www.atlantasymphony.org~/media/Sites/www.atlantasymphony.org/Newsroom/Press%20Releases/ASOBudgetCuts%20ORCHESTRA%20FINAL%204%207%2009.ashx, April 7.

Australia Department of the Environment, Water, Heritage and the Arts (DEWHA). 2005. *A New Era: Report of the Orchestras Review, 2005*. Available at http://www.arts.gov.au/__data/assets/pdf_file/0018/25083/ORCHESTRAS_Review_2005.pdf.

Australian Bureau of Statistics. 2009. *Arts and Culture in Australia: A Statistical Overview*. Cat. no. 4172.0. Adelaide: Australian Bureau of Statistics, October 21.

Ayer, Julie. 2005. *More Than Meets the Ear: How Symphony Musicians Made Labor History*. Minneapolis: Syren Book Company.

Baumol, Hilda, and William J. Baumol. 1984. "The Mass Media and the Cost Disease." In *The Economics of Cultural Industries*, edited by William S. Hendon, Douglas V. Shaw, and Nancy K. Grant, 109–23. Akron: Association for Cultural Economics,.

Baumol, William J. 1967. "Macroeconomics of Unbalanced Growth: The Anatomy of Urban Crisis." *American Economic Review* 57:415–26.

Baumol, William J., and William G. Bowen. 1966. *The Performing Arts, the Economic Dilemma: A Study of Problems Common to Theater, Opera, Music, and Dance*. New York: Twentieth Century Fund.

Bina, Vladimir. 2002. "Cultural Participation in the Netherlands." In *Proceedings of the International Symposium on Culture Statistics, Montreal, 21–23 October 2002*, 361–79. Montreal: UNESCO Institute for Statistics.

Bowen, William G. 2008. *The Board Book: An Insider's Guide for Directors and Trustees*. New York: W. W. Norton.

Brooks, A. C. 2000. "Public Subsidies and Charitable Giving: Crowding Out, Crowding In, or Both?" *Journal of Policy Analysis and Management* 19:451–64.

Bukofzer, Manfred. 1947. *Music in the Baroque Era*. New York: W. W. Norton.

Carroll, Robert, and David Joulfaian. 2001. "Taxes and Corporate Giving to Charity." In *Compendium of Studies of Tax-Exempt Organizations, Volume 3: 1989–1998*. Washington, DC: Internal Revenue Service. Available at http://www.irs.gov/pub/irs-soi/98eovol3.pdf.

Caves, Richard E. 2000. *Creative Industries: Contracts between Art and Commerce*. Cambridge, MA: Harvard University Press.

Connolly, Marie, and Alan Krueger. 2006. "Rockonomics: The Economics of Popular Music." In *Handbook of the Economics of Art and Culture*, vol. 1., edited by Victor A. Ginsburgh and David Throsby, 667–720. Amsterdam: Elsevier.

Courty, Pascal, and Mario Pagliero. 2009. "The Impact of Price Discrimination on Revenue: Evidence from the Concert Industry." CEPR Discussion Paper no. 7120. London: Centre for Economic Policy Research.

Cultural Trends. 1990:5. London: Policy Studies Institute, University of Westminster.

DiMaggio, Paul J., and Francie Ostrower. 1992. *Race, Ethnicity, and Participation in the Arts*. National Endowment for the Arts Research Division Report #25. Santa Ana, CA: Seven Locks Press.

DiMaggio, Paul J., and Toqir Mukhtar. 2004. "Arts Participation as Cultural Capital in the United States." *Poetics* 32:169–94.

The Economist. 2008. "Soft Power and a Rapturous Ovation." February 28.

European Commission. 2007. *European Cultural Values*. Special Eurobarometer 278. Brussels: European Commission. Available at http://ec.europa.eu/culture/pdf/doc958_en.pdf.

European Parliament. 2006a. *Financing the Arts and Culture in the European Union*. Policy Department Structural and Cohesion Policies. Brussels: European Parliament. Available at http://www.culturalpolicies.net/web/files/134/en/Financing_the_Arts_and_Culture_in_the_EU.pdf.

European Parliament. 2006b. *The Status of Artists in Europe*. Policy Department Structural and Cohesion Policies, IP/B/CULT/ST/2005–89. Brussels: European Parliament. Available at http://www.europarl.europa.eu/activities/committees/studies/download.do?file=13248.

Flaccus, Gillian. 2009. "Recession Is Bitter Music for Performing Arts in United States." Associated Press report, January 27. Available at http://www.breitbart.com/article.php?id=cp_glngvjosa13.

Flanagan, Robert J. 2008. "The Economic Environment of American Symphony Orchestras." Available at http://www.gsb.stanford.edu/news/packages/pdf/Flanagan.pdf.

Flanagan, Robert J. 2010. "Symphony Musicians and Symphony Orchestras." In *Labor in the Era of Globalization*, edited by Clair Brown, Berry Eichengreen, and Michael Reich, 264–94. Cambridge: Cambridge University Press.

Ford Foundation. 1966. "Millions for Music—Music for Millions." *Music Educators Journal* 53 (1): 83–86.

Ford Foundation. 1974. *The Finances of the Performing Arts*. New York: Ford Foundation.

Frey, Bruno S. 2000. *Arts & Economics: Analysis & Cultural Policy*. Berlin: Springer.

Frohnmayer, John. 1993. *Leaving Town Alive: Confessions of an Arts Warrior*. Boston: Houghton Mifflin.

Futterman, Matthew, and Douglas A. Blockman. 2010. "PGA Tour Begins to Pay a Price for Tiger Woods's Transgressions." *Wall Street Journal*, January 25.

Goldin, Claudia, and Cecilia Rouse. 2000. "Orchestrating Impartiality: The Impact of "Blind" Auditions on Female Musicians." *American Economic Review* 90:715–41.

Goudriaan, René, Wim de Haart, and Siebe W. Weide. 1996. "Subsidies, Productive Efficiency and the Performing Arts: A First Look at the Data for the Netherlands." Paper prepared for 9th International Congress on Cultural Economics, Boston, May 8–11.

Gramophone. 2008. "The World's Greatest Symphony Orchestras." December, 36–37.

Grant, Margaret, and Herman S. Hettinger. 1940. *America's Symphony Orchestras, and How They Are Supported*. New York: W. W. Norton.

Grossberg, Michael. 2008. "Criticisms of Orchestra Board Prompt Issue-by-Issue Review." *The Columbus Dispatch*, April 9.

Guillard, Jean-Pierre. 1985. "The Symphony as a Public Service: The Orchestra of Paris." *Journal of Cultural Economics* 9 (2): 35–47.

Hansmann, Henry. 1996. *The Ownership of Enterprise*. Cambridge, MA: Harvard University Press.

Hart, Philip. 1973. *Orpheus in the New World*. New York: W. W. Norton.

Heilbrun, James, and Charles M. Gray. 2001. *The Economics of Art and Culture*. 2nd ed. Cambridge: Cambridge University Press.

Ireland Arts Council. 2006. *The Public and the Arts 2006*. Dublin: Arts Council.

Kolb, Bonita M. 2001. "The Effect of Generational Change on Classical Music Concert Attendance and Orchestras' Responses in the UK and US." *Cultural Trends* 41:1–35.

Kurabayashi, Yoshimasa, and Yoshiro Matsuda. 1988. *Economic and Social Aspects of the Performing Arts in Japan: Symphony Orchestras and Opera*. Tokyo: Kinokuniya.

Kushner, Roland J., and Randy Cohen. 2010. *National Arts Index 2009*. New York: Americans for the Arts.

League of American Orchestras [formerly American Symphony Orchestra League]. 2009. "Audience Demographic Research Review." New York: League of American Orchestras.

———. Various dates. "Orchestra Statistical Reports" (OSRs). New York: League of American Orchestras.

Lehman, Erin, and Adam Galinsky. 1994. *The London Symphony Orchestra (A)*. Harvard Business School Case no. 9-494-034. Cambridge, MA: Harvard Business School Press.

Locke, Justin. 2005. *Real Men Don't Rehearse: Adventures in the Secret World of Professional Orchestras*. Boston: Justin Locke Productions.

Lubow, Arthur. 2004. "Orchestral Maneuvers in the Dark." *New York Times Magazine*, June 27.

Massy, William F. 1990. *Endowment: Perspectives, Policies, and Management*. Washington, DC: Association of Governing Boards of Universities and Colleges.

Melvin, Sheila, and Jindong Cai. 2004. *Rhapsody in Red: How Western Classical Music Became Chinese*. New York: Algora Publishing.

Mnookin, Robert. 2010. *Bargaining with the Devil: When to Negotiate, When to Fight*. New York: Simon & Schuster.

National Association of Schools of Music (NASM). 2006. "HEADS [Higher Education Arts Data Services] Data Summaries, 2005–2006." Available at http://nasm .arts-accredit.org/index.jsp?page=Catalog&itemId=8e9d9ddda7ab54587ce44eb 306f4cef8.

National Endowment for the Arts (NEA). 2000. *International Data on Government Spending on the Arts*. NEA Research Note no. 74. Washington, DC: NEA.

———. 2004. *2002 Survey of Public Participation in the Arts*. Research Division Report no. 45. Washington, DC: NEA.

———. 2007. *How the United States Funds the Arts*. 2nd ed. Washington, DC: NEA.

———. 2009. *2008 Survey of Public Participation in the Arts*. Research Division Report no. 49. Washington, DC: NEA.

Noonan, Heather. 2006. "Under the Microscope . . . " *Symphony*, July–August 2006.

Okten, Cagla, and Burton A. Weisbrod. 2000. "Determinants of Donations in Private Nonprofit Markets." *Journal of Public Economics* 75:255–72.

Opera America. Various years. "Fiscal and Operational Survey of Professional Opera Companies." Washington, DC, and New York: Opera America.

Organization for Economic Cooperation and Development (OECD). 2009a. *Employment Outlook*. Paris: OECD.

Organization for Economic Cooperation and Development (OECD). 2009b. *OECD Factbook 2009*. Paris: OECD.

Ostrower, Francie. 2007. *Nonprofit Governance in the United States: Findings on Performance and Accountability from the First National Representative Study*. Washington, DC: Urban Institute.

Peacock, Alan T. 1993. *Paying the Piper: Culture, Music and Money*. Edinburgh: Edinburgh University Press.

Peterson, Richard A., Pamela C. Hull, and Roger M. Kern. 1998. *Age and Arts Participation: 1982–1997*. National Endowment for the Arts Research Division Report no. 42. Santa Ana, CA: Seven Locks Press.

Ravanas, Philippe. 2008. "Hitting a High Note: The Chicago Symphony Orchestra Reverses a Decade of Decline." *International Journal of Arts Management* 10 (2): 68–87.

Recording Industry Association of America. "Key Statistics." Available at http://www.riaa.org/keystatistics.php?content_selector=2008–2009-U.S-Shipment-Numbers.

Rindfleisch, Terry. 2008. "226 Apply for La Crosse Symphony Orchestra Conductor." *La Crosse Tribune*, March 31.

Robinson, John P., and Geoffrey Godbey. 1997. *Time for Life: The Surprising Ways Americans Use Their Time*. University Park: Pennsylvania State University Press.

Rockwell, John. 1986. "Girl, 14, Conquers Tanglewood With 3 Violins." *New York Times*, July 28, A1.

Rosen, Sherwin, and Andrew M. Rosenfield. 1997. "Ticket Pricing." *Journal of Law and Economics* 40 (2): 351–76.

Sandow, Greg. 2007. "Rebirth: The Future of Classical Music." Available at http://www.artsjournal.com/sandow/2007/01/rebirth.html.

San Francisco Symphony. 2008. *Playbill*, March.

Schulze, Gunther G., and Anselm Rose. 1998. "Public Orchestra Funding in Germany: An Empirical Investigation." *Journal of Cultural Economics* 22:227–47.

Schuster, J. Mark. 1985. "Supporting the Arts: An International Comparative Study." Cambridge, MA: MIT Dept. of Urban Studies and Planning.

Seaman, Bruce A. 2005. "Attendance and Public Participation in the Performing Arts: A Review of the Empirical Literature." Working Paper 06–25. Atlanta: Andrew Young School of Policy Studies, Georgia State University.

Seltzer, George. 1989. *Music Matters: The Performer and the American Federation of Musicians*. Metuchen, NJ: Scarecrow Press.

Senza Sordino. 1994–2003. International Confederation of Symphony and Opera Musicians. Available at http://www.icsom.org/senzarchive.html.

Service, Tom. 2010. "Dutch Arts Cuts—What the Future Looks Like?" *Guardian*, October 5.

Sharpe, William F. 1985. *Investments*. 3rd ed. Upper Saddle River, NJ: Prentice-Hall.

Sheban, Jeffrey. 2011. "Contract Increases Base Pay for Columbus Symphony." *Columbus Dispatch*, February 26.

Smith, Thomas More. 2007. "The Impact of Government Funding on Private Contributions to Nonprofit Performing Arts Organizations." *Annals of Public and Cooperative Economics* 78 (1): 137–60.

Statistics Canada. 2000. *Patterns in Culture Consumption and Participation*. Ottawa: Statistics Canada, Culture Statistics Program.

Strom, Stephanie. 2007. "Big Gifts, Tax Breaks and a Debate on Charity." *New York Times*, September 6.

Swensen, David F. 2000. *Pioneering Portfolio Management: An Unconventional Approach to Institutional Investment*. New York: Free Press.

Taruskin, Richard. 2005. *Oxford History of Western Music*. 6 vols. Oxford: Oxford University Press.

Thompson, Helen M. 1958. "Report of Study on Governing Boards of Symphony Orchestras." Washington, DC: American Symphony Orchestra League.

Tobin, James. 1974. "What Is Permanent Endowment Income?" *American Economic Review* 64:427–32.

Triplett, Jack E., and Barry P. Bosworth. 2003. "Productivity Measurement Issues in Services Industries: 'Baumol's Disease' Has Been Cured." *FRBNY Economic Policy Review*, September, 23–33.

U.S. Bureau of Economic Analysis. 2006. "Local Area Personal Income." Available at http://www.bea.gov/regional/reis/.

U.S. Bureau of Labor Statistics. 2006a. "Local Area Unemployment Statistics." Available at http://www.bls.gov/lau/.

U.S. Bureau of Labor Statistics. 2006b. "National Compensation Survey: Occupational Wages in the United States, June 2005." Available at http://www.bls.gov/ncs/ocs/sp/ncblo832.pdf.

U.S. Bureau of Labor Statistics. 2007. "Employment Cost Index Historical Listing: Current-Dollar, 1975–2005." Available at http://www.bls.gov/web/echistry.pdf.

U.S. Office of Management and Budget. 2008. *Analytical Perspectives: Budget of the United States Government, FY 2009*. Washington, DC: U.S. Government Printing Office.

U.S. Office of Management and Budget. 2009. *A New Era of Responsibility: Renewing America's Promise*. Washington, DC: U.S. Government Printing Office.

Van der Ploeg, Frederick. 2006. "The Making of Cultural Policy: A European Perspective." In *Handbook of the Economics of Art and Culture*, edited by Victor A. Ginsburgh and David Throsby, 1183–1221. Amsterdam: North-Holland.

Wakin, Daniel J. 2010. "Talks Break Down at Cleveland Orchestra." *New York Times*, January 7.

Weber, William. 2008. *The Great Transformation of Musical Taste: Concert Programming from Haydn to Brahms*. New York: Cambridge University Press.

Wechsberg, Joseph. 1970. "The Cleveland Orchestra." *New Yorker*, May 30.

Wichterman, Catherine. 1998. "The Orchestra Forum: A Discussion of Symphony Orchestras in the US." In Andrew Mellon Foundation annual report.

Wolf, Thomas, and Nancy Glaze. 2005. *And the Band Stopped Playing: The Rise and Fall of the San Jose Symphony*. Cambridge, MA: Wolf, Keens.

Woodcock, Tony. 2011. "A Way to Move Forward." Available at http://necmusic.word press.com/2011/02/24/a-way-to-move-forward/.

Wyatt, Edward, and Jori Finkel. 2008. "Soaring in Art, Museum Trips over Finances." *New York Times*, December 5.

Yost, Mark. 2010. "The Outfitters' Lament: Too Few Kids with Guns." *Wall Street Journal*, February 10, D9.

INDEX

RECEIVED NOV 3 0 2012 50 02

DISCARD